SIZE DOESN'T MATTER

SIZE DOESN'T MATTER

My Rugby Life

Neil Back

First published 2000 by Milo Books Ltd

Paperback edition first published in Great Britain
in June 2002 by Milo Books Ltd

ISBN 1 903854 12 1

Typeset by Avon DataSet Limited, Bidford-on-Avon B50 4JH
www.avondataset.com

Printed and bound in Great Britain by
Cox & Wyman Ltd, Reading, Berkshire

MILO BOOKS LTD
21 Union Street
Ramsbottom
Lancs
BL0 9AN

To my beautiful wife Ali and our daughter Olivia.

Contents

Acknowledgements

The battle to achieve my dream, to play for England, was not an easy one.

Detailing that battle in this book has been almost as hard.

In order to make the case that I should have been part of the national side some years before I actually was, I have had to show that my selection would have been justified.

Doing this, inevitably, meant blowing my own trumpet. I have also quoted respected writers and players, past and present, who, as independent observers, were arguing for my inclusion before it happened.

I hope the resultant passages which praise my abilities will be seen in that context and will not be interpreted as conceit on my part. I am confident in my abilities but I do not profess to be the greatest rugby player ever.

I have had a great career, which is not quite over. But I spent many years trying to prove a few people wrong. I succeeded in the end. I hope that inspires other people to believe in themselves and to work hard to achieve their own dreams.

I would like to thank a lot of people, without whom this book – and, indeed, my rugby career – would not have been possible. Ali and my family have provided support and inspiration at the low points and helped me to celebrate the highs; the fantastic fans at Leicester Tigers and England's supporters; Dean Richards and John Wells at Leicester, Clive Woodward, John Mitchell and, now, Andy Robinson at England, and the Barbarians, together with the players and all the backroom staff behind each of those three sides, who are too numerous to mention by name but are no less important for all that; Jack Carnall, Peter Lloyd, John Smith and all the other junior club helpers and school teachers who put so many hours into helping youngsters develop; Fran Cotton, Ian McGeechan and Jim Telfer for making me a British Lion.

Thanks, also, to Jason Tilley for his cover photograph and to *The Leicester Mercury* for allowing the publishers access to their photo library.

Introduction
by Martin Johnson

What can I say about Neil Back?

He's short, he's losing his hair and he's got no front teeth – the falsies explain his lisp.

He is a neat freak who moans if you leave a tea-cup circle on his kitchen table.

And he's always first on the massage bench – not for nothing is he known as 'I'm Alright Jack' Back.

I first met him with England schools. My earliest memory is of a break in play during a game. The forwards huddled together and this little blond head poked in, grinning from ear-to-ear. He had just lost a tooth but wasn't at all bothered, which impressed me a lot (the illusion was ruined later, when I found out it was a false one).

Seriously, Backy is a superb player who should have walked into the England side as soon as Peter Winterbottom retired. He is one of the all-time great flankers but he is comfortable all over the field, which is important in the modern game. He isn't massive but he is very strong: you cannot play at his size and weight and not get smashed about without being hard. He is also very brave.

He has been around for ages – he was playing for the

Barbarians against England 10 years ago – and he has been easily the best and most consistent player in English rugby in that decade.

Off the field, he is a good friend and a popular bloke with club and country.

He has been a tremendous servant of Leicester, England and the British Lions in that time and his would be one of the first names down on any team sheet I wrote.

Well, at least he'd keep the dressing room tidy.

Martin Johnson,
Leicester, England and British Lions

CHAPTER I

In the Beginning

MY LIFE almost ended before it had begun.

My mum nearly died during the birth, too. She had been through the mill giving birth to my older brother Ian. Her labour had taken two days and the doctors had warned her she was in for another marathon session with me. I had other ideas, however. One minute, she was pegging out some washing. The next, the contractions started, she ran inside and I arrived.

On the blindside, for once.

It was 16 January 1969 and the birth took just 15 minutes from start to finish. No midwife. No doctors. Just my mum and my gran to help deliver me. My dad had rushed out to call the medics. In those days, we didn't have a telephone – it would have cost £20 to get connected, and that was a week's wages – and the phone box at the end of the road was out of order. Luckily, he found a neighbour who did have one and dialled 999. He was outside praying for the cavalry to arrive when he saw the upstairs lights flashing on and off as gran tried frantically to alert him to what was going on.

I had just been born in mum's bedroom. But she had been badly ripped apart inside and she was bleeding heavily. Dad raced upstairs to find her covered in blood from head to toe.

A few minutes later, two ambulances, a car load of doctors and a mobile-operating theatre arrived, together with a midwife.

It was touch and go whether my mum would live. Luckily, a surgeon was on hand and he set up a mini-operating table on the bed and worked on her as she lay there, basically bleeding to death. She's only five foot four, and really slim, and they had to pump pints and pints of blood into her. As a result of all the panic and pandemonium, though, no-one was paying much attention to me and I started going blue. I was icy cold. Eventually, a nurse thought to check on me and that was when they realised I was in trouble too. They warmed me up and did whatever they do to newborns and then handed me to my gran. She sat up all night with me, trying to get me warm. After an hour or so they stabilised my mum and, by the morning, the worst was over.

*

Mum and dad are great people – ordinary, traditional, British parents. My father, Keith, was a paint technician at Rover in Coventry. One of his jobs was to make sure that cars which were being lent out on test to motoring journalists were properly prepared. My mother Vanessa was a secretary at the sprawling car plant. They met in March 1964 and Dad used to walk over from his side of the works to her's in his lunch breaks. He must have had some good lines in chat because they were married just 16 months later.

When they started work, it was actually called Standard-Triumph. That was when Coventry was a major name in the motor industry. Humber, Riley, Chrysler and, of course, Jaguar all made the city famous across the world.

Nowadays, the car plants and the jobs they provided are pretty much a thing of the past, though Peugeot make their 206 at a facility in nearby Ryton and the Jaguar factory is still on the outskirts of the city. A lot of little factories exist just to turn out components for them and for the main Rover plant in Birmingham. But if the French pulled the plug on their Peugeot site and Rover was closed down, the whole area would be in real trouble. I thank God that rugby has given me a good living and a nice home but plenty of the guys I went to school with are out of work or just keeping their heads above water. It's sad. Coventry is my home city and I love the place but its people need work. They really struggle to make ends meet and it pains me to see the city decline like it has. During the war, the car factories had all been turned over to making munitions and tanks and Hitler ordered a Blitz on Coventry. Bombs fell everywhere, wrecking our famous cathedral and killing hundreds of people. The devastation was so complete that they coined a new verb for carpet bombing – 'to coventrate.' Out of the rubble, they built what was then a futuristic new city, made of concrete. Apparently, day-trippers came from miles around in the post-war years to see this fabulous new architecture. Unfortunately, a few years on the concrete was all cracked and grey and the place hasn't changed much over the years since then. I would love to see the city revived.

*

Life wasn't easy for my parents, early on. Rugby is widely perceived as an old school tie sport but you did not earn a king's ransom working at Rover and I went to the local comprehensive like everyone else in my area. Mum and dad always had to be careful with the cash when I was little. Having said that, as kids, we certainly never went without. We had all the sports equipment we wanted and three or four holidays a year – albeit under canvas, or in a caravan.

I'm one of three boys. Ian, a couple of years older than me, is now a hairdresser. Gary, four years my junior, works in assurance. They were both useful rugby players – Ian was a centre, a quick, strong runner, and Gary a mobile flanker, like me. Ian had to call it a day early on because he had to work on Saturdays and he couldn't fit in the matches. Gary still turns out occasionally now but he was never as keen as me. He has always had more of the amateur ethos about him; he loves to turn up and play, and enjoys the social side of the game, but he couldn't hack the rest of it. He has got a lot of talent but the training that modern players undertake would bore him to death. I think discovering girls removed some of his motivation too, though not before he had introduced a good mate of his to the sport. This lad was mooching around our house one day with nothing to do. He had never played rugby but Gary suggested he come along to our local club and try it. The lad ummed and ahhed before agreeing to have a go. It is a good job for England he did: he was Danny Grewcock, now one of the best young locks in the world.

I often wonder how many lads like Danny are lost to sport these days. On the one hand you've got cold, wet, muddy fields. On the other you've got comfy armchairs and Nintendo. It is not hard to see a modern Danny Grewcock opting for *Streetfighter* or *Command and Conquer* instead of bleep tests and scrum machines. The implications for British sport – not just rugby – are serious. Countries like New Zealand and Australia, with their relatively tiny populations, produce such outstanding sportsmen because they are outdoor people. The climate is so good that the youngsters over there are constantly outside and that's where you learn to play and you learn to win.

Back in the distant days of the late 1970s and early 1980s, computer games were pretty much unheard of and parents did not feel edgy about letting their children outdoors like they do now. So it was a constant diet of sport for me, my brothers and our mates.

We were very lucky in our local primary school, Park Hill. We had a games master called Mr Frankish, an athletically-built guy who was well into sport and spent hours with us, in all conditions, encouraging us, teaching us new skills and so on. He was not the only one. Another chap called Mr Briar, our football coach, spent hours of his own time with us. The headmaster, Ken Peach, was in charge of cricket and was another real enthusiast. In those days, sport seemed much more a part of school life and at Park Hill we really enjoyed ourselves. We played against a lot of the other local schools and beat them at most things. We won everything – rounders, football, touch rugby, cricket, you name it. And we loved beating the other kids. Being competitive was not frowned upon, as it seems to be now. Looking back, I seem to have spent half my time on the games field. I wonder how many primary schools today have games masters, or even sports fields? There are plenty of schools, and not just in the inner cities, where all the kids have is a piece of tarmac.

Away from school, there was plenty more of the same. Ian, Gary and I were always intensely competitive. If there was a ball and a gang of lads, we were there. We lived in a semi-detached in a quiet cul-de-sac in the Coventry district of Mount Nod. It was often invaded by hordes of small boys kicking, batting or throwing things. In the summer, we played cricket with a tennis ball, whacking it through clouds of midges until the sun sank over the rooftops. In the winter, we spent every spare minute splashing through the mud on the local school playing fields after a round or oval ball. Poor mum must have kept her washing machine on 24 hours a day cleaning our kit.

When she wasn't doing that, she was rushing me into casualty. No rugby injuries – just horseplay. One time I fell over in the bath and split my head open while I was getting ready to visit my gran. Another time, for some reason best known to myself, I did a forward roll down our stairs and crashed into the plate glass front door. Luckily, my mum's thick velvet curtain protected me from the shards. The curtain was ripped to shreds, though.

I was fortunate to be born with a knack for most ball sports. It's genetic, I think. Although I am the first member of the family to make a living out of it, we're all fairly sporting. My mum was a talented netballer, runner and long jumper and was also good at hockey. My dad was a reasonable schools rugby player and, later, a good golfer. He and his brother, my Uncle Colin, used to spend every spare minute on the golf course in the suburb of Earlsdon as kids, playing before and after school in all weathers. Colin was later Warwickshire Open Champion, in June 1967, and his picture is still on the clubhouse wall and his name on various rolls of honour. I play the odd round with my dad now and I can just about hold my own, usually getting round in the 80s. That's good enough for me. I am not massively into the game, though through rugby I have played in pro-celebrity tournaments on the best courses in the world, often without actually knowing at the time where I was. There have been some excellent golfers in my time in the England team, though. Nick Beal plays off something mad like three and Jerry Guscott, Austin Healey, Matt Dawson and Paul Grayson are all way ahead of me.

My brothers and I all seem to have inherited mum and dad's hand-eye co-ordination. That certainly helped me in cricket, where I played for Warwickshire schools as, I like to think, a hard-hitting middle order batsman and an acrobatic wicket-keeper.

Amazingly, given the controversy over my height, I also played basketball at representative level. I was a ball carrier, moving it up and disputing it, which is important in the game. Admittedly, I might have struggled professionally. Having said that, Alton Bird is only about 5ft 7in or so and he was one of the best ball carriers in the NBA, and a slam-dunking wizard to boot, so who knows? I even managed to get into the Coventry City high diving team.

But my two main loves were soccer and rugby.

I was bitten early by the rugby bug. I got into the game, like so many kids, through an adult who was prepared to spend time on me. In my case, it was a great guy who lived next door to my house. He was called John Smith and he played at Earlsdon, a good junior club side on the south side of Coventry. His son was a year or so older than me and John used to take him over to Earlsdon to play mini-rugby on a Sunday morning. The club was always on the look-out for new youngsters and John asked my dad if my older brother Ian and I could attend coaching sessions. I was five-and-a-half, the best age to start. My dad loves to tell the story of how, a couple of weeks later, John was back at the house begging him and mum to come and watch me because I was 'outstanding'. He was very perceptive! John meant an awful lot to me and I will never forget him.

Earlsdon RFC was a nice, family-oriented club and I stayed there for quite a few years. We used to have coaching most weekends, with little games of touch in between the practising and drills. It felt like there were hundreds of kids there and it was certainly a healthy environment in which to learn. Mum says we looked like a shoal of fish – everywhere the ball went, this gaggle of little boys would turn to follow.

Every now and again, we would get to play games of mini-rugby against other sides, some of them a fair distance away. I remember playing at festivals in Wales and Cornwall and one summer mum and dad hosted a couple of French kids, Ivan and Michelle, from Lyon, whose team came over on an exchange visit. Ivan still sends us Christmas cards now and I went to his wedding in 1994.

I absolutely loved those early years. I even enjoyed the contact, which some young boys don't. I can't speak highly enough of the people at Earlsdon. There were a lot of men and women who gave up almost all of their spare time, coaching kids, transporting them all over the country and even paying for equipment out of their own pockets. It was all done just for the love of rugby and for the enjoyment of seeing youngsters take up the sport.

One of the main people was Jack Carnall – 'Uncle Jack' to me and my brothers. He was a retired teacher who lived for the game. Earlsdon was not wealthy, though it is now, after selling off a large slice of its land for development, and although he cannot have been particularly well-off himself, Jack put a lot of his own money into the club to keep it going. He was very knowledgeable about the game and spent hours helping and guiding us. I particularly used to enjoy tackling practice with Jack. He would kneel down to make himself our height and we would run at him. Looking back, there is no way we could have knocked him over but he used to pretend, to keep our enthusiasm up. He was a stickler for technique. He was always careful to ensure we went in at the right angle, with the arms, head and shoulder in the right positions. It is saying something that the basic drills were the same as those we still do now at international level with Phil Larder, the England defensive coach.

Jack is a magnificent man who has been one of the key influences on my rugby career. He is getting on now but is still going strong. I invited him and his wife Dot, who used to make our teas, to my wedding. It just felt right that they should be there.

Like a lot of the parents at Earlsdon, my mum and dad did their fair share too. They were never the types to stand on the touchline shouting and bawling, living through their children. But they always came to watch and support and they, too, gave up weekends ferrying us and our friends all over the country.

I owe people like John Smith, Jack Carnall and my folks an awful lot for their time and effort in my very early days. You do not always recognise the support you receive and the sacrifices which are made for you when you are young. As a kid, you take it a bit for granted. I have a lot to thank them for. I hope they know how grateful I am.

Those Earlsdon days were great. We had a very successful team and we won a lot of cups and trinkets and, at that age, that is what it is all about. The club has raised a lot of useful players over the years. I think I am the only one of that generation who went on to become professional but a lot of them represented Coventry, Warwickshire and West Midlands at schools level and above. Some of them I still see. One guy called Robin Calloway, who went on to play semi-pro for Coventry in National Division Two, is a real top lad. He is another openside flanker and we had some positional tussles; he always claims I nicked his spot and that he is the one who should be playing for England. 'It could have been me,' he keeps whingeing. But he is half-an-inch shorter than me – far too small to be an international forward!

I stopped playing for Earlsdon soon after I moved to my senior school, The Woodlands Comprehensive in Coventry. Once again, I was lucky in my school. Woodlands was all-boys. There was an all-girls school half a mile away through the woods if you felt like some company but our main preoccupation was sport. Even more than at Park Hill Primary, it was important. Very important. For a state school, the facilities were excellent and we were taught, supported and encouraged by some fantastic teachers.

And I played everything, to a reasonable standard if that doesn't sound too big-headed. There was basketball and cricket – I could have been a professional cricketer, I think, and, who knows, Alec Stewart might have been able to carry on opening the batting for England. Let's face it, I couldn't have done much worse than our middle order has over the last 15 years or so. On the athletics field, I ran the 1500m in around 4min 40sec, was part of our 4x400m relay team and threw the javelin and discus. Of course, rugby played a big part. I was selected as captain and scrum-half for the Woodlands First XV in my age group. All my school and junior rugby was played at No 9, a position I liked. You get your hands on the ball more there and act as the link between the forwards and the backs. It is a good position from which to skipper a side because you are naturally having to make decisions about how to take the play forward. It was only when I stepped up to the representative level, from Coventry Schools on, that I started to play at flanker. I had always admired Jean-Pierre Rives and remember watching him in that fabulous French side as a kid. He was so arrogant and so talented. He was also blond, like me. It seemed only natural that I should switch to his position.

There was just one problem on the horizon. The school rugby teams played some of its games on Saturdays. That left me in something of a quandary. I could either play rugby all weekend or I could leave Earlsdon and fit a bit of footie in. I chose to play soccer on Sundays. At the age of 11, I had no idea I was making a decision which was to shape the rest of my life.

My Sunday football side was Mount Nod FC. They were happy days. A lot of my local friends were in the team and we were pretty good, beating most of the opposition fairly comfortably. Our grudge game was against our local rivals, Chapelfields Colts. We used to have some real mad battles, with studs and shinpads flying everywhere – even the odd fist. Chapelfields were always slightly better than we were, and probably won more matches, but we were harder, and the competition was intense and sometimes painful. My opposite number, Tony 'Dobbo' Dobson went on to become a professional, signing papers with Coventry City, although injury eventually forced him out.

Soccer was a real love. I was a midfielder but I took every opportunity I got to get into the box. I was a fanatical Liverpool fan. My mum gave me a Liverpool scarf one Christmas, while my brother Ian got a Coventry City one, and the loyalties were set there and then. I can remember standing there, pleased as punch, with this Liverpool scarf round my neck, a new leather jacket on and a new skateboard under my arm. Call me a glory supporter if you like, but Coventry City weren't exactly a glamorous team. My bedroom walls were covered in posters and articles cut out from the papers and magazines. Ian, who fancied himself as a bit of an artist, did me a big painting of the club crest. I loved Rushy, Dalglish and Souness – all of them, really. What a team they were in the late 1970s and the 1980s. I used to save my pennies and go to Highfield Road in Coventry every time they came to play City. There were some great games. Coventry usually got pasted and I would taunt the downcast, dejected Cov fans at school the following week. I remember one time we were going on a family outing to Blackpool Pleasure Beach and I managed to persuade mum and dad to do a detour through Liverpool so I could see Anfield. It sent shivers down my spine passing the gates. Earlier, we had stopped at a petrol station on the way into the city and I had got out of the car, knelt down and kissed the tarmac. I must have looked barmy but as far as I was concerned, we were on sacred ground.

Liverpool have been through a long lean patch, which started with the Heysel Stadium disaster and carried on through many disappointments on the pitch and the horror of Hillsborough off it. By their own high standards, they spent too long as a mediocre side. But I am glad to see that Gerard Houllier has them playing as a team again and I reckon they will be back as Champions in the not-so-distant future.

At that stage – early teens – I don't think I really thought my future lay with the oval ball, although I remember when I first went to Woodlands the teacher asked us all to stand up and tell the class what we wanted to do when we were older. I said I was going to play rugby for England. The whole room fell about, teacher included. The crunch came in my third year at senior school when I was 13 and I was invited to attend the Coventry Schools trials in soccer and rugby, held at the private King Henry's School in the city. I can't remember being nervous, although I suppose I must have been. I certainly recall being amazed and delighted when I was selected for both the soccer and the rugby sides. I couldn't play for both so I had to choose.

This was where my decision to play soccer on Sundays moulded my future.

Coventry's representative sides in both sports played on Saturdays. Because I was already playing football on Sundays I opted to play for Cov Schools at rugby on the Saturday.

It was my first taste of representative sport which really fired me up and if it had come in association football instead of rugby football I am sure I would have tried to make a career in that sport. I might never have been good enough, although if I had I would now be a bit less battered and a lot more wealthy. Even so, and even with all the money that's now flooding into the Carling Premiership these days, I have never for a moment regretted the way things turned out. But it is amazing how a seemingly unimportant decision made at the age of 11 can alter the course of your life.

From that point on, soccer became more a recreation. I still enjoyed it, but I started to get deadly serious about my rugby and I jacked in the footie after a year or so. It helped that Woodlands had a very good side with a number of guys who I consider could have gone a lot further in the sport. And there was plenty of competition, some of it with needle attached, in inter-school games in Coventry. It is very much a working class city but it has two private schools, Bablake and King Henry VIII. At that time, they prided themselves on their sporting traditions. We stuffed both of them at virtually every opportunity when I was there and we loved every minute of it.

There were a few cups on offer, like the Coventry FC Shield – an under-15 trophy presented by the once-mighty city club, which produced England players like the great David Duckham and Keith Fairbrother, to the local Schools Rugby Union in 1897. In 1984, Woodlands made it to the Shield final against Henry's, with me as captain. Bablake and Henry's had shared the spoils since 1970, with the former winning five times and the latter four. They had shared a draw in 1983. Woodlands was the only comprehensive school which had competed during that period, winning on the other four occasions.

There was always a buzz around the game, which was played at Coventry's Coundon Road ground in front of a decent crowd and a photographer from the local *Evening Telegraph*. The private school lads hated losing to us as much as we enjoyed beating them and it the 1984 game was as hard-fought a contest as any, until we pulled away in the second half. I managed to score a try, a conversion and two penalties in a convincing 19-6 win and a lad called Lee Jones got a pushover. We made it into the paper and there was a picture of me dwarfed by this huge shield with a boy behind me waving a bottle of cider. Smiles all round. I liked the feeling of winning.

The following year, we were in the under-16 competition playing for the Robert Askill Memorial Trophy, provided by the family of a promising lad who had represented Coventry, West Midlands and England schools before dying tragically young.

Once again, we faced King Henry VIII and, once again, we beat them, this time 16–0. Again, it was at Coundon Road and, again, it was a thrill playing on what felt like a big stage.

By then, I had started playing club rugby again, joining Barkers' Butts, a good junior side with a long history of producing players and teams of quality. Danny Grewcock and Leon Lloyd are two other Barkers' boys on the current England scene.

I know there were one or two people in the Earlsdon set-up who thought I had been unfairly poached but it really wasn't like that. The fact was, it was my decision. Most of my friends were playing for Barkers', a far stronger side than Earlsdon, where I hadn't played for three years anyway. To cap it all, Bob Coward, the club president, was a Warwickshire selector and I wanted to catch his eye.

I had a great two or three years at my new club. The rugby was hard and I was improving all the time, playing against good sides and really learning my craft: how to win the ball in broken play, how to ruck and maul, how to be first to the breakdown. Once again, there were plenty of people prepared to give up their spare time, coaching, advising, fetching and carrying.

I remember being most impressed by a lad called Jason Minshull. Jason was a year older than me and he got capped for England schools before I did. At that time, England used to have these hideous purple tracksuits – I mean truly hideous. You could only get one by being selected because there were no replicas and having one meant you had arrived. Jason used to strut round the club wearing his lurid purple kit, driving me mad with jealousy. It really spurred me on until I got mine. My selection for England schools also opened my eyes to the class system within rugby. Most of the guys in that side were from public schools. At one of the early games, my parents were approached by a very posh-sounding chap who wanted to know where I was at school. When they said 'The Woodlands' he looked a bit puzzled. 'Oh?' he said. 'I don't think I've actually *heard* of The Woodlands.' At other times, the bias towards privately-educated lads was less amusing. I had played extremely well in a game against Wales, scoring a try, but was dropped for our next match in favour of a lad with a double-barrelled name. There had been a behind-the-scenes deal that he ought to get a game because of his background. To be fair to this boy, he actually came up to me and said: 'You should be playing instead of me, Neil'. I kept my composure until I got into my parents car. As soon as we drove away, I cried my eyes out. It was the first time I had been dropped from any team. Thankfully, that sort of attitude has no place in the professional game.

In my early days at Barkers' I also discovered girls – lots of them. But I tried to avoid getting too serious. Girlfriends can come between you and sport if you are not careful. I have seen some potentially great players fall away from the game because they are getting grief over the training from their other half. I was always too dedicated to my rugby for that to be a risk to me, though. I can count my serious relationships on the fingers of one hand, though there were quite a few less serious ones along the way.

I met my wife, Alison, when we worked for AXA Equity and Law in Coventry. I fancied her from day one and pursued her for about six months without any joy. The trouble was, I had had the odd fling with other girls who worked there – hard not to, when 75 per cent of the workforce is female and aged between 18 and 30 – and I had a bit of a reputation so she played hard to get for a while. In the end, she agreed to come out with me with the idea that she would ditch me straight away if she didn't like me, proving that I couldn't have anyone I wanted (not something I actually thought, anyway!). Obviously, I was incredibly charming and she soon changed her mind. The rest, as they say, is history.

I had joined AXA after finishing my A levels. I considered university – I went as far as putting in my applications forms – but in the end I knew I wanted to play rugby and a degree doesn't help you do that. AXA have always been supporters of sport and the arrangement was that I could take time off to play in games. It caused some friction in the office. There were those people who felt it was unfair that Neil Back was allowed to miss days because he was playing a sport. They had no idea how much toil, sweat and sheer graft work I put in to my game. If they had been prepared to work like I did, who knows, they could have been in my position. By the time rugby went professional, I had been promoted to a managerial position, as had Alison. I loved the job, managing people and figures. I had taken maths at A level and really enjoyed calculating the end of month returns for my team of 10. Ali was well aware of the time rugby took up and her eyes were wide open when we started going out shortly after England returned from the 1995 Rugby World Cup in South Africa. She has always been incredibly supportive and has made my life a hell of a lot easier. I stick very closely to a diet and I spend a lot of time training. Alison backs me up all the way.

Back at Barkers', I met another guy who has had a tremendous influence on my life and to whom I owe a hell of a lot. Peter Lloyd was a club stalwart, a real gentleman and a great friend who did a lot for all us youngsters. He was involved seven days a week, taking kids to games, organising, keeping the bar in business. His son, Tim, played at Barkers' and his wife Anne was always there with him, too. When I was travelling all over the country for trials and so on, and mum and dad were at work, Lloydy used to drive me everywhere. He is very knowledgeable about rugby and he is a great scout, which is what, effectively, he has now become for Leicester. He recently introduced Leon Lloyd – no relation – to the Tigers and, as with me, he drove him everywhere in the period before Leon was taken on.

In 1990 and Peter had just retired from his job as a bank manager. Anne had also retired and they had plans to spend a lot of time together. Then, six months in, she died very suddenly. He couldn't go back to Barkers' Butts because he had spent his life there with Anne and it was too painful – in fact, he has never been back – so I spent well over a year taking him to Tigers games and training sessions with me to keep his mind occupied. It was the least I could do after all he had done for me.

He has become a legendary figure with a lot of the Leicester and England lads. He knows everyone and has travelled the world watching me and watching the side. He has been to Hong Kong twice for the Sevens, to Australia and he also went out to South Africa for the Lions Tour. We are very close and we talk all the time. Along with Bob Coward and Jack Carnall, he was an honoured guest at my wedding.

*

I was really growing in the game now, season by season. The soccer had fallen by the wayside and I was beginning to be known as something of a training fanatic. I had set up a gym in my mum's attic and bought a job lot of second-hand weights. I spent many hours up there trying to develop my physique and improve my fitness. I clearly had some ability, too. By 18, people were starting to suggest I should try for a move to a senior club. I had my doubts because, in a sport like rugby, even a talented teenager can struggle against blokes in their mid to late 20s. But deep down, I knew it was time to move on. It was just a question of finding a club which was interested.

Everyone thought I would go to Coventry. It was almost as though it was expected of me – there was even a story on the back page of the *Coventry Evening Telegraph* stating as fact that I was going to Coundon Road, when no-one had even asked me. In the end, they never made a move and Nottingham did, through Jim Robinson. He had been the Coventry coach and knew me from the local scene. He was going up the M1 with one of Coventry's players, Lee Johnson and he asked me to go with them. The East Midlands club was then a powerful force in English rugby, with major stars like Rob Andrew, Brian Moore and other internationals in the team's ranks. Importantly, the No 7 spot was occupied by Gary Rees, who shared the England openside duties with Peter Winterbottom. I agreed to join Jim. A major motivating factor was my desire to play for the England under-21 team. I had played at Schools and Colts level but the word was that to be considered for higher honours you needed to be playing for a senior club.

The first season at Nottingham went reasonably well and I did get chosen for the under-21s, making my debut against Romania in May 1989. I also made a few first team appearances at Nottingham, though most of the season was spent on the bench. That was fine. I didn't expect to kick Gary Rees out of the side and I was happy deputising for him, learning my trade on the sidelines.

By the second season, though, I wanted a full-time place in the first team. I felt I was a better player than Gary by that point and I raised the matter with the club. But it quickly became clear they were not going to pick me ahead of their local hero and long-standing club servant, which was fair enough. They did offer to play us left and right, which means you swap between open and blindside during the game, depending on the position of the play on the field, but this was no good to me. I was an openside, and that was it. Added to that, I was fed up with the hour's drive over from Coventry. I had a little MG sports car which was highly unreliable, so for two years I had shared lifts with Lee Johnson. But now he was quitting the club. I thought about that MG, those long, wintry journeys and the bench splinters in my shorts. For sure, it was time to be off.

It was around then that Dean Richards started making enquiries about me. The Leicester Tigers were a First Division club, a top outfit and Richards, at that time the world's leading No 8, was a rugby god. He called me at home one day and suggested I ought to consider the short move south, which was incredibly flattering. But it was Tony Russ, the England under-21 manager, and Matt Poole, a fellow member of that representative side, who really made the decision for me. Tony was taking over at Leicester as first XV coach and he and Pooley assured me that I would play in the main team from day one. Ian 'Dosser' Smith was retiring from the openside position and becoming forwards coach. While there were other guys at the club, they were actively looking for fresh blood. Playing at

Leicester would also put me in the shop window for an England B cap. It was closer to home, which meant shorter journeys, and it offered the opportunity of playing in a back row which contained John Wells and Dean Richards. It was hard to turn all that down.

'Hard' became 'impossible' when I attended a Tigers match ironically, against Nottingham for whom I had not been selected. I stood on the concrete terracing alongside 15,000 other Leicester fans. The atmosphere was fantastic and, as I left the ground, I knew I would be back.

In stripes.

CHAPTER 2

Endless Wait

CALL ME an eternal optimist. Call me over-ambitious, or a madman, but I expected to get my full England call-up a year or so after I joined Leicester. I had gone straight into the first team at Welford Road and had stayed there ever since, proving my ability alongside Deano and Wellsy. There were fewer bigger tests in club rugby. I had also had a good run in the under-21 side. I was sure of my own ability, to the point of arrogance some commentators felt. I thought I'd soon be chosen for the B team and that a senior cap would quickly follow.

There were three other genuine opensides in my way.

Nottingham's Gary Rees was a talented guy who eventually won 23 caps but he was already in his 30s and he would play his last Test, as it turned out, in November 1991. I felt I had overtaken him before I had left Nottingham. Peter Winterbottom had been the man in possession for most of the 1980s. A truly great openside, and a hard, uncompromising and skilful Yorkshireman who you would want on your side in a bar room brawl, he was a man I measured myself against. Again, though, he was at the tail-end of what had been a fantastic career, which eventually saw him claim 58 caps between 1982 and 1993. While I would hate to have been going up against Wints at the peak of his powers, he was inevitably on the downward slope. The third alternative was the Bath flanker Andy Robinson.

Robbo, now my coach with England, was another player I respected greatly and a genuine openside on whom I had modelled my game in my early days. He was a hell of a tough nut and a good player with a massive will to win but he had never quite established himself as the national No 7 (he went on to win eight caps spread between June 1988 and November 1995). He was also three or four years older than me, which surely went in my favour. Maybe it does sound arrogant, but I believe you have to back your own ability. I have to admit that I rated myself as at least his equal and maybe as having the better all-round game by that stage. As far as I could see, there was no-one else on the horizon. I ought to have been in line for a quick call-up.

But in the background lurked the issue that was to dominate the early days of my career: my size.

England manager Geoff Cooke had raised the question on the day I made my England under-21 debut, against Romania in Bucharest. Played on a baking hot, 100°F day in May 1989, there was a shimmering heat-haze distorting the concrete-hard pitch and you could have roasted turkeys in the bowl-like stadium which surrounded the field.

The senior England management were out there because the full side was to play Romania too and I was determined to impress. I did have a good game. A few critics agreed. Forgive me for quoting from one review in *The Sunday Times*, but it does help to paint an independent picture of my contribution. Describing my 'amazing' appearance as 'a staggering entrance to international rugby', the journalist added: 'He kept up a relentless, pounding pace in support, was electric while the others were sluggish' (something Matt Poole hotly disputes!). I also read later that Don Rutherford, the long-serving technical director at Twickenham, had described my showing as the 'finest piece of sustained forward play' he had ever seen. High praise indeed.

I scored a hat-trick of tries in a 58–3 victory, including two stolen from the aforementioned 'Ponty' Poole, my friend and future Tigers team-mate. The first one came from a lineout. As we won the ball, Pooley managed to break clear about 30 yards out. It is hard to imagine now, but in those days he could shift and he was fairly haring towards the line, head down, blowing like a bull elephant. I came up on his left shoulder and shouted that the Romanians were catching him. Being a good team man, and a somewhat trusting soul, he did not look but just offloaded immediately, only to watch me sail in under the posts with none of the opposition in sight. He was, naturally enough, hopping mad. Ten minutes later, he broke free from a maul and slipped the defence again. This time, he was around 35 yards out, on the other side of the field.

I sprinted up behind him and seconds from the line I shouted: 'Pooley, they're on you, pass it!'

He just yelled 'Bollocks are they, Backy!' and carried on.

'No,' I shouted, 'they really are this time! Quick!'

And poor old Matt, without looking again, offloaded it over his right shoulder. He turned his head just to see me go by, cackling so much I could hardly run. Another one, under the posts. Pooley was furious, though he would have done the same to me and he now dines out on the tale. After the game I was on cloud nine, having chalked up another score to make it three. I celebrated long into the night in a seedy Romanian nightclub, naïvely sure I had finally made it.

Admittedly, the wind was taken out of my sails slightly when Jerry Guscott, making his debut alongside Wints in the senior game, scored a hat-trick too. Three in an under-21 game suddenly did not sound *quite* so impressive.

However, I was on a high. I came down to earth with a bump a day or two later when I was chatting about the game with some of the boys and one of them said he had overheard Geoff Cooke talking. 'Back had a good game,' Cooke had said, 'but he is too small to make it in senior rugby.'

And that was it. Written off by the England manager in a few dismissive words, words that, typically I later discovered, he had not had the guts to say to my face. It was my first serious hint that further progress in life was not going to be easy.

The day after my hat-trick gave me another insight into the way Geoff Cooke's mind worked. I was walking towards the team hotel when I realised Cooke was coming the other way. We looked at each other and I thought I had better work out what to say to him. He was sure to congratulate me on my three tries and I did not want to make a fool of myself by mumbling back some gibberish. A second later, Cooke looked away and just walked straight by. It was an object lesson in how to ruin a young player's day. At the very least you would expect a nod and a curt 'Well done!': maybe you would even get a smile and a handshake. Not from Geoff Cooke. As I later learned, this was par for his particular course.

But it was his remarks about my size which really irritated me. It was only the second time this had been mentioned as a negative issue. The first time was back when I was 18. Before then, it had never been raised, probably because at 16 you tend to be all of a similar height, whereas at 18 there is a lot of difference between a lad who is going to end up 5ft 10in tall and one who is going to end up 6ft 6in tall. You do a lot of growing between the ages of 16 and 18. I had played England Schools and Colts and I had been attending summer rugby workshops at a college in Nottingham every year from about 16. They invited a few internationals down to coach and you were there for a week.

These courses were an absolute nightmare: they ran us ragged from dawn until dusk, 'beasting' us in the Army slang. You almost wished your mum and dad had booked a holiday which you had to go on so you would have a ready-made excuse not to go.

During one of these weeks, a Leicester and England schools coach called Chalky White took me on one side. I was 18, I was 5ft 10in tall and I weighed 12½ stones. I was pretty much as tall as I was going to be. Chalky looked me up and down with an earnest expression. It was obvious he had something to tell me but that he didn't like having to say it. 'Look Neil,' he said. 'You're not the biggest lad around and we think you should consider a switch. Back rows are getting bigger and bigger these days. Maybe you could try scrum-half?'

I was so gutted I had to turn away. I had played scrum-half all through my school days but my heart was not in a change of position. I had been selected to play for England at No 7 at every age level to that point and to my mind I was the best openside in the country for my age. Were they now kicking me out just because of my size? I felt sure that if I tried to change I would be walking away from a position I had made my own and, effectively, walking away from the team. Clearly, I was not the best scrum-half in England for my age and there were no guarantees of a place if I switched.

It was true that international back rows were taller and heavier. Some were monsters, probably four or five inches taller and two or three stones heavier than me, and that meant I could not be a back row. It was like a mathematic equation: 6ft 4in + 16 stones = openside flanker, whereas 5ft 10in + 12½st = half-back. The fact that these guys were often just big lumps didn't seem to enter Chalky's mind. He was a great coach at Leicester and I have the utmost respect for his record. But when it came to me it seemed he was ignoring the evidence of his own eyes. I am sure he meant well, though. I think he was worried I would suffer at the hands of bigger men later on in my career.

Now, from Cooke's off-hand remark a couple of years later, it seemed he was not the only one who doubted me. Hearing it from Chalky White at a youth training session was one thing. Hearing that the England manager felt the same way, after he had watched me against Romania, was another thing altogether.

For a few days, it was as though my world had fallen apart. All I had wanted to do, since the day I had stood up in front of the class way back in school, was play for England. It consumed my every thought, my every waking moment. I had all but turned my back on a social life, preferring to spend hours sweating and hurting in my mum's attic and in local gyms to be as fit and as strong as I could be. I had even passed up the possibility of a place at university, to study art, of all things, in the cause. To hear yourself being cast aside in two words – 'too small' – after all that effort and all that sacrifice was almost too much to bear.

I almost sought out Cooke and confronted him but somehow I calmed down.

It was not as though he would always be England manager. And anyway, I was sure I could prove him wrong.

And, in fact, it was not long before I was asked to take a further step forward.

My final game for Nottingham, on March 31 1990, saw me touch down twice as we beat Harlequins at The Stoop. A month later, I was part of an England XV which took on Italy in Rovigo. I played well in that game too, and I scored a try, even though Rob Andrew dived on top of me and tried to claim it as the senior pro! The only dampener on a fantastic day was that we were not awarded caps. That was very disappointing. The Italian players were capped, however, and, in my heart, I still consider that was my full international debut. The excuse for not capping us was that the game was only a friendly. In my opinion, friendlies are a nonsensical, and non-existent, concept in international rugby. I would like to have seen a few of the RFU committee men on the field. They might have changed their definition of 'friendly' with a 20st Italian prop's studs raking their heads.

After a while I became more relaxed about what Cooke had said. I had now been picked to represent England, after all. Maybe his words had been misheard? Maybe he had changed his mind? Maybe, just maybe, I would be selected again, this time for the Five Nations. Fresh from the Italy game, I was determined to make the No 7 spot in the England side my own.

Little did I know that precious first cap was four long years away.

*

That summer, I prepared for my move from Nottingham to Leicester. I spent every spare moment working on my fitness, training like a demon. I was determined to hit the ground running at Welford Road. And I did. On September 1, I made my Tigers debut, scoring a try against Bedford. I made my league debut against Gloucester three weeks later and played well again. I had made a dream start with my new club and felt confident that I would soon be noticed.

The year was capped when I achieved a personal ambition when I received an invitation to play for the Barbarians at the end of September 1990. What was more, it was to be against England, in the Ba-Bas' Centenary fixture at Twickenham. It is one of rugby's greatest honours to be invited, as a non-capped player, to turn out for this great old touring side. The Ba-Bas are steeped in history. A nomadic club, which has no clubhouse or ground, they were formed in 1890 by a Blackheath player and *bon viveur* called Percy Carpmael after a boozy night out. Their legendary black-and-white hooped shirts, bearing the Barbarian Football Club monogram on the chest, have graced virtually every rugby ground around the world since then. The roll call of world stars who have pulled on the Ba-Ba jersey is breathtaking, great names like W W Wakefield and David Duckham, Cliff Morgan and Gareth Edwards, Sean Fitzpatrick and Jonah Lomu. Their open, attacking, free-flowing play has won fans around the globe. It was a style I could fit into.

The England selectors would be among the 70,000 watching and I would be facing up to the best my country could throw at me. Impress, and I might win that place in the Five Nations line-up.

Some of my team-mates that day would go on to be true legends: guys like the Wallabies David Campese, Nick Farr-Jones and Michael Lynagh and the All Black Ian Jones. England played Peter Winterbottom at No 7, replacing him with Gary Rees during the game when he picked up an injury. I was a replacement too, coming on for the Frenchman Karl Janik. I managed to put on a reasonable display and had a hand in one of the all-time great tries, a 90-yarder touched down by Phil Davies and involving eight players. I was lucky enough to be in the right place twice – firstly to link between Eric Rush and Joe Stanley and then to receive the ball from Campo as he ran out of space on the wing, passing to Farr-Jones who, in turn, passed to Davies. I earned some nice reviews in the process. In *The Daily Telegraph*, John Mason said: 'Neil Back, the pocket-sized Hercules among English back row forwards, spent barely half an hour sprinting here, there and everywhere at Twickenham. The impact of his deeds in that period will resound for considerably longer.' Alan Fraser, in *The Independent*, wrote: 'Neil Back has a glittering career. He has genuine pace. Back is the future.' Tony Bodley, in the *Daily Express*, reckoned that 'Neil Back, a husky 21-year-old Coventry assurance official, has become an overnight star in a film epic that will run and run.'

We lost the match 18–16, but Geoff Cooke was also complimentary in the papers. He told Bodley: 'The game was tailor-made for Neil. He came on fresh after half-time and it was fast and furious. He is a talent we are pleased to have even though he did us considerable damage in that try.'

One telling footnote; John Reason's piece had gone on to say: 'Back, according to RFU figures, is a fraction over 5ft 8in tall and edging 13st.' Swiping two inches and about 10lb off me with the stroke of a pen, John, for all his well-meaning descriptions of me as a 'pocket-sized Hercules', was clearly another person who considered me a touch small for the international arena. That size issue would dog me for years to come.

Nevertheless, I was delighted after the game. The try was shown on countless newscasts that evening and analysed repeatedly on *Rugby Special*.

However, despite Cooke's words, the 1991 Five Nations came and went without me. But I had a good season for Leicester, racked up some England B caps and played for the Barbarians again in the Hong Kong Sevens in March of that year. My performances kept the pot boiling and there was even some talk in the media that I might make the 1991 World Cup squad. I would, frankly, have been astonished if that had happened but it was nice to be talked about by some good judges of the game. Instead, I ended up playing for Midlands, clinching the ADT Divisional Championship on the day England beat France. Afterwards, I was interviewed by a reporter for my local paper, the *Coventry Evening Telegraph*. He asked how I felt about my England future. I told him I was confident that I would be given a chance sooner rather than later. But I said it was obvious that England's victory over France, in which Peter Winterbottom had played well, had proved the selectors right in picking Peter, adding: 'I'm twenty-two and Peter Winterbottom is thirty-two so hopefully my time will come. I'll just keep on trying.'

It did not come that winter. And that 1991/1992 season was when I first really started to become frustrated by being ignored by England. More England B caps, including a 1992 summer tour to New Zealand, came my way, along with more Ba-Bas games. I had an excellent season with Leicester, proving myself against the best the country had to offer. I trained hard in the evenings and on Sundays and hoped for the phone to ring or the letter from the RFU to drop on to the mat. But not a whisper came from the senior England set-up. Instead, the papers kept harping on about my size and a few journalists implied that Cooke had told them it was a killer handicap for me.

The months of waiting dragged by. I was young and impatient and I feared I would never get my opportunity. My family and friends had to put up with hours of soul-searching.

The support I had during these years from fans and the press was fantastic and I am truly grateful for it. Brendan Gallagher, in *The Daily Telegraph*, was one who had some nice things to say about me in 1991, describing me as a 'prodigious talent' and predicting: 'His England call will come, as night follows day.'

I have boxes and boxes of cuttings at home, kept for me by my parents. Most journalists backed me. It kept me going when I might have fallen by the wayside. People said I was the most talked about non-international ever in terms of column inches. I was regularly selected in columnists' England teams before senior international fixtures and a lot of supporters and people in the game were telling me my time had arrived.

I desperately hoped they were right.

While it is a fantastic honour to play for England A, or B as it was beforehand, and it is almost an essential part of learning your trade, it is like low alcohol beer: it only has half the flavour of the real thing and it is barely a quarter as intoxicating. Eventually, you want to move on. You crave the big crowds that attend the senior side, the ultimate recognition of your hard work and talent. I watched lots of guys come and go out of the A team to the full side. Martin Johnson was the first, I think, because Wade Dooley had to pull out in the lead-up to a game against the French. We were in a meeting at Leicester when Johnno shuffled in, looking a bit embarrassed. He said, very weakly: 'I've got to go to Twickenham.' I will never forget that. So off he trotted and was, of course, outstanding. The likes of Tony Underwood, also from Leicester, and Tim Rodber, from Northampton, followed him while I sat on the sidelines, as frustrated as hell, destined, apparently, to end up as England's most capped A player.

When I sat and thought about it logically, certainly in the very early days, I could reconcile it in my head. For years, the three outstanding 7s in the country had been Robinson, Rees and Winterbottom. They were all older than me and had bags more experience, with a massive number of caps between them. As a 20-year-old, I could understand them keeping me out. As they and I got older, however, I could no longer accept it. I began to feel I ought to be stepping up and into their shoes.

Yet the 1992/1993 season came and went. I played for the Ba-Bas against the All Blacks in Cardiff (we lost 12–25) and against them again for the Midlands (we lost 6–12). I played for England A against France and Italy, and later joined the three-match tour of Canada with England A. The newspaper writers continued to press my case for inclusion. And Geoff Cooke continued to ignore them.

At the end of that 1992/1993 season, Peter Winterbottom was retiring. His final game was against me, when Leicester met Harlequins in the 1993 Cup final. We won the match and ruined Peter's swansong, which was a shame in a way. He is a nice guy, quite reserved, and still involved with the game with the Professional Rugby Players' Association. I have tremendous respect for him.

With Peter gone, and with my fitness, strength and experience improving all the time, surely my time had come? Wints certainly thought so. Speaking to *The Mirror*, he described me as 'the best openside flanker in England' and urged Cooke to pick me, citing my pace and ability to win the ball in the loose. Ex-All Blacks skipper Buck Shelford told *The Sunday Express* that I should be selected and nailed the size debated by saying: 'He may be a shortie but he's a flyer.'

In October 1993, just before the announcement of the England squad to play the All-Blacks the following month, Leicester took on Wasps at Welford Road. We inflicted one of their heaviest defeats ever, winning by 38 points to six. I scored a try and believe it was one of my best performances ever. One of those watching was the rugby writer Stephen Jones of *The Sunday Times*. He wrote: '(Back) had an astonishing game. He seemed to be first to every breakdown. He popped up in the midfield, around the scrum and even out on the wing . . . He contributed three kicks in contrasting styles, all effective. This was a classic effort for a flanker in the modern game.' David Llewellyn was of similar opinion in *The Daily Mail*, writing: 'If his performance against Wasps . . . is anything to go by, his will be the first name on Cooke's team sheet.' I was even described as 'a class above' some guy called Lawrence Dallaglio, then playing No 7.

They do not pick the team but unlike their sensationalist soccer colleagues, rugby writers are a serious bunch and they rarely seem far from the mark. On this occasion, though, they were wrong.

Cooke did not listen. Instead, he chopped and changed

between three Bath guys: Ben Clarke, Steve Ojomoh and Andy Robinson.

Ben was a converted No 8 or blindside who did not even want the job. He is a world class back rower but he's not a No 7. Because of his size he lacks the mobility which I believe is essential to the position. He played at openside for the Lions in 1993 and had a good tour but I still feel he was never a natural on that side of the pack.

Steve Ojomoh, another massive bloke, was potentially a marvellous player. No-one could question his mobility or pace: he was an explosive athlete who clocked 3.94sec over 30 metres against what was the then-England back row average time of 4.35sec. But I wondered about his ultimate commitment and felt he was even a little lazy. He wasn't even his club's first choice on the openside and had been kind enough to suggest in an interview that I should get the nod for that season's Five Nations.

Andy Robinson was the man keeping Ojomoh out of the No 7 spot down at the Recreation Ground. Robbo certainly had the edge over all of us in experience but, as I have said, I thought that by that stage I was at least his equal and certainly a better long-term bet because of my age.

None of the three really worked, a fact emphasised by the chopping and changing and by the fact Cooke was now considering trying Tim Rodber, another big guy, at openside.

In another *Sunday Times* piece, the highly-respected duo of Stephen Jones and Mark Reason summed up the issue thus: 'The key to the succession lies in the Great Back Debate. This house believes that size isn't everything. Or is it? Neil Back is the most discussed player in the whole of England, the David Gower of the sport. He would be the people's choice . . .'

Sadly, the people did not pick the side.

For the best part of a decade that job fell to two men who seemed dead set against me.

CHAPTER 3

Geoff Cooke and Jack Rowell

GEOFF Cooke and Jack Rowell robbed me of years of international rugby and the honour of representing my country on many more occasions than I have. I firmly believe I should have been playing for England from the early 1990s and their failure to select me deprived me of many caps.

Cooke gave me just two chances to prove myself, and Rowell three.

Not only that, on the occasions they had dealings with me, and other up-and-coming players, I found them narrow-minded, unimaginative and downright rude. They had no desire, it seemed, to create a happy atmosphere. They had little interest in listening to players' views about how we should play. I certainly never felt able to throw in my four penn'orth, anyway. My biggest complaint about the both of them is their failure to communicate with me, to take the time to explain their selection decisions. You accept the coach's decision – that's why he is there – but you can't accept the silent treatment.

In the wider picture, they lacked any kind of innovative tactical vision and they were weak when it came to selection. The issue about my size was blown up into such a talking point by the media during the early part of the 1990s that I think each one of them bottled it when it came to giving me a fair run. I feel their involvement in the game set English rugby back years in comparison to the Southern Hemisphere sides and it is only recently that we have started to claw back the lost ground.

*

My two chances with Cooke came when he selected me for my first two Tests in the 1994 Five Nations, against Scotland and Ireland. In desperation, I had started a new training regime designed to put on a stone – the details are later in this book – in an attempt to quash the size issue. It seemed to have worked.

Just as he had ignored me four years previously in Romania, he again made absolutely no attempt to make me feel welcome. As a young player, new to the international scene and nervous as hell, I expected him to help me settle in and explain how things were done.

Instead, he hardly even *spoke* to me in the time I spent with England under him.

I don't need leading by the nose but it seems only sensible that he would make the effort to shake you by the hand and say something like 'Well done, you've made it to international rugby. Now we want to make sure you stay there. This is what we are looking for from the team and this is what I want from you. These are your strengths, these are the areas of your game I feel you need to work on.'

At my first team meeting with him there was no tactical discussion to speak of – certainly none involving me, even though openside flanker is an important position tactically. His only reference to me was to say: 'Neil Back, seven.'

Even in training Cooke wasn't a hands-on motivator, like other managers and coaches I have come across. Forwards tactics were handled in a group, sitting round a blackboard with the senior players running things. That's okay, but why have coaching staff?

It seemed to me that he was more bothered about keeping those senior players happy and talking to them. A good manager identifies older and more experienced heads and uses them as sounding boards for ideas. But as soon as that becomes a five or six-strong clique you have got problems.

The record books show that I made just those two appearances in the '94 tournament before Cooke decided my services were no longer required.

Strangely, I had no nerves as I walked out for the first game against Scotland. The weather was fine and the pitch firm. It was a good day for running the ball: exactly the tactics we had decided on pre-match. I knew I was fit and I had confidence I could do my job. I felt as though I belonged.

Early on, we showed a lot of flair. In one move I had a hand in, we spun the ball wide to Tony Underwood in space but he was standing slightly flat and the pass went behind him. The momentum was gone and, with it, the possibility of a corner flag score. It would have been the perfect start but from then on we struggled, only winning 13–12 with a last minute John Callard penalty. I had a fairly good game – nothing to write home about, but I was competent and busy. Unfortunately we had departed fairly rapidly from the game plan. Every time we got the ball, we hoofed it at the Scots and they kicked it straight back. It was like ping-pong and I remember thinking as I watched another enormous kick sail overhead that if we were going to play like this Cooke might as well pick a big back row. I hardly touched the ball and I had no opportunity to use my abilities at all.

Before the Ireland game, we had a similar team talk. We would look for quick ball from phase, and use the width of the field, exploiting the pace of our back row. Instead, it was like Scotland all over again. The only difference was that this time we lost. Rob Andrew just sat back in the pocket and kicked up and down the field. Never mind cricketers bribing people to throw games, I would liked to have bribed the team to throw a few passes.

Again, though I hadn't played badly I could not shine in that type of game. Still, I felt that I was edging my way into the international scene.

In those days, the England senior side stayed at the Petersham Hotel in Richmond. There was a walk you never wanted to take and it was up the hill to the Richmond Gate Hotel where the A team was always billeted. I found out in the next team selection meeting, before the France game, that I was taking that walk, together with four other guys. I vowed to myself that we would get stuck in to the French and get back down that bloody hill but we were awful and we lost.

I also vowed not to get too downhearted. The mature thing is to accept the coach's decision. The one thing you do expect, though, is communication.

You might assume Cooke would place a fatherly arm around the shoulder of the disappointed young player, reassuring him he was not to be forgotten and maybe identifying an area or two where the guy might improve.

You would be mistaken. There was no explanation as to why I had been dropped and no words of support. He didn't even have a word with Dosser Smith at Leicester to explain the decision to him. He just announced it in our selection meeting in a matter-of-fact way: 'Back, A team.'

Maybe I should have made some sort of attempt to contact Cooke and ask him why I had been dropped. I would certainly do that now if Clive Woodward selected someone else at openside. But I didn't bother because, as a new cap, part of me did not want to overstep the mark and part of me was waiting for the call from him. It never came. I just expected that a man in that position would do the right thing and communicate with his players. Obviously, I was naïve.

When it eventually dawned on me that there was to be no letter or phone call, I concentrated on doing my best for Leicester, determined to fight for my England place.

But the newspapers were still full of stories that Cooke thought I was too small for the modern game and, after a while, I realised I was unlikely to make it back in while he was still at the helm.

Indeed, I did not play for the senior side again under him. But

I didn't have to wait too long for a new manager to arrive.

After the 1994 tournament, Cooke was gone, replaced by the Bath coach Jack Rowell.

Rowell had selected me at No 7 often enough during his time in charge of England B and A sides. At one point, he had even taken me on one side and reassured me that, as far as he was concerned, I was his first choice for those teams. He was going round telling everyone who would listen that he wanted his England to play a quick, expansive game. That suited my style to a tee. What was more, Rowell knew all about smaller flankers: the Bath openside, after all, was Andy Robinson.

Maybe, just maybe, my time had come.

Unfortunately, I soon discovered that, for all his fancy talk, Rowell was just another guy who seemed to be obsessed with my height. And he was another gem of a non-communicator. So at first the Rowell era was business as usual for me, as I played for England A all through 1995 Five Nations and heard hardly a peep out of the manager.

The 1995 World Cup was looming but I knew in my heart of hearts I could forget all hopes of going to South Africa. It was a strange contrast to my earlier, perhaps over-optimistic, self. I had really thought I'd be a part of the set-up for the 1991 tournament – I'd been selected in a few media squads and a lot of guys on the club circuit were telling me I'd be going – and was very down when I wasn't involved. Likewise, I missed out on the 1993 Lions tour despite a lot of people rooting for me. After these twin disappointments and given my non-selection by the new manager, I had steeled myself for another rejection. All of which made it all the more surprising when I made it into the 30-strong squad for the '95 competition. I received my letter in the post and two weeks later I was several thousand miles away. And at first, things went well. Rowell was a little distant but, largely through injury to other players, I made it into the side for the first three games. I played well enough to retain my place, I thought, scoring my debut senior try against Western Samoa. Unfortunately, I pulled my hamstring during that game.

It was touch-and-go whether I would be able to stay with the squad but some good work by our physio, Kevin Murphy, and something like 1,000 flexes of my leg muscles that evening helped stop the injury getting too bad. However, it was still serious enough to keep me on the sidelines as first Australia and then Jonah Lomu came and went, and it was our fourth place play-off against France before I was fit to play again. I thought that, given the crushing nature of our defeat by the All Blacks, we needed a change of personnel. I imagined I would be among those who got the call. But once again I was ignored and, as with Cooke, Rowell did not bother to explain why.

Despite this, though, I was not quite as down about it this time: I had three more caps, and World Cup caps at that. If I had been good enough to go to the best competition in the world, surely I was in the fold for keeps?

Once again, I was wrong. During the period post-World Cup '95 to Five Nations '97, Rowell hardly went anywhere near me. At first, though, it had looked as if things would work out okay, when he selected me in his squad for the clash with South Africa in the late autumn of 1995. It was a big game, against the new World Champions. I felt good during training and began to think that, if I had a good game and the team did well, I might have cracked it. But I was stunned when, just a few days before the game, Andy Robinson turned up out of nowhere and was picked to play in the Test. One day Robbo wasn't there and the next he was. Fair enough, Andy was a world-class player and these things can happen. But no-one said a word to me – ostensibly, the man in possession. It was a massive slap in the face and I was absolutely gutted. In recent years, they had been experimenting with different guys, chopping and changing all the big back row forwards as they tried to find an openside. I finally get a few games and it looks like I'm the man. Then along comes Robbo and I am back in the wilderness.

And there was no real change throughout 1996, when I didn't get a sniff of the senior side or even the A side. Admittedly, I was banned for six months but that came after the Five Nations so was an irrelevance to my non-selection.

It was the first time since my A debut that I hadn't been picked for either the As or the senior team – in fact, it was the first time I had not been picked for an England squad of some sort since I made my debut in 1985 for England Schools. I was very proud of my record of representing my country in every year and at every level apart from Student – and not having been a student, you can't count that.

The following year, 1997, Rowell ignored me again for the Five Nations. It was some sort of consolation that I played in the World Cup Sevens in Hong Kong that March but the shorter game does not carry the prestige of the XV-man version. Apart from the pride factor and the honour of playing for my country, there was now an additional financial issue. The game had not long turned professional and England A players and senior players were starting to get paid. That meant I was missing out financially, too.

Money is not everything. I would honestly play for England for nothing; I would probably even pay them. But there is a principle involved. I was, and am, a professional rugby player. That is what I do for a living, it's what puts food on my table and a roof over my head, and I don't have the option of retiring at 65 like most people. My working life, as a rugby player at least, would be over by 35 and I was conscious of the fact that I needed to make a decent living while I could. Those England A cheques were not huge – £1,000 a game if my memory serves me accurately – but I wasn't seeing any of it. Senior capped players also received £20,000 from EPRUC and I missed out on that too. Darren Garforth still taunts me with that payment every time I visit him at home. He built an extension on the back of his house with the cash and named it 'EPRUC' with a wooden plaque on the wall.

I couldn't understand it. A few months earlier, for God's sake, I had been good enough to get games at a World Cup. Now I was not even good enough for the A team.

Again, there was no chat – no letter, no phone call, no pulling me aside at a club game and telling me to keep my chin up. Instead, the old size issue began to rear its head again in the papers. It was like having Cooke in charge all over again although this time it was worse. Cooke had picked me at the end of his reign; Rowell had chosen me at the start of his and it could be years before a new manager came in. For some time, I waited, hoping, again naïvely, that there would be some explanation and a glimmer of light at the end of the tunnel. But when it became clear that Rowell had no intention of getting in touch with me, I decided to write to him. It wasn't physically possible to train any harder than I was doing. What had I got to show for it? Five caps. Then nothing. For all I knew, I'd never play international football again. I really considered jacking the game in. Instead, my personal trainer Darren Grewcock and James Gallagher, the chairman of my management company, persuaded me to send the letter. It was a hard few lines to pen. I had so much pent-up anger and frustration over the way I was being treated that I couldn't articulate what I wanted to say. Darren and James put it all into polite English.

The gist was simple: Why was I not being selected? Was there anything else I could do? Did he need me to work on any particular aspects of my game in order to enhance my prospects of being picked? All I wanted was a little glimmer of hope, something to build on, to motivate me.

Incredibly, I never even got a reply. Well, it's a measure of the man, isn't it?

If I was upset, Grewy was furious. Darren was just one of many friends who took the whole issue personally. In some ways, I think they actually felt the pain and disappointment during all my years in the wilderness more than I did. Peter Lloyd, my mentor from my younger days in Coventry, was another fervent supporter. He has met both Cooke and Rowell on separate occasions at internationals since I became an established member of the England side and given them both a hard time. Lloydy is only five foot three or four but he is as gutsy as hell and very passionate on my behalf. According to eyewitnesses, he marched up to Cooke on one occasion in 1999, prodded him and cackled 'Backy's not doing so bad these days, is he Cookey?' Cooke said something like 'It's a different game these days . . .' To which Lloydy cheerfully replied 'Bullshit!'

Meanwhile, another nail appeared to have been hammered into the coffin of my career.

After years playing big back rows out of position, Richard Hill had now been given the No 7 shirt for the 1997 Five Nations. Hilly was clearly a very good player and, although I felt he was more naturally a blindside, it was the first time I really worried that my chance might have gone for reasons other than coaching prejudice. He was younger than me, and while he was bigger than me, he wasn't some giant picked purely on size. He was playing No 7 for Saracens.

The media were talking Hilly up, too. I read several pieces which were saying 'at last we've found a successor to Winter-bottom', which they had not said about any other player, including me.

I honestly thought I had blown it and I genuinely considered retiring from the sport and taking up karate. Richard had a good Five Nations and I was very down. I had desperately hoped for a slot in that year's British Lions tour party to South Africa but how could I expect to get into that side when I wasn't being selected for England?

Ian McGeechan came to my rescue with an object lesson in motivation which Cooke and Rowell could each have learned from. McGeechan is, by common consent, one of the best coaches these isles have ever produced and a man whose boots Cooke and Rowell could not begin to lace. Not only is he a superb technician and tactician, he has fantastic man-manage-ment skills and knows just how to get the best out of his players. He proved that with Northampton and, even more so, with the British Lions. He must have sensed that I was at a low ebb and he obviously did not want me to lose heart. Tim Rodber called me to one side – I think it was probably after a championship game against Northampton at Welford Road – and said: 'Backy, I've got a message for you from Geech. He thinks you are playing outstandingly well at the minute. Keep it up and you're in with a shout for the Lions.'

That was fantastic: a massive, unbelievable boost. I felt like I was walking on air and I felt, too, that my hard work might eventually pay off. Virtually from that day on I would have walked over hot coals for Ian McGeechan.

My selection in the final tour party, and the tour itself, are dealt with elsewhere but I mention this now to show the difference that communicating with a player – letting him know you respect him, that you want to select him – can make.

Rowell was a successful businessman who was, supposedly, adept at man-management. But, like Cooke, he couldn't communicate, except with the 'senior' players like Will Carling, Rob Andrew and Brian Moore. He also allowed cliques to develop – Will, Rob and Mooreo was one, little club groups were others – which were bad for team spirit. Carling and his group certainly didn't go out of their way to make me feel welcome when I first showed up for England, which I think is totally wrong. They weren't overtly unfriendly, just stand-offish, and you were given the impression that they felt they were a cut above everyone else. At dinner, for instance, they would sit together because they were friends and had been together a long time. To be fair, they probably didn't even realise they were doing it. And it is quite possible that they didn't like what they had heard or seen of me. But whatever the reasons, it is one of the coach's jobs to stop this sort of thing happening. For the sake of the team you should bond together and put personal issues behind you but Cooke and Rowell did not foster that sort of attitude.

Rowell could not take criticism from the players. I remember an overhead projector session at the team hotel down in Marlow. He was running through team tactics on the white board with a pointer. Suddenly, a bluebottle landed on the projector, buzzing and moving about. Rowell takes his pointer and whacks the white board furiously, trying to kill this fly's shadow! He went on for a minute or two, looking very confused at how this cunning fly was managing to elude him. Eventually, everyone started grinning and nudging each other. So what did he do next? He looked *behind* the board, as though the fly was being illuminated through the plastic. Mark Regan yelled out 'Village!' – as in village idiot – at the top of his voice and everyone wet themselves laughing. Rowell went bright red. He was embarrassed, and angry at being made to look a fool. To deflect it, he picked on the first person he saw, who happened to be Graham Rowntree. He said something like: 'So, Graham, what are we going to do in this game?' Wiggy started to reply but after about three words Rowell cut him dead. It was as though he was trying to make us laugh at Wiggy instead and it was shameful, really . . . like a bullying teacher who could not control his class. It is very important that you are able to laugh at yourself in that sort of environment because you will have the mickey taken out of you whether you like it or not. Rowell obviously couldn't.

Not everyone in English rugby was as stiff and uncommunicative. In September 1992, for instance, having been disappointed at another non-selection – if only I had known how long it would take eventually to get established! – and nursing an injury, I was delighted to receive a lovely letter from the Vice President of the RFU, Ian Beer. In fountain pen and on his own notepaper, he wrote: *'Dear Neil, Not forgotten you . . . indeed, you have been much in our thoughts since the injury and as you may be in a 'bit of a low' at the moment we write to try to cheer you up. You have made such a fine name for yourself that you will not be forgotten and will be back I am sure. Remember how long Rob Andrew was in the wilderness between his first few caps and all the rest . . . Good wishes: keep cheerful and hope it is mending well . . . see you soon. Yours, Ian and Angela.'*

I can't speak highly enough of Ian for that. The coach has it in his power to write that sort of letter and failing to do so is a dereliction of duty. I had had five games for my country and had then been cut off. Rugby at the highest level is a combination of factors. Skill, tactics, fitness, strength . . . these are very important elements, naturally. But a player's mental state is also important. We're not all inhumanly confident about ourselves and our abilities – indeed I'm sure we have just as many doubts as other people – and being cast aside and ignored can wreck your confidence. I know of other players who have reacted very badly to being dropped. Luckily, my nature is different. Being kicked out made me all the more determined to prove Jack wrong.

*

It is possible to argue that, as coaches, Cooke and Rowell were successful. They got results, grinding out wins in the Five Nations and turning England into a force to be reckoned with, certainly on the European stage.

They were helped by having some excellent players – guys like Deano, Will Carling, Rob Andrew and Jerry Guscott – at their disposal but I think in both cases that the key to their success was that they were also able to recognise the limitations of the team as a whole. They knew that their strengths lay in a big, strong pack and good half-backs and that, Jerry and possibly Will apart, our backs were not as penetrative as Southern Hemisphere guys. So they built their game around the front nine, with Rob kicking for position.

But despite the wins, I believe Rowell and Cooke both failed as England coaches. Cooke is a very cautious man. Jack Rowell, I felt, was narrow-minded and shallow. Each carried these character traits forward into his position in charge of England.

In each case, these factors meant they lacked the vision and the guts to really go for it. They were frightened to try to compete with the Southern Hemisphere nations and instead were content for the England side to be a bully in its own backyard. The fans wanted to see England challenge the Wallabies and the All Blacks, to really be on a level with them, but we never really got anywhere near them. I believe we're still paying the price of their short-termist approach to coaching and management.

New Zealanders and Australians aren't supermen. Like anyone else, they spill the ball in contact, they pass forward, they miss tackles. But they are not afraid to embrace new styles of play, something you have to do as the rules of rugby evolve and as fitness, strength and endurance improves with better diet, more scientific training and increased professionalism. I believe the England of today would be more than a match for the Southern Hemisphere sides of a decade ago. The trouble is, the Southern Hemisphere has not stood still either. In their case, they have a history of evolving, of trying new things and striving to improve. Until Clive Woodward came on the scene, we were still stuck in the old small-minded Rowell and Cooke rut: this is how we play, we're good at it, sod the rest. It has taken three years for us to arrive at the position where we are as open-minded and willing to experiment as the Wallabies and the All Blacks.

CHAPTER 4
_____

One Little Push

I AM UTTERLY ashamed of what happened on May 4, 1996.

The date is engraved on my memory.

It was Pilkington Cup final day and we faced our traditional enemies, Bath. I am not sure where the fierce rivalry between the clubs originated, but it has been there as long as I can remember. Our fans always love to see the Bath boys suffer at Welford Road and we get a similar reaction from the friendly West Country folk.

On that May day four years ago, there was even more needle than usual. A week earlier, defending the championship we had won the previous season, we had seen our title ripped away in a narrow defeat to Harlequins. Horribly, that left Bath topping the table. That meant that they were playing for the league and cup double.

In the mid-1990s, Bath were an even stronger side than they are now. They had won the League championship in 1989, held it for four years between 1991 and 1994 and had now snatched it back once more. They had won the knockout cup five times in the 1980s and had also done so in 1990, 1992, 1994 and 1995.

We could not stomach the possibility of allowing them to grab that double.

There was a massive build-up to the game in the week beforehand. You could not move in Leicester for supporters coming up and slapping you on the back and the papers were full of speculation about the match, too.

We felt confident, even though we faced a great Bath side packed with internationals: Callard, de Glanville, Catt, Robinson, Sleightholme, Nicol, Dawe, Hilton, Ojomoh, Redman . . . the list went on and on. Our own XV was strong. We had the best pack in the country, led by Deano and fronted by the ABC club, with Martin Johnson and Matt Poole in the second row and myself and John Wells completing the back row. Our backs were not slouches: Rory Underwood was still in scorching form on the wing.

In front of a world record club crowd of 75,000 people, we played well enough to beat them convincingly. If it had been a boxing match we would certainly have won on points. We scored tries through Niall Malone and Matt Poole and kept them away from our line for most of the match. Our defence was awesome but by the final few minutes of the game, Catt and Adebayo had made some ground and they were putting pressure on us with repeated attacks a few metres out. We led, 15–9.

I say to this day, and so do all the other Leicester players and a few of the Bath lads, that we were just defending well, stacking up rucks. But the referee, Steve Lander, decided we were killing the ruck and awarded a penalty try against us. These had become a bit of a fashion with refs and Lander had actually informed both sides before the game that he would be awarding penalty tries for repeated infringement. With that in mind, there is no way we would have deliberately killed the ball and I think Lander ought to have taken that into account.

Five minutes to go. With the conversion, Bath now led 16–15.

We did not like the decision but we shrugged our shoulders and accepted it, reckoning we could still win if we got up the field. We threw everything into attack, recycling the ball again and again and getting ever closer to the Bath line. The fans were screaming us on and I felt we were a phase or two away from a score, when Steve blew up.

What happened next could have been the ruin of my rugby career.

Instead, in the same way Lawrence Dallaglio has come back stronger and better from his brush with tabloid infamy, it helped mould me into the player I am today.

The whistle blew, a red mist descended and the next thing I knew, Lander was lying winded on the turf. I had just pushed out at the nearest person to me – I actually thought it was Andy Robinson – and, unfortunately, it happened to be the referee. I honestly did not have any fully-formed intention in my mind to push him over.

Of course, as soon as I saw him lying on the floor I realised what I had done and regretted it instantly. But it had happened and there was nothing I could do to change that. Trying not to think about it, I just sprinted off the pitch, past the onrushing fans, down the tunnel and into the changing room, along with other Tigers players.

On top of losing the championship the week before, you can imagine the atmosphere in there. There was a lot of bitterness. We were all really disappointed about the result but it was really the manner of the defeat which rankled with the guys. We did not feel we had been outplayed. We felt we had been cheated. We were supposed to go and collect our losers' cups but only a handful of players did so. It wasn't a conscious snub – we genuinely were not aware of the post-match format for that year – but in retrospect it smacked of bad sportsmanship and we should have made an effort to find out what was required of us. To be honest, it was probably just as well we didn't all go. Someone brought in our glass runner-up trophies and most of them went against the wall, ending up smashed on the floor. Half a dozen more were just put straight into the bin. I never even saw mine.

As I do after every game, I had just taken off my shirt and boots and sat myself down, starting my stretching and recovery routine. I just wanted to forget the result, forget what had happened afterwards, get changed and get out of there.

The storm broke about 10 minutes after the final whistle when Deano and Dosser Smith came into the changing rooms. Deano was very quiet and sober. He walked over to me and said something like 'Why did you push the referee over?' Cocker followed them in. Apparently he had picked Steve up from the floor. He just stood there too. I could tell by the looks on their faces that they considered the matter serious so I stood up and went straight to the referee's room. I said: 'Look, Steve, I'm sorry mate. I didn't know it was you. I thought it was Andy Robinson.'

Under the circumstances, Lander was good about it. He said: 'Okay, apology accepted, no problem. As far as I'm concerned, that's the end of it.'

He later told the press: 'As the game ended, me and a player accidentally collided. I have no problem and there will be no further action on my part.' After the game Steve Griffiths, the national referees' development officer, reinforced that point, telling the press: 'Steve Lander considers the matter to be closed.' Someone also briefed the reporters that I had confused Steve with Robbo. I hoped that was the finish of the whole sorry saga. Had it happened on a parks pitch with no-one watching it would have been. But in hindsight, with TV cameras recording the whole thing for Sky and the BBC, a 75,000 crowd staring at me and 50 or so journalists watching I suppose I was rather naive to imagine I'd get off scot free.

A lot of the media were after me that evening but I avoided their attentions and spent the night at the team hotel in Leicester. After cup finals we usually stay overnight at a hotel in Leicester, either the Holiday Inn or the Hilton. If we have won, we get onto an open-topped bus the following morning and head for the Town Hall, where there are loads of people to greet us. If we have lost, we head for Welford Road to meet up with the couple of hundred fans who want to commiserate with us. As I opened the Sunday papers the following morning, it rapidly became apparent that Steve Lander's acceptance of my apology was not going to make the whole affair go away. Despite his magnanimous attitude, the papers weighed into me with enthusiasm.

One line of attack centred on the fact that Lander's jersey was a garish checkerboard design, quite different to Bath's stripes. Some guy on one of the tabloids wrote a column suggesting I ought to have my eyes tested if I could not tell the difference between Steve and Andy Robinson. Paul Ackford, the former England lock, wrote a piece in *The Sunday Telegraph*. Under the headline 'Unacceptable behaviour', he described it as an 'appalling' incident and said I had 'attacked' Lander. He, too, found it 'incredible' that I had mistaken the referee for a Bath player, given the differences in the kit.

Gloomy and worried, I joined the rest of the team for the short journey to Welford Road at about 10.30am. Gloom soon became downright depression: there were almost more journalists than fans hanging around the ground, and they were all after me. The combination of the headlines and the sight of these reporters buzzing around all over the place really jolted me and I realised I was in serious trouble. What was most worrying was the attitude the RFU would take in the face of the intense media storm which had developed. I thought it was entirely possible that they might be led by the nose by the press.

The Leicester committee men were all there and Tony Russ and Peter Wheeler took me on one side. They told me that the whole thing was taking on serious proportions and that there would almost certainly be a disciplinary hearing. They had initially leant towards disciplinary action themselves but then the club committee announced it was standing by me. I was grateful for their support and for that of the other players.

Even in the face of all this I still thought there was a chance everything would turn out okay. That all changed when I saw the footage of the incident shot from seven different angles, courtesy of Sky TV. My (then) long blond hair marked me out fairly distinctly and it looked like I had aggressively pushed Steve to the floor. In the context of the game, with the earlier penalty try having cost us the cup, people leapt to the conclusion that I had deliberately attacked him. I watched the footage with Brace and a few of the committee and I had to admit it looked bad. The expressions on everyone else's faces told me they did too.

The following day, the RFU disciplinary officer Ray Manock announced he was setting up a panel of three officials to deal with the matter. He had sought reports from the match officials and studied a video recording of the game and thought there was a case for me to answer.

The hearing was set for a few days later. The media interest was huge. People turned up at my house and were ringing me at all hours. In the face of this, the panel decided to hear the case at a secret location, a hotel near London, rather than Twickenham. I was driven there, head down, in the back of a car and, thankfully, there were no press in sight.

Dosser, Deano and senior figures from the club were there in support. It was the most nerve-wracking day of my life. By this stage, I had become only too aware of the seriousness of my predicament. I knew it was possible I could be banned from the game for life. An amateur player who had punched a ref in Cornwall a month before had suffered just such a fate.

The video evidence was reviewed again and the panel took an hour to go through my evidence. In the end, they barred me from the game for six months for bringing the game into disrepute – the first professional player to answer such a charge. I am convinced that it would have been a life ban if the panel had believed it had been an aggressive, calculated act. I was lucky that Steve had been literally a few feet away from me when he blew his whistle and that he had marched right across in front of me. It all happened in a split second: I did not even have time to move my feet towards him and the committee accepted that that showed a lack of premeditation.

They also ordered that the ban should run from the date of the offence, which was decent of them. It meant I only missed 13 games at the start of the next season instead of virtually the whole calendar. Importantly, the disciplinary committee announced: 'The panel believes that Back was telling the truth in his evidence.'

I walked away stunned and a little shaky.

The whole thing, I think, had been a product of the tension and frustration I had felt over the recent years. It all boiled up in that incident. That is an explanation, but it is not an excuse. What I did was wrong. Early in the 1999/2000 soccer season the papers were full of pictures of Roy Keane and a bunch of other Manchester United players surrounding a ref, jabbing their fingers at him, faces contorted with fury. I was sickened by that. Kids are looking up to these people. But kids were looking up to me, too, and my behaviour was inexcusable. It was almost irrelevant that I believed I had been pushing Andy Robinson: you don't push anyone on a rugby field. It was bad sportsmanship at the very least and I deserved my ban.

I think Steve genuinely accepted my apology and there is certainly no bad blood between us now, even if the Leicester crowd still gets on his back from time to time. He has asked me to autograph a few shirts for him for charity auctions, which suggests he can now look back with a wry smile at the events.

I took the summer off and did not return to the club until a week before my ban expired. In the meantime, Darren Grewcock and I had spent those months getting me into top shape for my comeback. I also took part in my own voluntary form of 'community service' organised by my agents: visiting over 30 schools to take rugby workshops with the children. I covered the whole spectrum, from public schools with tremendous facilities, to inner-city places with just a small patch of concrete and pupils doing games in their school uniforms. It was humbling experience and one I am glad I underwent.

On my return, I was a better man. I was fitter, stronger and very hungry for the fray. I was also a more mature, thoughtful person.

I wish I had found a different way for that to happen, but I am glad it did.

CHAPTER 5

Crying Lion

I WAS IN bed eating my breakfast when Ali brought in the envelope.

It was a letter from Fran Cotton, congratulating me on my selection to tour South Africa with the British Lions. For a moment, I just sat there, staring at it. Then I let it fall to the covers and burst into tears, sobbing my heart out. A huge reservoir of tension and passion and desperation had built up inside me in my wilderness years and those few words from Fran burst the dam.

All those years of self-denial, of sweat and pain, had brought me, finally, to my destiny.

By rights, I had no chance of being in the 35-strong party. When an original list of 62 possible names, based on those guys who had been suggested for inclusion by their Home Union coaches, had been released to the media in early March that year, there had been no mention of N A Back. That was crushing and I honestly felt that if I was not among the best 62 players in the British Isles I might as well give up the game. Added to that, I was not a regular international player at that stage while virtually every Lions player was. The only glimmer of optimism was that Tim Rodber had got word to me from the Lions' coach Ian McGeechan that I was in his thoughts. But it still seemed that I had two hopes . . . Bob Hope and No Hope.

Now, against all the odds, I was in.

There is a magic associated with the British Lions. To be invited to join a tour party made up of the very best players from these islands and to travel thousands of miles to take on the best that the other side of the world has to offer is a great honour. My generation was weaned on tales of the fabulous 1974 tour to South Africa led by the rock-hard Irishman Willie John McBride. The towering pipe-smoker and his band of brothers had stood toe-to-toe with the Afrikaaners and handed them a beating, mentally and physically, returning home without losing a match. To emulate those and other great British Lions achievements would be to become a rugby legend and I was ecstatic to have been chosen.

I spent a week or two with my head in the clouds, a permanent grin attached to my features. Little did I know that the tour would be the making of my career. Maybe I would still have secured a regular England place if I hadn't been selected but I believe my performances against what was a very tough set of sides helped to crystallise in people's minds that I had something to offer.

It was the first Lions tour of the professional era, and that was reflected in the meticulous preparation that went into its arranging and management.

Fran and the committee appointed Northampton's McGeechan as coach with Jim Telfer as his second-in-command. Together, they formed the main selection team. At one point, they had considered offering Telfer's position to Jack Rowell. Thank goodness they chose Jim for, like Geech, he was a fan of my style of play. I was not aware at the time but have since learned of the extent to which he pushed for my inclusion in the final tour party despite my omission from the first. In his book *My Pride of Lions*, Fran Cotton wrote: 'One selection that probably surprised quite a few people was the inclusion of Leicester flanker Neil Back. He wasn't in favour with the England selectors but I agreed to the change in our thinking because I was persuaded that he would provide us with flexibility in terms of back row play. There was still some doubt about Neil's lack of height, but Jim was our forwards' coach and he wanted him to go. In our view, his inclusion was a very important decision.'

The new professionalism saw McGeechan and Telfer looking in far greater depth at our opponents than had happened before. Geech saw video analysis as vital. He gathered tapes of every available Springbok international and provincial game and he and Jim spent hours and hours watching and studying. By the time the tour party left they knew more about the South African attacking lines and defensive patterns than their players themselves. Ian also appointed Harlequins coach Andy Keast as a video expert. Andy had the technical know-how to take on the task while we were away and his role – watching games and compiling video analysis for our squad meetings – provided invaluable help during our time away.

McGeechan also went on reconnaissance and fact-finding trips to South Africa and New Zealand. He spent a long time in the All Blacks camp, talking to John Hart and their then-skipper Sean Fitzpatrick. It was Fitz who advised him to take 35 players rather than the traditional 30. Sean pointed out that a 30-strong party meant that some specialist positions, like his own at hooker, had no cover. He would play on the Saturday and then also have to be on the bench for the midweek games in case of injury to his number two. That meant he got no effective rest, something which was vital in the modern era. Taking a third hooker – and spare props, locks and half-backs – gave cover in those key positions. It was a policy the Kiwis had already implemented to good effect and Ian noted the fact and followed suit. Importantly, during his time in New Zealand, he also drew on Hart's experience of the Southern Hemisphere style of play and refereeing. This provided us with valuable intelligence.

With Telfer and Cotton, he started drawing up the blueprint for the way his team would play: a mobile, attacking game, with quick ball being provided by the forwards to enable aggressive backs to penetrate defences. It was my kind of rugby.

They also chose my kind of captain. Martin Johnson was a surprise to some people, but not to me. Apparently, the final decision was between Ieuan Evans, Jason Leonard and Johnno. Ieuan and Jase were fine players but there was no doubt that Johnno was a leader of men. Playing South Africa, you must adopt a hard, uncompromising and physical approach or they will scent weakness and rip you apart. I had followed him into battle with Leicester many times and had never found him wanting. Selecting a 6ft 7in, 18 stone bruiser as skipper sent the Springboks an early message of our intent.

I also knew Johnno's personality – very straight, very fair, hard-working on the pitch and relaxed off it – would unite a side drawn from different nations. It was also important that the fans and the media would take to the captain. Selecting Will Carling, for instance, would have been a disaster because, rightly or wrongly, he was associated in too many peoples' minds with English arrogance. Everyone respected Martin.

*

My first week as a Lion was spent in Surrey. The Lions management had arranged for us to spend some time together at a hotel in Weybridge. The main purpose was team-building. Right from the start the management had been aware of the potential for cliques to develop. Clearly, there was a possibility that the Scottish lads would stick together, that the English contingent would do the same and so on. Then there were the club loyalties. The Leicester Tigers, for instance, had provided Johnno, myself, Will Greenwood, Austin Healey, Eric Miller and Graham Rowntree. Our East Midlands rivals Northampton had Nick Beal, Matt Dawson, Paul Grayson, Tim Rodber and Gregor Townsend on the trip. Would we form separate huddles, along with all the other little club groupings? It was important to prevent these cliques from setting, particularly along national lines. I was not there to represent England or Leicester, I was there to represent the British Isles. Any other attitude would have been damaging to team morale. Watch the video *Living With Lions* and you will see John Bentley, armed with his 'player-cam', gently chiding Scott Gibbs and some of the other Welsh boys for training together in the gym. Gentle as his mocking was, he was serious about it.

It was probably less of a problem than had been the case on previous tours. With the advent of professionalism, there had been far more cross-border traffic and a lot of us knew players from the other nations. Of the non-English players, 10 actually played for English clubs. Nevertheless, team-building was important.

We were split up into groups, with care taken to mix us together as much as possible, and put through our paces with a variety of exercises. In one, each team had an area to defend. We were given a few bits of equipment – sponges, wooden poles, elastic bands, rope – and the idea was to fire wet sponges into your opponent's area. Meanwhile, they were trying to keep the sponges out with home-made bats or even just their hands. The team who landed the most sponges won. Another games involved seeing who could build the highest stack of beer crates, with a player standing on them. The guy on top was wobbling around but couldn't fall because he was suspended from a pulley attached to a tree branch. I think the winning side managed something like 18 crates which was bloody high. Although you knew you couldn't fall it was quite scary and there was a lot of trust involved – your team-mates had to be very careful not to rock the stack. It was also a good way, away from rugby, of getting to know one another, of working together and communicating, and of establishing who were the leaders within each group. Another day we went canoeing on the Thames, which I found tremendous fun.

Fran also arranged some press practice for us. Two journalists – John Taylor of the *Mail on Sunday*, himself a former Lion, and David Norrie of *The News of the World* – came in to the camp to give us a few tips on handling the media. There were role play sessions, where they would fire random questions at individuals. They picked on Johnno because of his recent Five Nations record of giving away penalties for punching, asking him how he would react to the pressure out in South Africa. It was the sort of question he might well face and he had obviously prepared a good, stock answer. They came up with a scenario for Doddie Weir where he had been caught out in a nightclub. He claimed mistaken identity, which raised a titter.

And the third element of the week involved us coming up with a code of conduct for the squad. It covered everything from behaving with dignity while on tour to avoiding alcohol for 24 hours before a match. A disciplinary committee, comprising Johnno, Rob Wainwright, Geech and Fran, was set up and fine structures were laid down in case anyone transgressed.

At first, there was naturally a little caginess between boys who had not previously met each other except on the pitch, where they were battering hell out of each other for national pride, but it was not long before the banter and the jibes starting flying around. Within that week, the seeds of a fantastic squad spirit had begun to germinate.

On the last day, before we left, we all went down to the Swan pub in Weybridge and had a few beers – a lot of beers, actually. The next day, our wives and girlfriends came down to see us off. A few guys were the worse for wear but that pub session had really sealed the group together.

*

We flew out to Johannesburg first class courtesy of Virgin Airlines. One of the little treats they offer is massages on the plane. There wasn't time for everyone to have one so we all put our names into a hat. Mine was not drawn out so I tried to get some shuteye and was surprised when I awoke to find I had slept the whole way.

We disembarked briefly for a press conference before heading off again to Durban and the Beverly Hills Hotel in the resort of Umhlanga Rocks. Fran had flown out ahead of us on a whistle-stop tour of the country's facilities and he had certainly spent his time well: the hotel was fantastic, with stunning views over the Indian Ocean. We were introduced to the local press at a barbecue and also warned of the security problems in South Africa. The message was clear: don't stray from the hotel without a bodyguard. As the sun beat down on the turquoise sea and golden sands, it seemed hard to believe danger lurked outside the compound gates.

We trained at King's Park, just 15 minutes away. Jim Telfer rapidly proved what an outstanding forwards coach he is. He is the most emotional coach I've ever known. His speeches are exceptionally stirring and rousing and his delivery is second to none. His passion and fervour got everyone in the right frame of mind to play and contributed immensely towards our eventual triumph. Geech was different: more softly-spoken, more intellectual in his approach. The two of them together made an outstanding team. Ian is, in my opinion, a tactical genius. He was tremendously skilled at spotting weaknesses and working out ways to exploit them. He was also very methodical and he knew how to get the best out of his players. Telfer was technically excellent, too. For instance, he had looked hard at the ruck. The South African pack were all big guys and Jim reckoned that if we could get our body positions further down, so that we were entering the ruck nine inches below the Springboks, we would create an edge for ourselves. It worked well when we put it into practice.

The training out there was hard work. Some of the scrummaging sessions were murder in the heat. We would pack down 50 times, really grafting and straining. And Jim was in every scrum with you – not physically, but mentally. He exerted almost as much energy as we did by tensing his body as we hit every scrum. I have total, utter respect for the guy and I would like to think that by the end of the tour he respected me as well.

Defensively, we worked hard on our tackling, putting in the big hits on one another until our bodies ached. The backs were putting a lot into their attacking play and defence too.

We started the tour fit and, individually, talented. The task the coaches set themselves was to take this bunch of individuals and mould them into a team which was capable of beating the World Champions in their backyard.

The first opportunity to test their success came against an Eastern Province Invitation XV at the Boet Erasmus Stadium along the coast at Port Elizabeth. Guys who had played them before told me they were a punchy, mouthy and aggressive gang of Afrikaaners. The trouble for which the 1974 Lions tour had become famous had started with some deliberate punching by Eastern Province, and Tim Rodber had been sent off for fighting after he had been attacked during England's most recent visit there. Clearly wanting to kick our backsides in the first game of the tour, Eastern Province had drafted in international players like the centre Hennie Le Roux and the full-back Theo van Rensburg. They had a handy pack, too, with the fiery Kobus Wiese in the second row. He had been fined for smacking the Welsh lock Derwyn Thomas a year or two before and we knew he would take up any physical challenge.

From a personal point-of-view, I was disappointed not to be selected for that first encounter. Having said that, given the way things had gone with England, I did not really expect to get the nod. I hoped my chances would come later. The back row, Lawrence Dallaglio at blindside, Richard Hill at No 7 and Scott Quinell at No 8, played well in a brilliant 39–11 win. It was a cracking start, played at pace on a scorching hot day in which some guys lost 6lb in weight through fluid loss. Our defence was tight, there was good support for the ball carriers and my Leicester team-mate Will Greenwood, uncapped by England and playing in a Lions shirt for the first time, scored a try. Jerry Guscott grabbed two. Our front five had been under pressure from a combative pack but had held there own and there were no real negatives to take away. My overwhelming feeling was that I was going to have to work very hard indeed to break into the back row. Still, there was a lot of rugby ahead of us.

That night we headed to a nearby restaurant selected for us

by John Bentley. He was in charge of our entertainment committee and a better man for the job you could not find. He was a livewire character and a superb tourist.

The following day we headed off to East London for the second game against Border, four days later. When we arrived at our new hotel, the weather had changed. A foul storm, with lashing rain and gusting winds, was coming in straight off the ocean. We were supposed to be training on the pitch at the Basil Kenyon Stadium but they tried to keep us off it because of the water. It was sloshing around our ankles. The management held out, however, and we got in a good, long session on the field, helping us to adapt to the conditions. I hoped things would clear up for the match. I hoped, also, that I'd be selected.

Somebody, somewhere, was listening and my prayer was answered. I will never forget the moment I was handed that precious red jersey. Fran made a big thing about it with all the players, presenting the shirt to you in a rather formal, dignified way. It made the hairs stand up on the back of my neck and when I actually pulled it on the feeling was incredible. It was an unbelievable dream come true after my early international days with Messrs Cooke and Rowell.

Unfortunately, however, the weather did not clear up and I made my British Lions debut in a mud bath. It tipped down throughout the game and that acted as a real leveller. Bentley scored a superb try just three minutes in, after a midfield break by Scott Gibbs, and our handling and passing, at first, were sharp. We should have run away with the match. But with the ball getting greasier by the minute, we only scraped a win, 18 points to 14, to keep the momentum of the tour going. I hurt my shoulder in a tackle and had sand and mud jammed into every orifice by the finish. As we trooped off, someone from the stadium authorities had 'forgotten' to turn the hot water on, so we had a shivering wait while that was rectified.

By and large we played okay. I was satisfied, but no more, with my own performance. Austin had a poor first half at scrum-half and was replaced by Matt Dawson, who sparkled. Paul

Grayson had struggled with his kicks and it turned out he was carrying a thigh injury. The tour ended for him and he was sent home for treatment. Mike Catt joined the party as his replacement. In his book, Fran Cotton related how he called Jack Rowell in Argentina to see if Catty could be released from the England development tour over there. Rowell, according to Cotton, put up barriers and was reluctant to let Mike leave with a Test still to play. He wasn't sure about Alex King as a fly-half. Cotton made the point that England were on a development tour and playing untried players was supposed to be the point. Labelling Rowell 'narrow-minded' he said: 'The problem with Jack is that immediate results seem to dictate his selection policy.' That is criticism I can relate to. It is hard to believe anyone would stand in the way of a player getting a potential Lions cap in that way.

The following Wednesday, in Cape Town, we faced the first big test of the tour. Western Province had almost made the Southern Hemisphere's Super 12s competition and had won something like 15 or 16 games on the trot. They had an excellent side, with players like Robbie Fleck, Percy Montgomery and Corne Krige, and Gary Pagel and Fritz van Heerden who would later make their mark in England. Perhaps the most interesting name on their team sheet was the Springbok wing James Small. He was massive news in South Africa and he had a massive mouth to boot. He was full of it in all their press and on their TV, talking about how he was the man to put a stop to the Lions' bandwagon. In particular, the South African press were eating up remarks he had made rubbishing John Bentley. I must admit, I had my doubts about Bentos as a player. He had a fantastic swerve and sidestep and ran great angles, as you would expect of a guy who had spent time in rugby league, but I felt he lacked the out-and-out gas to be a world class winger. His defence was a bit suspect, too. I was not chosen for the match so, like everyone else, I watched from the stands in the magnificent Newlands stadium, overshadowed by Table Mountain, to see who would win the clash. My heart said Bentos but my head said Small. He had pace to spare and he also had that touch of arrogance, of self-belief, which marks out the really top players.

In the end, though, my heart was right. Bentley had a storming game, scoring a pair of tries himself and helping to make another for Alan Tait. It was Small whose defence looked weak. At one point, his frustration boiled over when there was contact between the two of them and Bentley just threw him off the pitch. Small came back at him with loads of attitude. After the game, which we won 38–21, he refused to shake hands with John. That was a bit unsporting but it was a pleasing sign that we had got under the skin of one of their nation's top players.

The back row was Lawrence and Hilly, with Tim Rodber at No 8. Again, it functioned well. But I was less concerned about my own chances. It looked very much as though there would be a rotational system and that I'd be getting a game every other one. That left one question burning away in my mind: would I get on for the Tests?

*

Three games and three wins, and the South Africans now knew we were a good side and that we meant business. Now it was time for us to move our sights higher – literally and metaphorically. Rugby in the high veldt – high field – is a real challenge. Most of it is at 5,000 feet above sea level or above. That has several effects. Firstly, oxygen is much scarcer at that altitude and you can feel your lungs burning as you struggle for air during a match. The ground is rock hard, too, baked by the almost ever-present sun, and that means the matches tend to be played at pace, which doesn't help matters. Secondly, you dehydrate quicker at altitude and this is something you need to keep your eye on. Thirdly, because there is less air there is less resistance against the ball and kicks can travel an amazing distance. An added factor was the locals. The area up there around Johannesburg and Pretoria – in what used to be called the Transvaal – is strictly Afrikaaner territory. They like their rugby played hard and they like their rugby players big and aggressive. We had a squad meeting to discuss the implications of our move north. We would certainly be at a disadvantage in terms of the oxygen – our opponents had lived and played at that altitude all their lives. Arriving on the Sunday, we only had three days to acclimatise before our clash with Mpumulanga Pumas on the Wednesday. There was not much we could do about that fact and we would just have to live with it.

Tactically, we expected them to kick long balls at us – longer than we were used to - in the thin air. As a squad, we agreed that we would not kick it back at them, but would try to continue with our running game, emphasising possession, passing and continuity.

Their forwards would be imposing – Mpumulanga were said to have the biggest and best pack in provincial rugby. There had been some criticism of our scrummaging in the previous games and it was true to say that it was the one area of our game which could have improved. On the Monday morning, Jim took the chosen pack – I was among them – out for a really brutal scrum session. The ex-England lock Nigel Horton had brought his Predator scrum machine on tour. It was a huge piece of kit, with hydraulics which enabled it to measure your output and also fight back against you. We attacked this machine, putting in 46 big hits on it in almost an hour of sustained grunting and shouting (from us) and clanking and hissing (from the machine and its hydraulics). It was unbelievably intense stuff and as I lay on the grass at the end I knew that, no matter how big the other eight were, we would have the measure of them. Our general squad sessions, under Geech's eye, involved lung-bursting passing and handling moves, at high pace, for three minutes at a time. He was working on the basis that if we could manage that we would be able to keep it up for half as long in a match situation. That ought to keep us in touch with anything the locals managed.

And it worked. If anything, we were the faster, fitter outfit and that was reflected in the fantastic 64 points to 14 score line. The front row of Paul Wallace, Keith Wood and Tom

Smith – known as 'The Boston Strangler' because of his supposedly serial killer-like quietness on tour – faced their opponents down superbly. A local paper later wrote: 'They said these Lions had forwards who were soft and fatally deficient. We now know that is a load of garbage.' Rob Wainright certainly showed no deficiencies, scoring a dream hat-trick, and the backs had a field day too. I was delighted with my own performance, which was one of the best I turned in during our time out there. Jerry Guscott later said of me in that game: 'His work rate was simply phenomenal – he was always there. If you had not seen it with your own eyes you would not have believed it.' High praise from Jerry, who I feel is one of the all-time greats.

Our elation, though, was reduced by some thuggish behaviour on the pitch by the Afrikaaners. Once the game was gone from them – and it went inside 15 minutes – they set out to maim and injure us. The worst incident came when the lock Marius Bosman deliberately stamped on Doddie Weir's knee while it was braced against the ground. Doddie instantly collapsed in agony and had to leave the field. It later transpired that the whole of the interior of his knee was wrecked – the kick almost dislocated the joint. We were told that, had blood vessels been broken, Doddie might have lost his leg. As it was, it was touch and go whether he would ever play again. Thankfully, he has now made a full recovery. Earlier in the match, Bosman had stamped on Rob Wainwright's head – immediately after his second row partner Elandré van der Bergh had done the same thing. That kind of senseless thuggery has no place on the rugby field and men like Bosman and van der Bergh – a repeat offender – ought to be banned from the game.

It was really tough seeing Doddie leave. We had all really bonded together by this point and it was like saying goodbye to a brother. He had become an immensely popular member of the touring party, known for his good humour and hard work, and had also shown himself to be a tremendous second row. He had been looking forward to his mum and dad flying out to watch the later stages of the tour and it was a shame that pleasure had been denied his family.

Northern Transvaal's Blue Bulls awaited the following Saturday. Fresh from the Super 12s, in which they had finished eighth, this was always a big Lions fixture and one the Bulls had won just once before.

Played in front of a big crowd at the imposing Loftus Versfeld Stadium in Pretoria, it was a game we lost through making mistakes. The losing margin was only five points, at 35–30, and they were gifted those five with an intercept from a rare slack pass by Gregor Townsend. A top boy, Gregor is the kind of player who can literally produce a stunning piece of genius one minute and a mind-blowing error the next. Unfortunately, this was more a day for the errors. Having said that, we came back strongly and would have won had the game gone another 10 minutes. It was a bit of a shocker – our first loss – and we were all a little down about it. I was disappointed when the selectors decided to play Eric Miller at openside for the game. Eric was not an openside and he proved that by not having the best of games. For the first time on tour, I felt that a selection decision had been made against me. There was no point in complaining, though. I had to make it impossible for them to ignore me.

Scott Gibbs had more cause for complaint than me, anyway. He had become the first player in Lions history to be suspended, after an alleged punch during the match. It didn't look like a punch to me. I thought the South African player had just been injured by one of Scott's trademark big hits but a disciplinary committee made up of local worthies banned him for a match. It was ridiculous when you compare it with what happened to Bosman. He got fined a pittance – hardly even enough for Doddie's airfare home. Meanwhile, Scott Quinnell became our third injury drop-out with a groin problem.

All through the tour, where possible days out were being organised to help take us away from rugby. The one I most enjoyed was when we went 'sharking'. The sea off Durban is teeming with monster great whites and tiger sharks – there are plenty of beaches where you are not advised to swim. We were taken out on a boat to a point a few miles offshore where the shark activity was high. They 'chummed' up the water, throwing buckets of fish blood and guts all around the boat to attract the great whites. Then we went down, two by two, in shark cages. I was in with Mark 'Ronnie' Regan and I was feeling really seasick. As our heads bobbed above the water I threw up all over him. Luckily, he was wearing a mask – and is not the sharpest tool in the box – he just thought it was chum being thrown from above. Even given my nausea, it was fantastic, if a little frightening, seeing these five metre fish close up.

The Richmond pair of Allan Bateman and Barry Williams were down together and a big shark charged their cage. Bateman pushed Williams towards it, which must have done wonders for their relationship.

These sorts of days were rare, though, and they got rarer as the Tests approached. I was desperate for a Test slot. So far, I had played only Wednesday games and I felt as though I was being seen as a mid-weeker. Logically, this was nuts. The concept of a mid-week side means nothing until the Tests start. At that point, the Saturday fixtures – the internationals – do become the focal point and the mid-week Wednesday matches inevitably take on slightly less importance. If you are playing Wednesday games then, you are a true mid-weeker.

That is not to say you should not try your best. It is hugely important that the mid-week side performs well. Playing in that side can be disheartening. You can't avoid that. You have pride and ambition and you want to play in the first choice side. But if you let your head go down, if you give up, if you sulk, you cannot help but allow that to feed through into your performance. If the Wednesday side starts losing, that lifts the opposing nation and damages your camp's morale. The idea is for the mid-week guys to kick their opponents' backsides, to boost your squad's morale and wreck theirs. Despite the importance of that mid-week side, though, I'd be a liar if I said I didn't want a Test berth.

Following the Blue Bulls defeat, we had three more matches before coming up against the Springboks for the first time.

Gauteng Lions was the first of the three and I was in, with Rob Wainwright on the other side of Tim Rodber. Training went well, with some crisp handling and good line-out and scrum sessions by the forwards. One unfortunate incident happened when a few of the guys raised the question of how to clear the ball in contact. The backs wanted technical advice from the forwards on the best approach. I told Jerry to get down on the floor so I could show him how it was done. But as I went to pick the ball up and drive over him, I smacked him in the eye with my knee. There was blood everywhere and a big split. Jerry took it very well but insisted on going to the best surgeon locally so he could have 'invisible' stitches put into the cut. Well, he is a part-time model.

Gauteng were a hardened Super 12 side and both they and the media expected them to win. Ellis Park is a huge and intimidating stadium but for some reason it was not much more than half full. Still, there was 38,000 people there and they were baying for their heroes. They started well and we were nine points to three down at half-time, Mike Catt having hit the posts a couple of times with penalty attempts. After the break, Austin Healey touched down and then John Bentley scored one of the most memorable tries of all time, running it home from 15 metres inside our own half. Bentos set off on this amazing, mazy run, turning five or six of their defenders inside out with his jinking and twisting and changes of pace. I shadowed him home for the final few yards but he didn't need to pass and went over the line with a couple of their guys hanging on to him. The whole crowd, most of them locals, were on their feet cheering a fabulous score. The flanker André Vos scored a consolation try but the game finished 20–14, despite some bizarre refereeing which favoured the home side, and we were back on track. Bentos was buzzing like mad and was later overheard on the phone to his wife telling her 'Love, you won't believe how famous I am in South Africa!' It was something he was ribbed unmercifully for.

Again, I was pleased with my own showing. Jerry Guscott again had kind words to say about me in his *Lions Tour Diary*: 'Another player whose tour was made against Gauteng was Neil Back. Throughout the tour, Backy was sensational. His performance out wide against Mpumulanga had been one of the best by an openside I had ever seen. He doesn't get this freedom with Leicester because they don't play like the Lions. Nor do England play in a way that makes Neil Back look the world-class player that he is. But with the Lions, every time he played and the ball went out wide, or anywhere for that matter, he was there. The bloke is the link – the missing link – for anyone who wants to play 15-man rugby. You can't play in that style without players like Backy. He was so good that size was a non-issue.' I certainly hoped that the England management back home were watching the games in which I had played because I did think I was playing well and making my point.

CHAPTER 6

The Real McCoy

WE CELEBRATED that evening and awoke to favourable head-lines. 'British Lions the Real McCoy' thundered the *Pretoria News*. The Springboks, however, had sounded a warning note of their own by thrashing Tonga by 74 points to 10 at Newlands.

Two games to go before the First Test. Natal at Kings Park in Durban was the Saturday game and I was not among those selected. I must admit that at that point I started thinking I might not make the Test side. On the principle that you would want that team to be rested, I thought the management would probably play them the week before and put out a different XV on the Wednesday. As things stood, I was likely, therefore, to be facing the Emerging Springboks in four days' time.

And that is how it went.

Natal were brushed aside by 42 points to 12, with the back row of Hill, Dallaglio and Miller performing well. Keith Wood had a cracker and perhaps the highlight of the game was a massive hit by Scott 'Snake' Gibbs on the 20-stone prop Ollie Le Roux. Snake, who had been out through injury and his suspension, was fearfully pumped-up for the match and smashed the huge Springbok to the ground as he charged through the Natal defence like a snorting bull. You don't see too many centres treating Ollie like that! The big downer was the shoulder injury to Rob Howley, which ended his tour. We all felt that losing him was a major blow. He took it very hard, and was in tears when the doctors told him he was out. I rated Rob very highly as a scrum-half – he had pace, awareness, an excellent, quick pass and was strong in defence. Kyran Bracken was tracked down on holiday in the West Indies and came out as his replacement.

The Emerging Springboks contained several names for the future – guys like Percy Montgomery and Deon Keyser – and we expected them to put up a good fight. They were also playing for places in their Test team, after all. The Boland Stadium in Wellington, a farming community an hour or so from Cape Town, was a cauldron of noise and colour and there were many red Lions shirts among the crowd. They had obviously started to come out in numbers, with the Tests about to start. Nick Beal didn't disappoint them, with a hat-trick, and Tim Stimpson scored with all of his six kicks to create a finish score of 51–21.

The Test team was announced to us early in the week via white envelopes slid under our doors. Fran Cotton had signed the letters personally. Mine said that, sadly, I had not made the side or even the bench. I was disappointed but not really surprised. Richard Hill would wear No 7. I honestly thought I had been playing as well as, if not better than, Hilly but you just have to take selection knocks on the chin. As I've said before, there is no mileage in letting it fester. I immediately congratulated Richard on his selection and wished him all the best for the Test.

We headed out on the Thursday to the Stellenbosch wine region for a really hard training session. For the first time, it was a little flat and I felt that some of the disappointed guys were struggling with their motivation. I knew how they felt. When we got back we found that the Irishman Eric Miller had been replaced with Tim Rodber at No 8 after coming down with flu. The incident was reduced to farce after it was revealed that Eric's dad, out following the side, had been to the local chemist and bought his son some over-the-counter cold remedies which Eric had promptly taken. We all knew – at least, we thought we all knew – that this was madness. A lot of prescription medicines contain trace elements of substances which are proscribed under the rules and if Miller had been tested he would have faced a year's ban from the sport.

This was all typically Eric. He was not known as a full 100 watt bulb and the stories about him from his time at Leicester are legion.

Lots of food tales spring to mind. He often cooked himself pizza with it still on its polystyrene base – and then wondered why it tasted funny. He was also a Pot Noodle fan – hardly the ideal food for a professional athlete but his cooking method was unusual: he emptied the contents of the pot into a saucepan, added cold water and heated it for five minutes. Then he poured it all back into the pot. Apparently he had not quite understood the concept of the Pot Noodle. Another thing he often did was buy a bag of potatoes, cook them all, eat a few and freeze the rest.

There's plenty of non-food tales, too. When he first moved to Leicester, he rented a room off Leon Lloyd. Unhappy with the bedroom furniture, he took himself off to MFI and bought a huge wardrobe . . . which he proceeded to assemble downstairs. It took him two hours and a load of wrecked wallpaper to get it upstairs. Perhaps my favourite Eric anecdote, however, came when he was weighing himself. The scales registered a certain number of stones and pounds and Eric decided to try doing it naked to get a more accurate reading. He couldn't understand why there was no difference until someone pointed out he was holding his discarded clothes in one of his hands.

The cold remedy incident therefore came as little surprise to the Leicester contingent but did cause hilarity among the rest of the squad.

Before the first Test, the Springboks launched a media offensive clearly designed to intimidate and unsettle the boys. The papers were full of how they were going to be bigger, harder and more skilful than us. Mark Andrews shot his mouth off about how he was going to deal with Johnno – never a wise move.

The Friday before the match I concentrated on relaxing and trying to offer support to guys in the 21. Geech had arranged for a video to be flown out to us from the UK. It contained snippets of news and sports coverage from back home, detailing how the tour was being followed and emphasising to us the support we had from millions of people thousands of miles away. It was a clever psychological ploy and one which stirred us all. Hundreds of messages of support were flooding in and a few of these were shown to us too. Geech also produced a local newspaper flier reading: 'Lions in Town – the Pansies have arrived'. That steeled a few of the boys just a little more.

Our side was: Neil Jenkins (Pontypridd and Wales) at full-back; Ieuan Evans (Llanelli and Wales) and Alan Tait (Newcastle and Scotland), a centre playing out of position, were the wings; Jeremy Guscott (Bath and England) and Scott Gibbs (Swansea and Wales) at centre; Gregor Townsend at fly-half with Matt Dawson (Northampton Saints and England), in for Rob Howley, at scrum-half; the front row was Tom Smith (Watsonians and Scotland), Keith Wood (Harlequins and Ireland) and Paul Wallace (Saracens and Ireland); Martin Johnson (Leicester Tigers and England) and Jeremy Davidson (London Irish and Ireland) were the locks; the back row saw Tim Rodber (Northampton Saints and England) at No 8, Lawrence Dallaglio (Wasps and England) on the blindside and Richard Hill (Saracens and England) on the openside. A formidable side, in anyone's book.

The replacements bench was John Bentley (Newcastle and England), another who was disappointed and unlucky to miss out on a full place; Mike Catt (Bath and England), who could play stand-off or centre; Austin Healey (Leicester Tigers and England), another chosen for his versatility, with the capacity to play to international standard at scrum-half and wing; the second-choice hooker Barry Williams (Richmond and Wales); Jason Leonard (Harlequins and England) and Rob Wainwright (Watsonians and Scotland). I did feel that last spot, at least, should have been mine.

The Springbok side was littered with world-class performers, many of them World Champions two years earlier: James Small, Henry Honiball, Joost van der Westhuizen, Mark Andrews, Os du Randt, Naka Drotske, Ruben Kruger, Japie Mulder . . . the list went on and on.

Newlands was a superb venue for the first meeting. It has a capacity of under 60,000 and many of those seats are taken up with corporate hospitality. Lions supporters had flooded the area with a vengeance, buying up every spare ticket, and while they were outnumbered they were never out sung.

The game plan was to continue with our 15-man rugby, getting the ball wide as often as possible and taking the play to the Springboks. In the end, it didn't work out quite like that. The South Africans killed the ball at every opportunity and kept the play close. They threw everything at the boys but fantastic defence, particularly by the likes of Scott Gibbs and Lawrence Dallaglio, pushed them back. Pinpoint kicking by Jenks gave us a nine points to eight lead at half-time. A Russell Bennett try shortly after the break gave them the lead but Jenks replied with his boot and the game was still evenly poised after 70 minutes, with the score 15–16 in their favour. Then we were awarded a scrum just inside their 22-metre line. Matt Dawson picked up and beat Ruben Kruger for pace off the mark. Hurtling down the right touchline, he made as though to pass inside – and Teichmann, Venter and van der Westhuizen all bought the dummy, leaving Daws roaring with delight as he screamed over their line to make it 20–16 to us. It was a superb try and we were all on our feet in the stands. At that moment, there was no disappointment at not being on the pitch – just elation that we had taken the lead.

Finally, there was another burst away from the scrum by Daws and Tim Rodber, which led to a ruck. The ball was recycled and Scott Gibbs carried it up for a number of yards, sucking in the Springbok defence. Rodber and Jenks got it out to Alan Tait and Pidge – named because he was said to have had a pigeon chest during his rugby league days – raced over for the try. He soared around the dead ball line firing imaginary shots into the crowd with his six-gun hands waving in celebration. The scoreboard glittered in the night, reading 26–16, the Lions fans in the crowd went berserk and the players, on and off the pitch, followed suit.

Later that evening, we all went out to celebrate the win at a restaurant called the Cantina Tequila. I was pleased but, understandably, a little subdued. Two Tests left and I now had to break into a winning side.

We soon calmed down and began to assess the situation. One down, one won. We had two to play and we could still lose the series. There was to be no taking the eye off the ball.

The South Africa media reacted in typical fashion – as if the end of the world had come. They take their rugby very, very seriously, which is why it is such a big deal to beat them on home soil. They seemed, though, to be taking the view that it was Springbok errors, rather than Lions excellence, which had caused the defeat. Right from the word go, in team meetings, we had seen this arrogance as something we could capitalise on. They thought their monster pack would steamroller our much lighter eight. They were wrong. They underestimated our defence, which was superb. And they thought they were fitter than us, when the reverse was clearly the case. As long as they continued with these false theories, and did not address the real problems – their tactical inability to find ways to unlock our defence and their inability to cope with the rapier thrusts of our backs – they were not at the races.

A hard training session on the Sunday was followed by a split in the camp. The First Test side headed off to Durban, where the Second Test was to be staged. The rest of us relocated to Bloemfontein, where we were due to meet Free State. It was the first time on tour that we had been divided like this and it added to a sense of gloom in my mind that I was not going to get a Test berth. Other guys felt the same way and although Fran and Geech assured us that this was not the case, we all felt a little down.

Our answer was to try to put on a good showing against Free State, the strongest of the South African provincial sides. What transpired, on the rock-hard turf, was probably the best game of the tour. Fran Cotton later described it as the best-ever performance by a mid-week Lions side between two Tests. It was certainly the best game of rugby I have ever played in. Tim Stimpson opened our account with a penalty and followed this by converting his own try, scored in the corner after a clever, cross-field kick by Mike Catt. Our second try came a few minutes later, when Austin threw out a long pass to Bentos. A man on a mission, he scorched round two defenders to touch down, again in the corner. Kicking superbly, Stimmo slotted that one over too. With the Free Staters clearly bewildered by the pace of our attack, they opened up again for Bentley to score his second, the result of an excellent break by Will Greenwood and some great support play by Catty. Allan Bateman also got on the score sheet and, although they came back into it with a score before half-time, at the break we led 31–13.

After the break, Will Greenwood was involved in one of the worst accidents I have ever seen on a rugby field. Tackled by a one of the Free Staters, he was thrown to the ground and concussed by the hard turf. We gathered round as the doctor and physio ran on, but there was no movement from Will and we began to fear the worst. Eventually they took him off to the side and then on to hospital, where he was examined by one of South Africa's top neurosurgeons. He had recovered consciousness and was allowed out of hospital the following day, but was ordered to play no rugby for two months. We later discovered that he had basically died on the pitch – there was no sign of life for four minutes. It seemed a miracle that he had survived and a tragedy, at the same time, that he would now miss out on England's tour to Australia a few weeks later. He had shown himself to be a superb talent during his time as a Lion.

When play restarted, the Free State boys came back hard at us and notched up a converted try and a penalty. But Bentley grabbed his hat-trick, after a move in which Bateman passed to me and I sent him through. Jenks also scored near the death and then Tony Underwood galloped over to put us over 50 points for the third time on tour. We had won 52–30 and I felt that our performance, and perhaps more importantly our attitude after being left out of the Test side, meant they might look against at one or two of us for the next encounter with the Springboks.

Tests after the game revealed that Ieuan Evans was out of the tour with a groin injury. That meant Bentos was named in his place on the wing. The selectors also added new names to the bench – among them, that of N A Back.

The feeling of being named in the 21 was fantastic. It is hard to describe. My trials and tribulations with the England set-up have been well-rehearsed and just to get on the Lions tour was a major achievement for me. It had been a surprise to many people and now, with the way I had played, I had forced my way into the Test set-up. I still wanted to start, but this was a step in the direction and I felt as though I was walking on air for hours after getting my envelope.

It was a must-win game for the Springboks. The whole country had been stunned by the almost uninterrupted victorious nature of our progress through their land. The unthinkable had happened – we had beaten the Springboks. The unimaginable – that we might win the series – loomed over them. They were not helped by having to replace a number of first-choice guys, injured by the ferocity of the tackling they had experienced at the hands of the Lions 'Pansies'. Out went James Small and the centres Japie Mulder – his shoulder wrecked in a challenge on Dallaglio – and Edrich Lubbe. They brought Percy Montgomery in at outside centre to give them a new goal kicking option.

You might imagine that the tension in our dressing room before hand would have been massive. It was anything but. We were relaxed, focused and calm. We knew the job we had to do. We knew they would throw everything at us or the first 20 minutes, desperate to avenge their defeat. We collectively agreed that our bodies, even our lives, would go on the line to stop them coming through. Fran and Geech made speeches and Jim Telfer also stepped up with one of the most stirring pieces of oratory I have ever heard. 'Kill them, boys!' he yelled at the end. 'Kill them till they're dead!' Johnno and Woody led the forwards into the showers where we huddled round for our own psyching-up. Then it was time to run out.

Kings Park was jam-packed and around 10,000 Lions fans had managed to find tickets. The atmosphere was thrilling. I headed for the bench, hoping I would get on at some point.

We kicked off and they did throw everything at the boys. Massive, earth-shaking tackles went in time and time again, as Scott Gibbs and Tim Rodber led the way in battering the green and gold hordes backwards. Gibbsy smashed through one tackle attempted by the massive Os du Randt. As he ran back, du Randt was still sprawled on the floor and Snake, eyes bulging with passion, yelled 'Get up, you fat ox!' at him. The Springboks had the lion's share of the possession and managed to plunder three tries, two of them through mistakes by Tait and Bentley, but Neil Jenkins' boot kept us in touch.

With 10 minutes of the second half gone, Geech told me to warm up and five minutes after that I sprinted out onto the pitch in an adrenalin haze for my first-ever Test appearance in a Lions jersey. The cacophony of noise was unbelievable as I tried to concentrate on slotting in to Richard Hill's position and raising the tempo. It was already fierce, with the South Africans attacking us as though their lives depended on it. The game was still there to be won or lost but the pendulum was definitely swinging towards the home team. Two minutes earlier, André Joubert had gone over for their third try to make it 15 points to 9. Another score then, and the game would probably have been lost. But it was we who made the next inroad, with a 66th minute penalty by the ice-blooded Welshman which made it 15–12. Still the Springboks battered at us and still we kept them out. On the 73rd minute, Jenks notched another three points to level the scores and the banshee wailing and howling of the crowd went up another level. At 15–15, many of the guys on both sides were running on near-empty but Keith Wood intervened. The ball came loose and the bald-headed Irish hooker fly-hacked it down field, sprinting after it like a demented winger. He made so much ground so quickly that the full-back Joubert had to side-foot the ball into touch, twenty five yards out. We won the line-out and a maul was set up. As the Springboks waited anxiously, watching for our runners to take their attacking lines, Matt Dawson flung the ball out to Jerry Guscott, who had drifted into the fly-half pocket. Cucumber cool, Jerry pinged the ball between the posts for one of the most famous drop goals in rugby history.

The clock ticked on for three agonising minutes but the agony began to show more on South African faces as the seconds elapsed. When the whistle blew, pandemonium erupted. Players sank to their knees or hugged each other and tears of exultation flowed freely. Around us, the Springboks were a dejected, wrecked team, lying on the turf or standing with head in hands. Lions players ran towards our tremendous fans and saluted them for the support we had received while the home supporters were muted in their shock and dismay.

For my part, I was proud to have been on the pitch when the series was won. I felt I had contributed well throughout the tour and so I was able to share in the joy and triumph of the victory with a clear conscience.

That night we shaved Geech's head. Early on, he had promised we could if we won the series and the crew cut was duly administered. We all had a boozy evening – a few of the boys went out on a monumental bender – and there were some sore heads the next day. An hour or so before sunrise, for some reason, Keith Wood, Tom Smith and I thought it would be a good idea to go back to the hotel and take a duvet and a flat pack of beers down onto the beach. It was freezing that night and I remember the three of us cuddling up under this one duvet – without touching a tin – and waking up at about five o'clock in the morning as the sun came up. We looked around and found the beer gone and lots of footprints in the sand. Fifty yards away a group of hotel security guards was watching us. They were part of the plainclothes team who followed us everywhere. I never did find out if it was they who had our beer.

There was a chance that, after the second win and with the series in the bag, guys would start to relax. Job done. It didn't happen. And, speaking for myself, I certainly didn't see things that way. There was still a Lions starting place up for grabs in the Third Test and I was determined to do everything in my power to secure it. The Tuesday saw us travel to the mining town of Welkom for the final mid-week game against Northern Free State. I was in the side. Those guys who were not decided to come out to the match to support us. That was typical of the team spirit and bond which had grown between us. It was freezing when we arrived – they had been threatened with snow – and Northern Free State were bang up for the match. They ran in a stack of points against us but were not the strongest side in defence and we were able to put our own mark on the score board almost at will. The final score was 67–39 in our favour – which was both the highest number of points we had scored and also the highest number we had conceded. I managed to plant the ball down for my first try in a Lions shirt, which gave me a lot of pleasure. It was a tough, physical game for the wrong reasons – they took a few guys out off the ball and the pitch was another rock-hard affair, with the grass cropped as close as a US Marine's hair. There was precious little protection if you hit the deck.

The side for the Third Test at Ellis Park in Johannesburg was announced shortly afterwards. Tony Underwood had grabbed a hat-trick at Welkom and, since Alan Tait had been injured in the Second Test, he had booked himself a spot in the third. Gregor Townsend and Keith Wood were also crocked and Mark Regan and Mike Catt were handed their Test jerseys. The other change was momentous, as far as I was concerned. I had just edged ahead of Hilly to snatch the No 7 shirt for the final game. Fran Cotton later said: 'Richard Hill had been terrific in defence in the first two Tests but we needed someone who was a little more streetwise on the ground, and who could start winning us some ball. Neil Back had already demonstrated how effective he could be in that department and he had produced another outstanding display against Northern Free State. We were pleased that Jim Telfer had insisted on having Neil on board.' I think those remarks were a little unfair to Hilly who, in my book, is extremely 'streetwise' and also wins a lot of ball. However, I was not about to quibble with Fran and was ecstatic to have achieved my dream of a Lions start. The other change was Rob Wainwright. He was in for Tim Rodber, a late flu victim, and would play at No 6, with Lol going to No 8.

A massive roar from the 60,000-strong crowd greeted us as we ran out onto the pitch, Johnno throwing aside the cuddly, stuffed Lion mascot for the final time. At our team meeting beforehand, we had agreed that it was essential that we continued playing the 15-man game. The Boks would be playing for pride and were likely to hit us every bit as hard as they had in the previous meeting. And so it proved. They claimed first blood with a couple of penalties inside the first three minutes which were kicked by new boy Jannie de Beer, a man a few of us were to run up against a couple of years later. Then a converted Percy Montgomery try made it 13–0. By the interval we were back in the game after three Neil Jenkins penalties had made it 13–9. Jerry Guscott had to be replaced by Allan Bateman after breaking his arm and Tim Stimpson was on for Tony Underwood on the wing.

Both sides tried to open the game up, the South Africans having belatedly realised they were not going to bully our pack. A van der Westhuizen blindside break earned them a try which de Beer converted and a 61st minute penalty made it 23–9. Two or three minutes later we were back in it with a sniping Matt Dawson try which Jenks converted: 23–16. For five or ten minutes, each side thrust and parried. Had the pace of Guscott and Underwood been available, we might have done it. But the Springboks killed us off with two tries inside the final five minutes and our dream of a whitewash was itself washed away.

I was disappointed not to have been on the winning side in the match but elated to be on the field when Martin Johnson went up to collect the series trophy and to join in the triumphal procession around the touchline. That night, we hit the booze in a big way and the session continued the following day at a bar called the Bushranger. British and Irish players don't get too many opportunities to celebrate series wins against Southern Hemisphere sides and we were not going to let this opportunity pass us by. There were many drunken renditions of our tour song *Wonderwall*.

People have suggested the final Test was a match too far. I don't agree. We were just as fired up before that game as any other and we wanted to win it. Perhaps subconsciously you relax a little because the hard work has been done. I don't know. I do know we had done fantastically well on the back of a season in which most of the guys had played something like 45 games of rugby. The Springboks played more like 25 games in their season so I thought it was an outstanding effort by us all.

We had certainly struck a major blow for Northern Hemisphere rugby. Written off by the South Africans as 'pansies' with no stomach for the battle, we had shown ourselves to be every bit as fit, strong and skilful as them over the course of the seven weeks. We had taken the words of big mouths like James Small and Mark Andrews and rammed them back down their throats. The media, home and abroad, which had all-but written us off as we left the British Isles had also been proved wrong and was now hailing us as one of the great Lions sides.

I felt that I had come through well, too. My 'end-of-term-report' in Fran Cotton's book reads as follows: 'Neil forever put to bed the ridiculous theory that he isn't big enough. They don't come any bigger than South Africans but Neil made his mark and had a quite outstanding tour. I was delighted when he got into the final Test because he thoroughly deserved the honour. His footballing skills opened everyone's eyes as to just how good a footballer he really is.' In a jibe at Jack Rowell, he added: 'Had he been in the right environment in the last couple of years he would have been outstanding.' It was humbling to be spoken of so well by such a man and after I had spent so long in such illustrious company.

Jerry Guscott had more complimentary words too: 'Six years ago, the public perception of 'Backy' was that he was a little upstart who had a very high opinion of himself and too much to say. However, he had already made a favourable impression on me with the way he handled himself during the 1995 World Cup. He surprised me because he was easy to get along with, a good tourist who will mingle and mix with anybody. The way he plays the game I've got to be a fan because he makes the backs' job so much easier. I feel really pleased for him because he answered all his critics so completely that he earned the right to walk away from the tour smiling inwardly and outwardly. All I know is that whoever manages England is in a dream position with two opensides of the calibre of Backy and Richard Hill.'

With Jack Rowell set to quit his England post, I was certainly hoping the new incumbent would see things the same way. I haven't asked Clive Woodward but I am damn sure the Lions put me on the map.

And who were my tour heroes?

Every one of those 35 players was a hero. Johnno was a superb captain. As he does with Leicester, he led from the front, with bravery and skill, and was never intimidated by the Springbok aggression. By the end of our time together, the Scottish, Irish and Welsh lads would have walked on hot coals for him, which speaks volumes for the man. He handled the pressure from the media very well and behind closed doors with the rest of us he was his usual dry, sarcastic self. He is an intelligent and witty man – unusually for a second row – and it is perhaps a shame that that is not widely known.

Of the rest, Scott Gibbs, Rodber and Lol stood out for their monster tackles and Jenks for his kicking and his ability to soak up alcohol and mickey-taking to no apparent effect. Keith Wood was great: as mad as a hatter and a dreadful snorer, but a real character who was full of passion. John Bentley was another superb guy to have on tour. He spent every waking moment jabbering away in his broad northern voice, winding people up either deliberately or by accident, and could have had his face filled in a few times. That he didn't was proof of how much he was liked and respected. Geech, Telfer and Cotton made a brilliant job a managing and coaching us. The back-up team were fantastic, too.

Perhaps my ultimate tour hero, though, was a guy who will, for obvious reasons, remain anonymous. Picture the scene. It's an early morning training session at the beginning of the tour. The guys are working hard, sweating and grunting, but the focus isn't quite there. Then this character strolls over, just showered. 'Lads,' he says sternly, surveying the panting players. 'We've got to sort this out. There have been one or two of you out on the piss, one or two having late nights, one or two out misbehaving in discos. I don't want to hear any more stories like that. From now on, it's commitment all the way. We're pro-fessionals so let's act like bloody professionals.'

And off he strolls.

He'd been up until six that morning entertaining a local barmaid!

*

The next Lions tour, to Australia in 2001, will be a hell of a tough one to crack. There will be no Bentos and no Ieuan – in fact, a few of the older lads have called it a day in the last two or three years. The Aussies, like the Springboks, are World Champions, and Tri-Nations winners, too. They have a host of big, powerful attackers who will test the Lions defence like it's never been tried before. Their own tackling is ferocious too, so the Northern Hemisphere boys will have to find new ways of reaching the line.

No Geech or Jim, either. There has been a lot of controversy about Graham Henry's appointment. People say that because he's a Kiwi he can't possibly understand the mystique and the passion behind the British Lions. That's garbage. The only criteria for a Lions coach is his ability to select, mould and inspire 35 guys from four different countries and to come away with a series win. Henry has proved himself as a coach with Auckland and with Wales. Now he has to produce the goods with the Lions.

I hope he makes Martin Johnson skipper. Johnno knows what it means to win a series Down Under and he's got what it takes to ensure it happens. The guys, whoever they are, will follow him over the top.

I desperately hope, too, that I'm selected. It's a huge honour. But there will be stiff competition for places. All I can do is play as well as possible and keep myself fit. Rest assured, I'll be doing all I can to be on that plane.

Footnote: Things have obviously moved on since those last few paragraphs were written for the original hardback edition of this book, but I have kept them in so you can see my thoughts before we went on that ill-fated Lions tour. For an account of what happened – and my views on what went wrong – see Chapter 20.

CHAPTER 7

Clive Woodward

CLIVE WOODWARD took over as England coach in 1997 and has since given me 30 caps I probably would not have had. Much more than that, in his era things have been totally different.

He has a great understanding of the psychology of players and of teams and he knows how to get the best out of both. He knows the importance of communication and he recognised, too, the need for both the team and back-up staff to be as professional as possible. We get the best of everything.

When he was appointed, I knew next to nothing about him except that he had played at centre for Leicester, England and the Lions. His pedigree was fairly impressive, which was an early factor in his favour with the players. He had been there and done it at a higher level than most of us had so we had to respect that. But no-one knew whether he had the vision to see what was needed to be done to make England competitive on the world stage and whether he had the guts and drive to see it through. He has answered those questions pretty emphatically, in my view.

He has changed the whole system. There is now plenty of communication. He has told all the players that he is available seven days a week, 24 hours a day. In his autobiography, *In Your Face*, Richard Cockerill criticised Clive for being 'gutless' because of his reliance upon e-mail. Cocker's implication was that Clive did not have the courage to tell a player to his face if

A rugby player in the making – practising my handling skills in the garden of our Coventry home, aged two.

Above An early outing for the Back fists: my brother Ian lies on the turf as our friend David Smith raises my arm. *Below* Challenging for a high ball in my days with Mount Nod FC. I loved soccer and it was hard giving it up for rugby.

Above Earlsdon RUFC under-eights, with me, aged six and with the ball under my arm, in the centre of things. My brother Ian is third from left in the front row. *Below* In action for The Woodlands School against King Henry VIII, doing my best to imitate Jean-Pierre Rives.

Above Celebrating winning the Coventry FC Shield. My mate Rob Calloway stands immediately to my right with a bottle of cider at the ready. *Below left* About to set off on tour with England Schools. *Below right* Posing in my purple England Schools tracksuit and red cap – the colour scheme left a lot to be desired, but I was as proud as could be.

Above Back the Lad – my Schwarzenegger impression, aged fifteen, in the gym I set up in my mum's attic. *Inset* The real thing – hitting the bag under the unforgiving eye of training partner Darren Grewcock.

Above In Tigers colours – on the charge for Leicester, ball in hand. *Opposite page* In a monkey suit – Ali and I on our wedding day. Doesn't she look gorgeous?

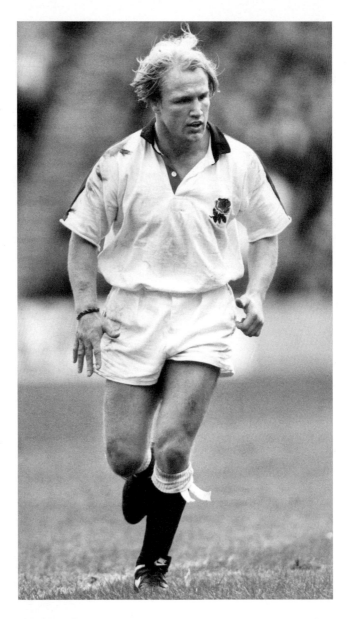

Above At last I have made it! Twenty minutes into my first game for England, against Scotland. The feeling was unforgettable – and, sadly, rare for me in mid 1990s. PICTURE WWW.RUGBY-HEROES.CO.UK.

he had been dropped and that he did not want to talk about it afterwards. With respect to Richard, I think that is nonsense. For instance, Mike Catt was very disappointed with non-selection during the World Cup. He took his concerns to Clive and I saw them having a number of conversations at the side of the pitch during training sessions. Clive was always ready and willing to explain his decision. Catty might not have agreed with the selection but at least he knew what he had to do to get back in. He took it on the chin and bounced back in the 2000 Six Nations to play some of his best international rugby so far. The fact is, e-mail is just another way of talking to people. It has not replaced the phone or the face-to-face conversation, just supplemented it. I have been lucky in that Clive has yet to drop me. But if, or when, it happens I will certainly feel comfortable ringing him or calling in on him to discuss his motives. He and his wife Jane operate an open-house policy. You can turn up any time to chat about rugby, or anything else. Recently, for instance, Ali and I went out for a meal with them in Marlow with Martin and Kay Johnson. It is good for the players to know that they can call Clive any time and it is so different from the Cooke and Rowell era. He treats you like an equal and like an adult. It is not just a question of communicating with the players. He and Jane have gone out of their way to get to know our wives, girlfriends and families. They have tried to create a 'family' atmosphere about the squad, recognising that if you are happy off the pitch you are more likely to play well on it. Jane is particularly good with all the girls. She knows only too well what it is like for players' families, with all the weeks we spend away on tour and at training camps. At matches, she always makes a point of giving them a hug and a kiss, asking how they are. I doubt Jack Rowell's wife even knew their names.

Before one of our World Cup games, all the girls went round to Clive's house and Jane took them out for a Chinese, paid for by herself and Clive. She even arranged for transport to take them back to their hotels. Ali cannot speak highly enough of them. Tiny babies are not allowed in the stands at

Twickenham. During the World Cup, when Ali had just given birth to our daughter Olivia, Jane and the RFU president Geoffrey Addison arranged for her to watch a game from the President's Box, for which I was very grateful. Jane was always on the phone, checking up on mother and baby, and Clive allowed me to leave our camp a number of times to spend time with the two of them during the competition. He's got young kids himself and he's a human being, not a robot.

We invited the Woodwards to our wedding. I wouldn't have invited any other England coach: even if I had done so I doubt they would have bothered to reply. It is not just wives and girlfriends. Clive and Jane have got to know my parents and brothers, too. Before games, Clive's obviously busy but Jane always makes time to chat to my parents. She makes them feel involved and special, whereas before they were totally ignored. Allowing the families to get too close can backfire, however. Before and during the 26–26 game against New Zealand in December 1997, my brother Gary had dived headfirst into the hospitality, celebrating my first cap against the All Blacks with a little too much enthusiasm. He was well beered-up as half time approached and thought it might be a good idea to wander down to where Clive was sitting watching the game for a chat. He tried to shake Clive by the hand, shouting 'Great game!' and other perceptive comments. Clive, who had more important things on his mind than humouring this lunatic rugby 'naus' – nauseating git – told him to f*** off. Fair play to Gary, he f***ed off.

Importantly, the environment now is one where you feel you can speak your mind and have input, something I never felt confident enough to do before. It also means there are none of the cliques of yesteryear. For instance, when Hilly was brought in at No 7 by Jack Rowell, I certainly did not feel able to talk to Richard about what had happened. In those days the management fostered, whether accidentally or by design, a culture in which players did not really speak to each other. Under Clive, the players and the management together designed new rules of conduct. One of them dictates that a non-selected player will speak immediately to the selected player in his position, to wish him luck for the game ahead. I think this is an excellent idea and I will happily do it if and when the roles are reversed.

This atmosphere has made it easier for new players to come in, too. There is none of the slightly frosty attitude which was exhibited towards incomers before. Now, we all make a point of welcoming new guys and try to make them feel a part of it. We are a team, after all.

However, I think the biggest change has been in the professionalism of the modern set-up. There is a tremendous attention to detail, with every base covered as far as possible. Simple things can made a lot of difference. For instance, we have altered the hotel England use before home internationals and now use the Pennyhill Park at Bagshot. It is a country club in a good location, with all the facilities we need on site – even a rugby pitch. For relaxation, there is a permanent team room with a pool table, a couple of TVs and sets of video games, papers and magazines and a fridge full of drinks and snacks. Outside, there is clay pigeon shooting and a golf course. With all this at hand, we don't have to travel off site, so we stay fresher.

Team England's new-found professionalism has extended to the staff we now have in place around us. John Mitchell was an excellent forwards coach who combined his England duties with those of Director of Rugby at Manchester Sale. He was given the responsibility of ensuring the pack lived up to and surpassed the reputations of previous England packs. It was a shame when he decided to go back to New Zealand at the end of his contract but Andy Robinson has stepped into his shoes almost seamlessly and his will to win and technical know-how are just as strong as Mitch's. Phil Larder, the defensive coach, was an inspired introduction. Phil had been a centre in both codes of the game, starting in Union before heading north to League. He coaches at Leicester and has been a factor in our two recent championships. He brought in new ideas and methods to England and has helped to make us one of the best teams in the world defensively.

Dave Alred has worked with Jonny Wilkinson as kicking coach, applying some lessons from his days coaching American footballers, and his results are there for all to see. Other guys like backs coach Brian Ashton and scrummaging Phil Keith-Roach have contributed massively too. Dave Reddin, the fitness coach, has also had a big impact. I don't think many people would argue with the assertion that we are now one of the fittest sides in world rugby. Away from the training ground, Clive brought in Steve Lander to advise us on referees' interpretations of the laws of the game. The team doctor Terry Crystal, physiotherapist Kevin Murphy and masseur Richard Wegrzyk are also first class.

When Clive first came along, all the players were given a large, black leather Filofax, embossed with the English Rose, which is the squad's bible. It set out our team objectives, details our code of conduct and provides all sorts of supplementary information. Chief among our objectives is to create an attacking style of play which emphasises pace, excitement and the scoring of tries. We want to have the Twickenham crowd on its feet and we reckon we can do that by playing attacking rugby with quick, flat ball at all phases.

Equally, we place particular emphasis on our defence, spending 50 per cent or more of our training time on this area. We also work hard on our fitness and power, on kicking strategy and on strength under the high ball.

Off the field, we have tried to improve media relations. There have been role-play sessions with journalists to help us deal with what will be thrown at us. For post-match interviews, we have agreed that players will be straight-talking, but that no one individual will be singled out for blame in the event of defeat. It is all a part of building our team spirit, where the players are united and can trust each other.

Our selection criteria is now far fairer than it was. The emphasis is on class. Our 'bible' quotes Ian Botham: 'Form comes and goes . . . class lasts forever.' Clive had tried to establish the team around guys who had proven themselves international performers over recent months and years.

He has also put in place far better video and statistical analysis, examining both ourselves and every player and team we were likely to meet.

Clive is very open-minded about training methods and he draws on ideas and theories from all over the world. For instance, he tried to drill home in us how easy it was to see the obvious, to take situations for granted. He set us a little teaser, showing us the following sentence and asking us to say how many times the letter 'F' appeared in it:

'FINISHED FILES ARE THE RES-
ULT OF YEARS OF SCIENTIF-
IC STUDY COMBINED WITH THE
EXPERIENCE OF MANY YEARS.'

Nearly all of the players only saw three 'F's. It was a way of making the point that the human brain and eye are essentially lazy and will only scratch the surface, will not look deep enough, and will not find what they are looking for, unless they are disciplined. Clive told us: 'The whole philosophy of the England team is exactly the opposite. We want to leave nothing to chance or ignore any information or ideas that might make a difference. This means continually looking for six F's in everything we do, which our competition haven't spotted and which might make the difference.'

Above all, the players are now able to set their own objectives and to be heavily involved in everything we do. There is none of the schoolmasterly attitude which characterised earlier eras. Clive and the coaches are big on discussion between the players. At one meeting we were asked to name the qualities we would expect to find in a high-performing team. Words and phrases like 'open minded', 'high energy levels shown', 'support for others' and 'willing to sacrifice' came out and from then on we have tried to play by those ideals.

Of course, no-one can get everything right. Coaching, like playing, is the art of the possible, cutting the mistakes down to the minimum. I feel Clive maybe gets *too* enthusiastic, *too* caught-up in the atmosphere and the emotion. He's almost too positive, if that's possible.

*

Were Cooke and Rowell right not to pick me? Does size matter? You often hear people talk about this new rule and that old law and how the game was different in the past as they try to explain why I was kept out of the England side.

What a load of rubbish. I played for one of the leading clubs in the world under all the old rules and no-one questioned my contribution there. The fact is then, as now, size doesn't matter, within reason. If you are good enough, you are big enough. In fact, I believe my height is actually of positive benefit to me, I can get down to the ball and up again a hell of a lot quicker than a big guy like Ben Clarke.

I am not saying Ronnie Corbett, however talented he might be, could be an international back row – though he might make a half-decent scrum-half – but at 5ft 10in tall and 14½ stones, I am hardly a midget. Added to which, I am a lot stronger than some guys twice my size. In the gym, I am moving weights that they don't even want to look at.

And the fact is that time and time again, playing at every age level for my country, I have proved I am good enough.

I hope that doesn't sound arrogant. I am not suggesting I am the best No 7 ever to walk the earth. At their peaks, Peter Winterbottom and Andy Robinson were just two England players who had as much going for them as I have. I am not even suggesting I am necessarily the best in the world at this moment. I have gone on record as saying Josh Kronfeld is the man to beat. The gritty Frenchman Olivier Magne and Scotland's Channel Islands-born Budge Pountney are also excellent players.

What I do firmly believe is that I am currently England's best openside flanker and I have been for some years.

Can I win the ball? Do I help continuity? Is my defence good?

Does my game add an extra attacking dimension to the side? Most commentators would answer 'Yes' to all those questions. How tall I am is not the issue – or, at least, it shouldn't be. It certainly is not for me. On the pitch I feel as big as anyone else. I have never felt intimidated or overshadowed.

Looking back, I actually wonder whether the size issue obscured Cooke's real reason for leaving me out. Maybe it was just a convenient excuse, when really his decision was being made on personality grounds.

My somewhat outspoken approach when being interviewed probably didn't help. I have no doubt that some people saw the things I said in the papers and immediately assumed I was an arrogant, big-headed loud mouth. I am certainly confident in my abilities as a player but I am actually a quiet and fairly shy person. I just tended to give an honest, straightforward answer to a question. Example. Journalist: 'Neil, are you the best openside flank forward in England?' Back: 'Yes.' While I would honestly believe that to be the case, it might not, in hindsight, have been the most sensible answer. A better answer would be something like: 'I certainly think I am up there in contention but there are a lot of talented guys around and I am going to have to work hard to win a place.'

I had had no media training – something I firmly believe young players should now receive as a matter of course – and this tendency towards honesty earned me enemies.

I did not realise how the things I was saying would look in black and white. I spoke to *The Daily Express* in February 1993 and was asked about my England future after I was dropped to the bench from the then B team, in favour of Steve Ojomoh, for a game against Spain. I was quoted as 'rapping' Geoff Cooke and saying: 'You cannot be outstanding and too small at the same time. Unfortunately, team manager Geoff Cooke doesn't seem to share that opinion.'

Apart from the spin the journalist put on this – I don't think I was really 'rapping' Cooke, because whatever I felt privately I was careful always to be respectful to him – that was logical enough and, I think, fair enough. But, looking back, I can understand how Cooke might have been rubbed up the wrong way by someone he perceived as a junior player making fairly outspoken remarks. Sometimes it was just the way articles were slanted.

On one occasion, I chatted to Steve Bale of *The Independent*. Steve kicked off his article by saying: 'If – or more likely when – Neil Back plays for England, it will be despite, rather than because of, Geoff Cooke, a noted sceptic.' Steve also referred directly to Cooke's 'occasional inference' that I was being ignored on size grounds. Straight away, that seems to set up an opposition between me and Steve Bale on the one hand, and Geoff Cooke on the other. Steve then quoted me as saying: 'For the game I play my size is a massive advantage in that a bigger guy would have to be extremely agile to get up and down and make all the tackles I get through during a game. I just can't see why this should place a question mark over my ability to perform at international level. You're either good enough or you aren't, and if you're good enough you're big enough. I'm on top of my game at the moment and all I need is a break.' So it now seems like I'm basically saying Geoff Cooke has got it all wrong. Steve then goes on to write: 'Even when England's loose forwards struggled to keep up in last year's Test in Australia, Cooke refused to accept that a player of Back's speed and uncanny positional sense would have made any difference in exploiting the incisiveness of Will Carling and Jeremy Guscott.' By now, he is making Cooke sound like an imbecile for not picking this amazing player on the completely erroneous grounds of size.

In the England set-up of the time, you were supposed to put up and shut up. It was like they wanted you in short trousers off the pitch as well as on.

If I had recognised this a bit earlier, maybe my career would have been different.

CHAPTER 8

In Training

I WENT into the World Cup – I think we all did – knowing we could win it and believing we would. It was the first time, I feel, that any England side had really been given the opportunity of winning a serious competition. Previously, we had not had the correct preparation for any tournament.

The last World Cup I had been involved in was in 1995, before professionalism. The selected players finished the season, rested for a couple of weeks and a fortnight later we were in Durban playing our pool games. The only concession we had was to be limited to 25 games for our clubs – which, incidentally, led me to miss the game in which Leicester secured the League title that year, against Bristol. I had to sit up in the stands wearing my club Number Ones – our formal suit. I've never been a good watcher of rugby and I found this very frustrating and a massive anti-climax to what had been a hard-fought campaign. When the England squad joined up, we had time to do a little training and to work on a few tactical plans but it was nothing like enough, and that probably told in the end.

The 1999 World Cup was different. Coming on our own turf and timed for October, it gave us four months to prepare and we knew there could be no excuses. This was far longer than the Southern Hemisphere sides had and it gave us a fantastic chance to attain peak fitness and to gel together as a team. You could argue the Kiwis, Springboks and Wallabies benefited by coming fresh from playing hard Tri-Nations fixtures week in, week out. Their dilemma was whether they picked up any major injuries which would upset their squads. That was not a problem for us, although Kyran Bracken did get injured while training down in Australia, and unfortunately went on to miss the World Cup. There were benefits to each approach but I preferred ours.

It started in paradise.

South Stradbroke is one of only 15 sand islands in the world and it was our home for just over a month as we worked on our fitness in the summer. A long bar of semi-tropical rainforest and golden beach, bound together by mangrove roots, sitting in the South Pacific just off Queensland's Gold Coast, it is miles from anywhere and incredibly beautiful – a land of dazzling pink and orange sunrises and sunsets. In the strangely-shaped gum trees, cabbage-tree palms and eucalyptus, sacred kingfishers, kookaburras and rainbow lorikeets flitted from branch to branch. On the golden beaches we saw five-foot lace monitor lizards basking in the sun and wallabies scampering to escape the huge, foaming, turquoise breakers. The sea teemed with shoals of brilliant fish, sharks and dolphins. Generations of Aboriginal tribespeople knew it as a haven and made regular trips over from the mainland, gathering oysters, edible molluscs and other shellfish and – somehow – using dolphins to herd mullet towards the shore for easier netting.

'South Straddie', as the Aussies know it, is best known now for Couran Cove, a 151-hectare slice cutting straight across the centre of the island. In this dreamland, the former Australian Olympic runner Ron Clarke has created a beach and sports resort which rivals any in the world. Clarke was a superb athlete who set 18 world records during his career. Some years ago, with his wife Helen, he set about developing Couran Cove. It is a cleverly-designed village of beachfront lodges, apartments and villas with excellent sports facilities: indoor and outdoor gyms, running tracks, swimming pools, climbing walls, tennis and basketball courts and golf courses.

While you couldn't ignore the stunning backdrop to it all, we were there to work. We needed to build up a base of endurance fitness and to work on team spirit if we were to have any chance in the World Cup.

It was the perfect place to start that tuning-up process.

A few of the Leicester guys and I actually arrived five days late. There had been a couple of weddings – my brother's and Richard Cockerill's – and we had permission to stay behind in England.

Our itinerary suggested there would be two weeks of general recovery before we cracked on. I don't know what Clive's idea of general recovery is but within an hour of landing the fitness coach Dave Reddin had us all on a six kilometre run. I didn't mind. I wanted to get into it, to feel part of the squad. I had been missing the boys and it felt great to be with them again, making up for lost time. I actually felt guilty for staying behind to see my brother get married.

The whole time out there we were pretty regimented. We were up at 7am every day. First thing, we drank a protein shake to help us build muscle. At 7.30am we would be on weights or endurance work, depending on the day. Endurance meant timed six or seven kilometre cross-country runs, up and down hills in the rainforest. These would vary: some were steady-state, maintaining a good pace and a heart-rate of 165 bpm, while others involved sprinting for two minutes and recovering for one until you had covered the distance. Afterwards, I would drink a recovery agent which helps you get carbohydrates into the body. It is important to take carbs on board immediately after exercise. The food we ate was very strictly low in fat, high in protein and with a solid base of complex carbohydrates. Each player had his own course of supplements, broken down and designed to meet his specific needs. From 10am until 12 noon we did rugby training: tackling, ball handling, set pieces. More recovery agent, more pills and lunch, with a rest in the afternoon to avoid the heat of the day. Around 4pm, we would train again, taking on more pills and another protein shake. All the time, we were hydrating, drinking six or more litres of water each day. Dehydration is a serious problem anywhere but it is obviously accelerated when you are training in tropical climates. The heat means you lose a lot of fluid through sweat so we had to be on our guards. By 9.30pm most evenings, I found I was exhausted and I needed some kip, taking on another protein shake if I woke up in the night.

It was a tremendous way of preparing the ground for what was to come, though some of the guys were not as enthusiastic as me. In one article which was drawn to my attention, someone described as a 'very senior member of the England party' was quoted as saying: 'Bloody place. You can't smoke, you can't get a drink and you can't get a round of golf. We're all up at six and in bed by nine and it's driving us all mad. All except Backy, of course. It's right up his street. But then, he's been mad for years.'

We didn't let up even in the days before the 'friendly' Test match which had been arranged against Australia, towards the end of June. Ordinarily, before a big international, you would tailor your training programme so that with three days to go you are just doing light aerobic work to maintain fitness but avoiding heavy work to conserve your strength for the game ahead. But we were out there to get fit for the biggest test of our playing lives, not just for that one encounter: it was just an obstacle in the way and we were focused well beyond it. Having said that, it was good to face them. It gave us a reminder of the physical intensity of the Southern Hemisphere teams.

For the first hour in Sydney we were the better side, certainly up front, but we were tired from all the activity and we didn't put away our chances. In the end, we went down narrowly, losing by 22 points to 15 to a good outfit who we knew would make tough opponents should we face them in the coming tournament. We handled their pack well but the backs gave early notice of how punishing Southern Hemisphere running can be. I thought Tune and Herbert were outstanding and Joe Roff showed what a dangerous finisher he is.

Despite the loss, we didn't feel too low. We were focused on the World Cup. We went back to the resort and straight back into the training. It wasn't all graft, however. There was one legendary fishing trip on an afternoon off. About 30 of us went out on a huge boat. The sea was really choppy and an hour and a half into the journey I started throwing up and I carried on for the entire afternoon. I wasn't the only one – out of all of us, only a couple of guys weren't ill. We were trawling our lines out at the back of the boat and loads of players were being sick and hauling in fish at the same time. I lost three kilos in bodyweight, I couldn't eat for a day and I was badly dehydrated. It was a poor idea for a day off. I've been sea-fishing before and I've been Okay but that's definitely my last go.

One thing I and a couple of other players and coaches noticed was the change in body shape that was achieved out there. Some of the lads came out overweight and unfit. I had always trained hard, even before professionalism, and I found their condition hard to believe. The coaches were asking what was happening at club level. I agreed with them. Four years into professional rugby, what had some of the players been doing with their time? At Couran Cove, the Leicester contingent, the Bath guys and a few others were already pretty fit but some people just weren't. The physical demands in Australia shocked them and they simply weren't up to it at first. Phil Greening was one example, as he has admitted himself.

I'm not necessarily blaming the guys. I think it pointed up a problem with English club rugby in general. Most clubs have improved now but you can still get by in the Premiership. You don't have to be 100 per cent fit. It is still too soft. International rugby is different. Talent is not enough. You need to have a bit extra.

I feel Leicester have got it right. We have a dietician and fitness advisers. We, as players, have an input into the training and it's run by blokes who have been there and done it at the top level – men like Dean Richards, John Wells, Pat Howard and, at that time, Joel Stransky – and they know when to push you and when you need a rest.

But fair play to Phil and one or two other guys, they realised they had a problem, knuckled down and beat it. Greening is now one of the fittest players in the England set-up – testament to the hard work and sheer effort he has put into his career in the last 12 months. I am, however, waiting to see the six-pack he promised to develop. He even had a rather fetching sun tattooed around his navel ready to draw attention to it when it arrived. The effort which everyone put in during those four weeks was outstanding. The possibility of playing in the World Cup was a pretty good incentive. We all improved but some improved vastly and it enabled them to catch up by the time we ran out against Italy in October.

On our return from Australia, we got three weeks off. But we were given a training schedule. Ali and I went on holiday with my parents and my brother and his new wife. Ali was expecting Olivia at the time so she couldn't fly and we rented a cottage down in St Ives. I went out at 7am every day for an early morning run to keep my aerobic fitness levels up. There was also weights one day, endurance the next, with some speed work as well. Despite that, I really enjoyed the break. I needed to spend time with Ali and I needed time away from the England set-up to recharge mentally.

Soon, though, it was time for camp. The last two months before the World Cup, we were to spend weekdays at the Petersham Hotel, with weekends off seeing our families and so on. During that period, we had our much-publicised outings to train with the Marines at Lympstone

I had seen TV programmes about the Marines and the punishing training they put their recruits through, and I was really looking forward to spending time with them. They treated us like officers, putting us up in the officers' quarters. The first morning, the ice was well and truly broken. Clive Woodward was sitting out on the Mess veranda having a coffee with all the top brass, anxious for his boys to make a good impression. Matt Dawson arrives in his flashy Porsche Boxster – personalised registration plate MBD-something-or-other – with Nick Beal in tow. Daws gets out and he is wearing shades, shorts and sandals. What's more, he reaches into the back and pulls out his golf clubs. Then he proceeds to stroll casually up to the Mess, grinning all over his face, clubs clinking behind him, looking for all the world like he has arrived for a relaxing vacation and a gentle round or two of golf. The top brass's eyebrows are somewhat raised. Clive's gone red and his eyes are popping out of his head. He says 'Daws! What are you doing?' Matt replied: 'Bealy just bet me fifty quid I wouldn't walk up here with my golf clubs like I was on holiday.' There were a few chuckles among the top brass and it certainly broke the ice. It was typical of the spirit we were developing.

The Marine NCOs were strict and punctual but there was no barracking or dressing down, something I had expected. I thought they would try to show us that they were not impressed by who we were. Tim Rodber, an army officer, felt he would get particular stick because of the Forces rivalry, but they were fine with all of us.

It was a fantastic experience. We were really spoiled. Twickenham covered part of the expenditure but it must have cost the MoD a fortune. For instance, one day we were all taken up onto the moors in helicopters, which are not cheap to fly. It was exhilarating. The pilots hedge-hopped us, batting along at ground level, scaring cows and popping up to get over hedges as they would if they were carrying Marines into battle. We had been kitted out with the new recruit's 'rig' – all the clothes and equipment a real Marine would have – because if the weather had closed in on the moors we would have had to dig in for the night. We had a few exercises up there. We climbed up a 30 metre rock face and abseiled down. The only thing stopping you falling is the Marine above you holding the rope. I found it pretty scary,– even for someone who has bungee-jumped off the Victoria Falls bridge, but you soon built up a great rapport and trust with these guys. We did their assault course, split up into six-man teams. Mine included Cocker and Jason Leonard and our team came first, completing the course in 14 minutes, which was only 30 seconds behind the Marines' best team. We were two minutes ahead of the nearest England bunch, which led to plenty of banter.

Another day they kitted us out with rifles and we simulated an assault on a fort. The SBS – the Special Boat Squadron, who are the naval equivalent of the SAS – took us onto a beach in their high-speed inflatable raiding craft. We had to go ashore in the formations they would adopt if they were under fire. They had gathered together a load of young recruits and painted them up with Scots, Irish and Welsh flags on their faces to represent the enemy. It was great fun, just like being a kid playing soldiers. We were given machine guns and thirty blank magazines and guys were putting them on rapid fire and blazing 30 rounds off in a couple of seconds. Some of them were really getting into it. A few passers-by stopped to watch what was going on. This one old chap did a double take as a saw one of the players yelling and screaming and charging along the sand. He turned to one of the officers who was standing watching nearby and said: 'I say! I didn't know Victor Ubogu had joined the Marines! Good show!' We were all face-painted up but Vic was still clearly recognisable. He's pretty hard to disguise, I guess.

Those SBS guys were really impressive. They are more 'special' than the SAS but less well-known. At least, that is what they told us, and I was not going to argue with them. A few players got the chance to meet up with them in a bar on the base and a list was sent round asking what drinks we would like. For a joke, Will Greenwood wrote 'A bottle of champagne and six glasses'. We were sitting next to the most senior officer and when the drinks came back the waiter said to him: 'Is the champagne for you, Sir?' We just cracked up. I don't think anyone drank it. We were not drinking much at the time. I only touched alcohol twice or three times all year. A few of the other guys were having the occasional pint but nothing more. It was all too serious for that.

We did some simulated battle emergency exercises, too, designed to build up communication and leadership skills. One involved groups of us in a steel room that was filling with water, to mimic a ship which had been hit by enemy fire. We were told how to block off the holes to stop the water pouring in and how to get everyone out. We all failed. In fact, I don't think they let anyone succeed in there. They control the water pressure and they are monitoring you all the time. I reckon if they see you might win they just pump it full more quickly. Eventually, no matter what we did, the water got to the roof, and you have to use the escape hatch to get out. If you get stuck, you just have to hold your breath until they can drain it – a maximum, they said, of 60 seconds, though no-one was anxious to test them.

In another room, we had to go in to put out a diesel fire. We were wearing asbestos gear and breathing apparatus but it was still red hot. It was pitch black and you had to feel your way around. No-one panicked in my group but Neil McCarthy and Phil de Glanville bottled it when they were in there. They got lost and they were in longer than they should have been. 'Blouse' – Phil de Glanville, as in 'Big Girl's' – started squealing: 'Sir, Sir, let me out, let me out'. It was hilarious. He was not allowed to forget it. You are never in any real danger – the Marines are watching you with night sights and they know exactly what's going on at all times – but the mind plays funny tricks when you are under pressure. In our group we had a bit of a communication problem. Cocker thought we were all ready to fire our extinguishers, so he let his off. Unfortunately, we weren't ready. You're supposed to crouch down because spraying onto a fuel fire can cause a big explosion – a back flash – where the fire shoots up all along the roof before it dies out. One of the instructors was still standing up and he took the full blast in the head. He was okay because he was wearing protective gear but he was very warm and not at all amused.

They gave us a stress test, too. They put masks on us so we couldn't see and led us into a what you thought was a dark room. It feels like you are going through an air-ducting full of water. There is all this banging and yelling and fire extinguishers going off in your face. You are part of a group of six, so you have to wait for people. It was really confined and you feel as though you might get jammed in. Cocker was one guy who really suffered in there. For some reason, it stressed him out, though he didn't lose control because he knew there was someone in front of him at all times. It was the one I feared the most, too. I am not one for tight spaces. But I coped simply because Danny Grewcock was leading me: he is a lot bigger than I am and if he was not going to get stuck, neither was I. Jason Leonard was behind me so I felt pretty safe there, too. When we saw it afterwards I was amazed. It was brightly-lit, the water was only about six inches deep and the 'ducting' was just a few obstacles– a table and planks of wood. It was an interesting exercise, though. It really showed how your mind can become confused.

I have to take my hat off to the Marines. They are very fit, wiry guys. They can run all day. Our instructor, Coops, was a top man. At one point on an obstacle course, we had to carry a stretcher with a dummy weighing 100kg through 150 yards of thick, wet mud. The bigger guys were going in up to their knees and by the end of it we were all absolutely hanging. Coops was on the back of a stretcher and he just zipped round, not a moan, not a word, in there till the end. His mental attitude was spot on. They just never give in.

The time we spent with the Marines, before the World Cup and since, was really useful in terms of building team spirit, learning to work together and just maintaining fitness levels in an interesting way. And they were an inspiring, outstanding bunch of blokes. We got on with them all and had a laugh together. It wasn't revealed at the time but they were invited to all our World Cup games. They all stood just by the tunnel as we came out, dressed in security vests to blend in, and it gave us a buzz knowing we had their support as we ran onto the pitch. Coops was told he was being sent away on a short tour of duty but he went to his CO and said 'I can't do it, I've got to be with the England boys' and they let him miss the tour so he could get to Twickenham.

They respected us and we respected them. It was a bond none of us will ever forget.

*

After saying farewell to Lympstone, we began to focus on the task ahead. We knew time was getting shorter and that, within a matter of weeks, we'd be facing New Zealand, Jonah Lomu and all.

The problem we had was a shortage of real build-up games. Like I said, the Southern Hemisphere sides had spent the summer locked in combat. They had had some classic Tri-Nations battles, between genuine World Cup contenders, played out at high-speed with full-on intensity. In training, we had a lot of tough inter-squad matches but it can never be the same. You hold back, you don't have the atmosphere and you don't have match officials, although Steve Lander worked with us a great deal. He went to pre-tournament refereeing meetings and reported back on what they were saying and on how he felt the laws would be interpreted. He reffed a few training game and was very strict but it is still not the same as a game.

Our prep had all been about fitness and team-building. From that point-of-view, it was unsurpassable. But there is no doubt that we were not as match fit as our rivals.

There was nothing we could do about that. There were no international games of any stature to be had in the run-up months before the tournament started. So we had to make do with some weaker opposition, Canada, the United States Eagles, and a Premiership All-Stars side, than we would have liked.

It wasn't a question of not being up for the All-Stars games, certainly not in my case. I always play as though my place is on the line. I never take it for granted because it was so difficult to get. To give you an idea how much it means to me, I remember one training session down at Inver Court before the World Cup began where John Mitchell had just quickly chalked up two teams, under the words 'One' and 'Two', on a blackboard. He said: 'Right guys, these are the teams for today.' I felt physically ill because I was in Team Two. Team One had Corry, Hill and Ben Clarke as a back row. I was with Lawrence and Joe Worsley.

Lol had just returned to the side after his run-in with the *News of the World* and it was still not certain he would play in the competition. Joe was a young guy who was still very much on the fringes. I looked at the other team. It was full of seasoned, experienced hands, people like Jase Leonard, for instance. Even though Darren Garforth and Richard Cockerill were with me I felt we must be the seconds. It wasn't logical but my mind would only register 'Team Two'. I said nothing and trained anyway but it just wasn't there. The next day, we came back for training and the same names were still up on the board, the same way. Catty was in my team and I went over to him and said 'We've got the bullet, mate.' He said 'I'm thinking the same way.' I warmed up and then individually spoke to Garf and Cocker and they felt the same too. I couldn't stand it any longer so I went up to Mitch and said 'Mitch, do I have to read anything into these teams?' He looked at me, completely mystified, and said 'What are you on about, mate?' I said: 'Team Two. Is it the Second Team?' Mitch just laughed at me and said: 'Mate, I just stuck some names down at random. You'll be in the other team today. I just haven't changed the board yet.' Then Clive came over and read out the names from a list and, sure enough, I was in Team One. I had been worrying over nothing. But it was 24 hours of gut-churning misery.

So that gives you an insight into the way I approach my England duties. It is the greatest honour of my life to have played for my country and I never want to let myself or my team down. I can't stand the thought of being dropped so, even against a thrown-together side like the Premiership All-Stars, I give it 100 per cent. I get up for every game. I am extremely competitive by nature anyway and I don't play any non-competitive games now, apart from the odd Barbarians appearance – where I still want to win. I have never played for the Leicester seconds and I never want to. The day it happens I will retire.

The All-Stars tried to get themselves up for the challenge, to avoid being embarrassed, but they were well beaten. Canada and the United States were brushed aside fairly easily, too. The Eagles we thrashed 106 points to 8, with me grabbing a pair of tries. The Canucks were made of sterner stuff but still went down, 36–11.

But none of these games were anything like Test matches. For one thing, the Twickenham crowds were really poor and the atmosphere was non-existent. The RFU played one of the games at Liverpool, where I was able to live out a boyhood dream by touching the 'This Is Anfield' sign as I ran out onto the pitch, but the rest were at HQ. They should have played those games at club grounds. They would have filled every seat with England fans who can't find the time or money to get to London or simply can't get their hands on tickets.

On the plus side, we came out of these warm-up games with no real injuries. On the minus side, however, Richard Cockerill's form continued to dip. In 1998, Cocker was Mr Consistency at the lineout. Our mastery of set pieces was one of our key measurements of success and we had been brilliant, in terms of the accuracy of Cocker's throwing, and the speed and the regularity with which we crossed the gain line. But he would be the first one to admit that he suffered in those run-up games. His form and confidence went and his throwing went awry. In one of the All-Stars matches, for instance, he gifted them an early try. He picked himself up and actually went on to have a decent game but you just knew people were thinking 'What if that happens against New Zealand?' It might easily be one score that turned a game like that.

We would find out soon enough.

CHAPTER 9

In Business

IT WAS the biggest moment of my life but, in a round-about way, it almost led to one of the worst. My wife, Ali, had been expecting our first baby and she was due to give birth around the start of the World Cup. Great timing, eh? As it was, I took her into hospital at 12.45pm on Sunday afternoon, September 26.

It was actually only a routine check, just to see how the baby was. But it transpired that her waters had started to break three or four days before and she had been losing a trickle of fluid. The doctors took the decision to admit Ali and to induce her contractions, which meant, at least, that I could be there.

At 1.41am on Monday 27 September, our daughter Olivia Grace was born, healthy and well. Having watched the birth, I'll never complain about pain again. Believe me, being stomped on by the ugliest, nastiest front row ever doesn't come anywhere near that. Ali went through the whole thing with just gas and air – she wouldn't have an epidural or any other pain relief – but I think if she has another child she'll have everything possible. Olivia weighed in at 6lb 12oz, a good size, and, thankfully, she took after her mum. Straight away I started worrying about young lads calling round for her in 16 years' time!

Ali was exhausted and I was very tired and, of course, I couldn't even wet the baby's head. But it was a fantastic lift to see them together. Shattered, Ali drifted off to sleep in the small hours and I finally went home to bed myself at 5am. But the adrenalin was such that I was up a couple of hours later at 8am, wanting to get back to the hospital. I went out to buy some flowers and a card and collected my parents before taking them to see their new grandchild. It was a very emotional occasion. I stayed with her as long as I could but at around 8.30pm I kissed them both goodbye and set out for the Petersham Hotel in Richmond to meet up with the World Cup squad.

I arrived, utterly zombified, at around 10.30pm. Some of the guys were still up and about so there were a few smiles and handshakes of congratulation. But I was desperately tired and headed for my room. I was actually half-dreaming as I unpacked my bags. Finally, I collapsed into the bed. I was just drifting off when the phone next to me started ringing. Drugs test. Come down straight away. Nightmare. Fifty per cent of the squad, selected at random, had to have a drugs test during the World Cup as part of our participation agreement. A bit different from the original contest in 1987, when there were none. That says a lot about professional sport in the modern era, I guess.

Being tested would ordinarily have been no problem. Right now, though, I needed to sleep. Cursing, I got dressed and headed straight down into the medical room. There was just one problem. As soon as I'd arrived at the hotel, I'd gone straight to the loo. I had nothing left and I just couldn't pee.

I asked if I could take the test the following morning but they refused so I drank plenty of water, trying to rehydrate so my bladder would refill. I waited, half asleep for about an hour, before trying again. I was very proud of my efforts – 50ml. Unfortunately, that wasn't good enough. They wanted 70ml. I was mentally and physically exhausted and that was it. There was no way I was going to wait there any longer. I said: 'Sorry. That is all I can give you. I'm off to bed.'

The medical guy replied: 'I'm sorry Mr Back. We need 70ml. You can't go, you've got to stay.'

I shook my head and he formally cautioned me. 'That is a refusal to produce then?'

I said: 'Yes it is,' and signed the form they offered me agreeing that I had refused to produce a sample.

As soon as my name was on that paper, the place went ballistic. Phone calls were made – 'One of your players has refused a drugs test' – and within minutes half the England management were in the room. It was almost an international incident. Refusal to produce a sample meant, officially, ejection from the competition. Plus certain disgrace and, possibly, the end of my career. You can tell how tired I was. They were talking very seriously about banning me. Defensive coach Phil Larder arrived to mediate for me and eventually, the testers agreed to split my sample on the understanding I would produce another the following day. I said: 'That's fine. I'll give blood or take a test every day for the rest of my career if you want – I've just got to get to bed now.'

Next morning, urine sample duly handed over for one of 300 tests that players would give during the tournament, I slipped into my first World Cup team meeting. There was a lot of banter for the new dad, particularly from Jerry Guscott. Jerry has three daughters himself and I had always ribbed him about what it would be like when the first boyfriends come calling. Now he got his own back in spades. Everyone was very congratulatory. The first thing which came up on the overhead projector was 'Welcome Olivia' and I was presented with a bottle of Möet and Chandon champagne.

As I took it, I was praying that I'd be using it for things on November 6: the first wetting of my daughter's head and toasting our World Cup win. Hopefully, I'd be drinking the champagne out of the Webb Ellis cup.

But that was all in the future.

Clive announced the side to play Italy that Saturday. I was in, which was great news. There were no real surprises in the team selection apart from the centre pairing of Will Greenwood and Phil de Glanville, which left Jerry Guscott on the bench. Jerry had been injured over the last couple of games and had not played but even so I felt Phil and Will had done extremely well to keep a world class player like him out.

The pressure of seeing Guscott on the bench would spur them on to give 100 per cent, I felt sure. He must have been disappointed but straight away he went up to the other guys and shook their hands and wished them well, which is the mark of the man. I think at the back of Clive's mind he was probably saving Jerry for the New Zealand game on October 9, our big game in qualifying.

Later that day we completed our first training session. There was a great buzz in the squad. Everyone was up for it – 'mad for it' as the Oasis brothers like to say. It was an intense session, a tough scrummaging workout, but, on the down side, I felt there was a little too much talking in the camp. Guys would make one mistake and then have to have a big debate about it. My view is that you haven't got time to do that in a game. You have just got to get on with the job. As far as possible, we should strive to replicate that attitude in training. I wasn't sure if I qualified as a senior player, but those old Rowell and Cooke hierarchies had been swept away anyway, replaced by an atmosphere in which we were encouraged to share our thoughts. I let the guys know how I felt about the chit-chat and they took the point well.

At that day's media conference I revealed my happy news to the assembled pressmen. I figured that if the newspapers mentioned the birth it would at least let Ali know I was thinking of her and the baby. Obviously, I called whenever I could but it was hard for her to be without me and tough for me too.

Clive – a father himself – must have known how I was feeling because he took me on one side and said he'd let me pop back to our home at Balsall Common, near Coventry, to see them both on the following Friday, our day off before the first game.

That evening, the boys relaxed with a *Question of Sport*-style quiz sponsored and arranged by Tetley's Bitter. It was no surprise when Johnno's team romped home to win. He is the ultimate sports trivia naus. Ask him who won the Outer Mongolia Women's Darts Championship in 1963 and he'll tell you. The management team came last, which caused some amusement.

Wednesday morning's training session went like a dream. The day before, we'd spilled a few balls as the nerves got to the guys. Those nerves seemed to have settled and we had an outstanding afternoon.

Everyone was looking forward to our big night out. Once a week we were allowed out to go and eat somewhere different, to get away from the confines of the hotel and to get away from our very strict diets. Our choice was the local Chinese restaurant, where we were able to eat as much fatty food as we wanted. My own favourite was crispy duck. If you spend a lifetime denying yourself something, the enjoyment is heightened when you do get it. That duck skin tasted fantastic.

During the day my mobile phone had been going mad. Ali and Olivia had been released from hospital and were now back at home, where the baby was settling in nicely. Family and friends were ringing me to check if I needed anything doing and the press were calling, too. I flicked on Teletext to check out the sports and was surprised to see Olivia's birth mentioned. *The Sunday Mirror* and the Midlands-based *Sunday Mercury* had arranged to take a picture of us when I was at home on the Friday. I was really looking forward to spending some time with my new family.

I had had time to reflect on Clive's selection for the Italy game. I wasn't sure I agreed with the bench he had chosen. There were four forwards and three backs – Martin Corry, Phil Greening, Darren Garforth, Graham Rowntree, Jerry Guscott, Nick Beal and Paul Grayson. It was really the forwards that concerned me. My view was that that bench would have been fine in the old days when you could come on for injury only, but now the players could come on and off at will. So-called 'impact players' were all the rage and I thought we were missing a trick not selecting Victor Ubogu in that role. Victor was by far the quickest forward over 10 metres and was actually quicker than most of the backs. He was a very powerful and athletic guy and while his lack of stamina meant I didn't think he should necessarily start a game, when it came to finding someone to break the gain line and smash holes in a tight defence in the last 20 minutes, he was the ideal man for the job. Garf and Wig – Rowntree, so named because of his bizarre schooldays hairstyle – were great set piece players and have contributed massively towards making Leicester the team it has been over recent years. I thought Darren, in particular, was unfortunate not to be starting because I thought Phil Vickery had struggled with a shoulder injury he hadn't really shaken off. But their game wasn't about breaking the gain line and distributing the ball.

Cozza and Phil Greening I had no quarrel with as both were perfect impact players. Since Couran Cove, Phil had dug deep to up his fitness levels tremendously and Cozza is a very strong, explosive guy too. I thought Phil, Vic and Martin, coming on to replace Cocker, Phil Vickery and one of the back row in the last 20 minutes would have a major effect on a tired opposition.

Grays and Jerry were fine. I thought Mike Catt had been very unlucky, though, and might have placed him on the bench ahead of Bealy. Catty is a quality player, with speed, power and great footballing skills. In my view his all-round skills just shaded those which Nick Beal, himself a tremendous talent, had to offer. I thought Mike would be able to unlock defences, especially when the other side were tired at the end.

But these were fairly minor tactical questions and all they really did was point up the essential fact: the great thing about *not* having to select the team is that you can't be proven wrong.

Our final training session before the Italy game went superbly well – even though some jobsworth denied us access to the Twickenham turf for some line-out work. It is the sort of attitude you can get occasionally at headquarters. Another example concerned David Rees. Reesy had been one of our key players in the run-up to the World Cup but had, unfortunately, been sidelined though injury. Some time either just before or during the competition, there was a players' reception at Twickenham and David was among the guys who were invited. He turned up at the Rose Room only to be denied entrance because he had forgotten his pass. I mean, hello? This is David Rees, a current

England player, not some guy off the street. It is a strange attitude but it has pervaded rugby for years.

Putting behind us our annoyance at not being able to train on the pitch, we got on with things. Not a ball was dropped, not a mistake made. It was our best session for a long time. The team spirit and confidence was high and I felt the tone was set for the World Cup. All the hard work had been done now, everything was stored away in the bank and I just couldn't wait to get on with it.

With Clive's permission, I spent the evening at home, 100 miles literally and a million miles in my head away from the World Cup hotel. It was great to see Ali and Olivia, who looked absolutely beautiful.

The following evening we had a final team get-together, a bit of a line-out session and a bit of a run out on the Twickenham pitch. There were no visible nerves. We just wanted to get into it. The mood was quiet as it always is before a big international. Some guys were in the team room watching videos, others were playing with Gameboys. You try to switch off and rest your mind as well as your body, but it isn't easy. Everyone was getting their last-minute rubs in the massage room. I arranged to have my whole body massaged, so I felt relaxed and sleepy as I turned in to bed at around 9.30pm.

I slept soundly. There was a big day ahead.

*

We battered the Italians, 67–7.

It was a top start to our World Cup campaign and I got on the score sheet with a typical Backy score, the catch-and-drive at the lineout.

Early in the day, I had watched a video of the opening game of the competition, Wales against Argentina at the magnificent new Millennium Stadium. Wales were perhaps the form team of the tournament, having gone into the match on the back of nine or 10 straight wins put together by Graham Henry. I expected them to win reasonably comfortably, albeit while undergoing a stern examination from opponents who back their skills with a lot of forward power, heart and aggression.

But the Welshmen found it difficult to get continuity and phase play together and ran out winners only by 23 points to 18. Their performance was stuttering and error-strewn and they gave the Argentinians six penalties. It looked to me as though Rob Howley's men had frozen a little in the headlights. I have to admit that I was worried that, under the spotlight and with the weight of expectation which was upon us, we might run into the same problems against inferior opposition.

I don't know what I expected before our first game – more animation, or a maybe the complete opposite, a dead silence – but the changing room was hardly different from any other international we had played recently. Personally, I knew we had put all the hard work in and that physically, to a man, we were in great shape. The confidence, the determination, was palpable. There was some apprehension, given the occasion, but there was enough experience in the side and enough old heads to keep everyone together and focused.

It was a fantastic win. The Italians handed us a stack of points by giving away pointless penalties. We kicked them all, bringing a few boos from the heaving Twickenham crowd. I was surprised at that. We wanted to win well to send out a signal to the All Blacks, clearly our main rivals in the group, and that meant destroying Italy, not just beating them. I understand that people want to see tries, but we gave them plenty of those too. In the end, a win is a win. If you snatch victory by a point with a last-minute kick in the World Cup final, who is going to complain then?

There were a few injury concerns, which took some of the gloss off the day. Will Greenwood had a slight hamstring tear, though we were hopeful he would be alright for the following week. Danny Grewcock was injured, too.

Importantly, the line-outs went very well. Richard Cockerill's position had been the subject of intense media scrutiny in the run-up to the tournament. But he is not a bottler and, like the big match player he is, Cocker was bang on target with his throwing and back to his best.

Jerry Guscott came on to a massive cheer from the crowd and within a minute he was diving in and winning the ball in a ruck. That sort of commitment and guts from a back lifts the side and makes my job a lot easier. That is one of the distinct changes between the amateur and professional game. It is no longer down to the forwards to win the loose ball. It is down to the nearest man and, quite often, that means the nearest back. Phil de Glanville, another guy who is full of heart, was also outstanding in this phase of the game. Both he and Jerry enabled us to get a lot of continuity and a lot of phases together and that led to us scoring some fabulous tries.

For my part, I thought I had a good game. I was delighted with my try but more pleased that my tackle count was 100 per cent. I didn't miss a man.

And the chat between the boys on the field was outstanding. No-one lost concentration and we did not ease off once we had the Italians beaten. A poor side relaxes once it knows it cannot be caught. A good side grinds the opposition into the dirt.

Some guys stood out. Young Jonny Wilkinson, just 20 years of age, was superbly composed, scoring an English Test record 32 points – including a try – to eclipse Rob Andrew's best of 30. His passing was fast, flat and accurate, his kicking out of hand was tremendous and his tackling devastating. Lawrence Dallaglio was magnificent at No 8 and Richard Hill played outstandingly well on his side of the back row, making it on to the score sheet too. We seemed to have formed a cohesive partnership, reacting well together and feeding off each other's strengths. I hoped the unit would continue to function as well throughout the tournament.

The mood in the dressing room afterwards reflected what we thought was a job well done. But it wasn't over the top. We knew we had bigger games to come. The All Blacks would have been looking on and thinking they had to play well to beat us. And that game the following weekend presented my biggest challenge in world rugby: head to head against the man I considered to be the best openside flanker in world rugby, Josh Kronfeld. His form was outstanding and I knew I needed to lift myself a level higher if I was to compete.

CHAPTER 10

Up Against the All Blacks

THE WHOLE squad was given Saturday night off after we beat Italy to get a break from the relentless mental pressure. Eating, sleeping, thinking and dreaming rugby can leave you stale. The Marines turned up and spent the evening with us, having a laugh and sharing a few beers with those guys who were drinking. It was a valuable moment's pause, a reminder of normality in an unreal world.

The following morning, I headed back to the Midlands for another precious few hours with Ali and Olivia, reporting back at the Petersham Hotel sharp at 6pm for the squad meal. We had a team meeting at 9pm during which we looked ahead at the New Zealand game. Clive ran through their formidable strengths and their few weaknesses. They were such a fine side it was hard to find anything. But Australia had punched some holes in their defence around Mehrtens at 10 and their outside centre area in a recent Bledisloe Cup match, running out winners. We hoped to emulate them.

Will Greenwood and Jerry Guscott were the major injury concerns, Danny Grewcock suffering nothing more serious than a dead leg. Clive told us he was delaying the announcement of the team until the Thursday, so I crossed my fingers and hoped mine would be among the 15 names. After years on the outside, I wanted to stay in. I reassured myself that there was no reason to make changes apart from those which might be forced by injury.

Tuesday morning saw a little light entertainment, organised by the social committee, laid on for the squad. Up at 8.30am, we were split into three teams for a combined clay pigeon, cross bow and axe throwing competition at the nearby Hampton Court. I won't dwell on my performances.

Back at the hotel, the squad session that afternoon was outstanding – in fact, I thought it was the best we had ever had. We started off with some speed-agility-quickness (SAQ) work which was really crisp. This was followed with handling skills. As before, not a ball went down. Then the forwards grouped together for line-out practice. Following his top-drawer performance against Italy at the weekend, Cocker was, once again, outstanding.

Afterwards, confidence was really high. We'd been struggling with getting the team runs error-free but it felt to me that we had drawn a lot of positives from our good performance first up.

The session was followed by a press conference in Twickenham's Rose Room. The All Blacks had overcome Tonga and all the media attention was now looking forward to the big game that weekend. As far as the English papers were concerned, it *was* the World Cup.

The reporters only wanted to talk about one man. Jonah Tali Lomu. He became rugby's first global superstar when he almost single-handedly destroyed a stunned England during that devastating defeat in the 1995 semi-final. It had left an apparently indelible scar on the face of English rugby. There is no doubt he is an extraordinary physical specimen, perhaps even the 'freak' that Will Carling labelled him. At 6ft 5in and 18st 8lb, he's built like a big No 8 but he runs like the winger he is, generating tremendous pace with those giant legs, and is very hard to stop. His stride is so big that people have trouble getting their arms around his huge thighs.

In the run-up to the match, it seemed as though every

newspaper you read and every TV sports show you watched was looking back at that game. I had been on the tour but I was injured for the semi and had to watch from the stands. I admit I was shocked by what unfolded in front of me. Lomu was pretty much unknown before that day in Cape Town. Afterwards, he became a household name.

He literally ran over Mike Catt to score their first try inside two minutes and from there the avalanche of points just kept on coming. No-one really managed to work out a way to halt him. My poor Leicester team-mate Tony Underwood's career was effectively wrecked there and then. At around 13 stone, he was tasked with stopping this monster and he did not fare too well. After the tournament, he was reduced to making a humiliating pizza commercial which dwelt on the difference in size and power between himself and Jonah. But it was unfair to single out Tony. We had watched videos as a team beforehand and we thought that, while Lomu was big, strong and quick, we'd be able to stop him. As Will Carling later admitted, we were simply wrong: 'Tony Underwood carried the can for the four tries that afternoon, but Superman on a steamroller would have come off second best. They tore us to pieces. We were in shock, I could see it on the faces of our players. After the second score (four minutes into the match!), I gathered the team round and told them not to panic. After the fourth try I was unable to convince myself. New Zealand were touched by genius that day. They were untouchable. It was like 15-year-olds against a men's side. Embarrassing.'

This was the sort of morale-boosting stuff which newspapers were running as the 1999 match approached. One quoted Brian Moore: 'We relied on first-time tackling. But Lomu simply battered his way through three tackles to score. It was not a strategic collapse on our part. There were three players covering and he just ran through all three of them.' He added: 'These were devastating blows, stunning and bewildering. At any moment you expected to wake up, sweating but safe, in your bed.'

I maintain that tackling Lomu is the same, in essence, as tackling anyone. I go back to my days in junior rugby as an eight-year-old when I was taught that the area to attack is the eight to 12 inches between the ribs and the thighs. If you take a man there, hold on and you continue your leg drive, he will eventually fall no matter who he is. That is the theory. In practice, obviously, it is a damn sight harder. Given his weight and pace, the margin for error is cut down dramatically. The best way to stop him is to get to him before he builds up any momentum.

A few of us in the 1999 camp had been there in 1995. Some of the guys knew first-hand what it was like to try to stop Lomu, and to fail. We had to be very careful not to let negative feelings creep into our heads and to pollute the camp. In an atmosphere where ex-players' memories are being dredged up by a media which is ever-anxious to tell you that you cannot possibly win, that's a hard task. To our credit, we managed, largely, to ignore the press fever over Lomu.

Clive Woodward made it pretty clear what he thought of the fuss surrounding the giant winger. 'It's all hot air, all history,' he told the press conference. And that was the right attitude. We had plenty of other threats to keep our eyes on. Tana Umaga, for instance, had actually overshadowed Lomu. Jonah spent a long time out of the game with a potentially lethal kidney complaint and Umaga had lately kept him on the bench. I guessed, correctly, that his potential as a psychological weapon meant Jonah would start against us. But the other backs they had at their disposal were equally dangerous. Andrew Mehrtens and Justin Marshall were perhaps the best half-back pairing in world rugby. Christian Cullen was probably the most dangerous counter-attacker around. Jeff Wilson was thriving at full-back. Centres like Gibson and Ieremia, either one playing in tandem with Cullen, were massively imposing guys who could smash holes in your defence and suck in guys to stem the breach. And the All Black pack was not exactly poor. Lurking opposite me was Kronfeld.

And all of the front five were highly mobile and had good hands. Arguably, though, their front row might prove one fruitful point for us to probe. Players like Carl Hoeft, Anton Oliver and Kees Meuws had an average age of 24 and only around 10 caps each. It was unlikely they would dominate us.

One other controversy arose at the press conference. Plans had been laid for an official rendition of *Swing Low, Sweet Chariot* to be sung pre-match. The idea was that it would act as some kind of riposte to the All Black *haka*. Someone in the All Black camp had kicked up a fuss, saying it should not be allowed. Clive was asked his opinion. And he was typically bullish in his response, telling one reporter: 'I don't give a monkey's about *Swing Low*. It's an irrelevance, as is the *haka*.'

I disagreed with Clive on that point. I wasn't too concerned about the song. I took the view – as did all of us – that if it entertained the crowd and if it was what they wanted, sing it. If it wound New Zealand up at the same time, so much the better. But from a player's point of view, it was irrelevant. I was not going to play any better for having heard some operatic tenor belt out an old spiritual song. The *haka*, however, was a different matter altogether.

In my opinion it should be banned from the international rugby field. It gives the All Blacks a precious minute to bond themselves together and make an aggressive statement to the opposition. Fine, if you are allowed to return the gesture. Cocker had come the closest I've seen when he had wandered up to the halfway line and stared out one of the Kiwis during the *haka* before an earlier confrontation. The fans and the media loved it, but not the powers that be, who castigated him for disrespect. Instead, you are supposed to stand there and take it. It is not intimidating but I believe it does give some sort of psychological edge to the All Blacks. They are the only major nation allowed to carry out any sort of ritual before a match. That cannot be fair and it cannot be right. It is not as though it is some genuine tradition. As I understand it, it is some half-translation of a Polynesian fishing chant. Not content with stealing half their players from the islands, the Kiwis have appropriated their tune too.

*

The Wednesday after the press conference saw a flurry of headlines and a rare poor day at the office for the England squad. Our training session went badly. It was all a bit frantic, balls were dropped and the odd temper mislaid temporarily. Things got heated and a few of the players had words with each other. It can get like this before really big games and I felt the pressure was beginning to get to some of the players, particularly those who had been reading a lot of the newspaper coverage and speculation about the match.

If we won it would mean an easier route to the quarter-finals, perhaps facing Scotland. If we lost, it meant an extra game to get to the quarters where we would probably come up against South Africa. If we won that game and kept winning, we would then meet Australia in the semi-final and New Zealand again in the final.

That extra game, and the tough opponents we would face thereafter, were playing on a few minds. I took one or two people on one side and told them we had to beat the best to be the best. If we had to go through all three of the Southern Hemisphere sides to victory, so be it. It would just be a fantastic story. As the hard training tapered off for the rest of the week, I thought things would probably calm down.

That night we went out for our normal out-of-hotel dinner. I had my usual crispy duck, complete with more fat in one sitting that I was eating in the whole of the rest of the week. As I hoped, some of the composure which had been lost earlier on had been regained and there was a lot of banter between the players. A number of our fellow diners came over to wish us good luck. I'm never rude to people who make themselves known in such circumstances – it is nice to know you have supporters and fans backing you – but I rarely know what to do or say. If I were ever to show signs of becoming big-headed about it, though, Ali would soon bring me back down to earth. I remember on one occasion just after the World Cup we were in a restaurant in Coventry and there was a queue of teenage girls outside waiting to get into a bar. A few of them started gawping over at me. Obviously they vaguely recognised me as someone half well-known but weren't quite sure who I was. 'Look at that lot,' says Ali, indignantly. 'It's not as though you're David Beckham.' Thanks, love.

On the Thursday, there was no return of the previous day's fractiousness. We'd had a big team talk, at which we had agreed that we couldn't possibly be better prepared physically and our confidence and our spirits were really high. The Lomu chit-chat was written off as paper-talk. When a headline in *The Times* of all papers compares an opposing player to The Incredible Hulk and warns you not to upset him – 'You wouldn't like him when he's angry' – what can you do but smile and shrug it off? As a team, we were fitter, stronger and faster than our 1995 incarnation and we were also forewarned about the big man from South Auckland.

We knew their backs were dangerous but we were sure we had the beating of them up-front. Control first-phase, secure possession and you are half-way there. We were playing well and, given that vital possession, we had the firepower to out gun the New Zealanders. I think it was the first time that any team bar the Lions that I'd been a part of really believed that it would beat New Zealand – or any Southern Hemisphere side, to be frank. Prior to that, the England sides I have been involved in have been committed and talented but lacking in genuine self-belief. We felt that *possibly* we could win *if* things went well *and* we had a bit of luck. This time, no ifs, buts or maybes. We honestly thought we *would* win.

Despite their Lomu-blindness, surprisingly, many of the pundits also had us as slight favourites. Nick Mallett was one guy I saw interviewed who thought that way. Even John Hart was praising the English team to the skies. That we didn't listen to. We knew the wily old fox was trying to lull us into a false sense of security. But there were definitely points in our favour. Home advantage gives you a tremendous boost, though for many years Twickenham was a soulless, almost hushed place, with more seats given over to corporate clients who tend to be more restrained than fans who have paid. I'm happy to say that, in recent appearances, our play has brought the supporters to their feet more and the noise levels have gone up. At least we had not had to follow the Scots, who got it badly wrong up at Murrayfield during the World Cup. Attendances were shocking and they had resorted to playing piped crowd noise to boost the atmosphere. That would be dodgy at the best of times but to make matters worse they often seemed to have the tapes running when there was nothing to cheer.

Another point was the fact that New Zealand had struggled against Tonga in the first half of their opening game, only pulling away to beat them 45–9 in the second half. We had annihilated Italy.

During the day, Clive announced the side. I was in. Jerry Guscott and Will Greenwood had been the only injury doubts. Will had struggled and failed to overcome his pulled hamstring but Jerry had recovered after quietly sneaking off to have some treatment to his groin. If we couldn't field a full-strength team I also rated our back-up. Mike Catt was very fit and sharp, as he had showed in the warm up games, and Phil de Glanville had been in solid form. He got the nod over Catty.

I was allowed home that night to spend much of Friday with my wife and Olivia, as I had been prior to the Italy game. While back in the Midlands I had to pop into my local Co-op for some nappies. I was amazed by all the people who saw me in the street and in the store and came up to wish me and the team the best of luck. To get that in my home town was a wonderful feeling. We had also received tens of thousands of faxes and e-mails at our hotel. The support was tremendous and it brought home to me what a big thing it was that I was part of. English sport had been in the doldrums for years and we had a chance to do something about that.

After those few precious hours away, I reported back at 5pm for some line-out spotting, which we did on Twickenham. The groundsman who had refused to allow us onto his precious turf a few days earlier had relaxed his policy somewhat and we had a good session.

I always feel it is a good idea for the forwards to go through a few spotters the night before a major fixture, testing and honing the hooker's ability to find his men. It is an art, a skill, which requires hours of practice. Brian Moore, a suit-and-tie solicitor in the amateur playing days, used to infuriate the partners in his legal firm by throwing a ball against the wall of his office every spare moment he got. Thump, thump, thump, all day long. Allegedly, they threw a party when they learned he was retiring from the game. Cocker and Phil Greening each threw quickly and accurately, which was reassuring. We pencilled in another session for noon the following day, before our pre-match meal, but we felt that the line-out was functioning well.

We had our team meeting prior to training at 5pm and a few of the coaches said some emotive words. They were definitely more nervous than the players. Tactically, we had gleaned some intelligence on the All Black plans. They had been working on disrupting our line-out. All the work we had done in that area would help. They had also come up with a ploy to disrupt our scrum which would see them push, halt for a second and then push again. The aim was to upset Lawrence and his pick-up at No 8. They obviously saw Lol as a big threat and the pack in general as our most potent weapon. Robin Brooke had given an interview in which he said he had played in three All Black packs against England in the 1990s and had lost five out of the six halves. The scorebook said one game all and a draw, the 26–26 thriller at Twickenham in 1998, which showed we could compete with them. I felt that we would dominate the forward play and that when that happened they would start asking questions of themselves. They were used to being in a comfort zone, where they win first phase ball quite easily and then spin it wide for their powerful backs to capitalise on.

There were a few important individual one-on-one battles to be won. Andrew Mehrtens and Jonny Wilkinson was one. Mehrtens had been on top of his game for the last four years but we felt he was maybe defensively a little weak. Wherever he was, we aimed to attack. The outside centre spot was another one. Christian Cullen, an outstanding attacking player, looked set to play there. There were slight question marks over his vision and passing. Only slight, but they were there.

The confrontation between Taine Randell and Lawrence Dallaglio was another mouth-watering prospect. I felt Lol was the best No 8 in world rugby but that Randell would play with a lot of heart and pride. He was an unpopular choice as skipper and had a lot of critics back home to silence.

And there was myself against Kronfeld. Most critics rated us one and two in the world. Usually he took top spot, although occasionally the positions were reversed. Josh is a superb player. He looked the part, with a beat-up face and hard eyes glowering under that black scrum-cap. More importantly, his work rate, bravery, speed and hands really aided his side's continuity. That job is made easier if your side is going forward and I hoped our bigger, stronger scrum would give me a little edge. I also felt that I had the beating of him out wide, with a touch more pace. Defensively, I needed to stop their backs from crossing the gain line. That would also make Josh's job a whole lot harder.

After training, a few of the guys ventured out to the cinema to watch a comedy called *Big Daddy*. Others played with the Nintendo machines which had been provided for us. One favourite was a James Bond 007 game which allowed four players to shoot the hell out of each other. That went down really well. The cinema-goers would be late back but they were not in the 22 for the following day's game so it was a good idea for them to get away, enjoy themselves and just relax. By 10.30pm, the rest of us were in bed.

The morning of the match was a time for quiet contemplation. I ran through my mind what Steve Redgrave, the four-times Olympic rowing champion, had said to us earlier in the week. He had come in to lend a hand with motivation and had delivered an inspiring, off-the-cuff speech. You have to listen to a man who has been to his level of competition, in a punishing sport which requires utter dedication and total fitness, and triumphed as often as he has. He made the point that in some races he has been exhausted – absolutely hanging. But he looks inside himself, remembers the work and conditioning he has carried out to that point, and reminds himself that if he is knackered then the other rowers will be feeling just as bad. I knew that I'd be able to look at Josh later that day and see that he was as bushed as I was. He could not possibly be any fitter. The same went for all our opposite numbers. We had become an 80-minute side and I knew we'd need to be against New Zealand.

Kick off was at 4.30pm.

*

That Saturday was one of the most disappointing days of my life. I will never forget the hollow anguish as we trooped away from Twickenham. The All Blacks had beaten us by 30 points to 16. And we were in the game, too. We could have won.

We started full of fire, although the early points went their way. A penalty and then a converted try by Jeff Wilson gave them a 10 points to nil lead. We battled our way back into it, conceding another couple of penalties but knocking one or two of our own over. Then, with 49 minutes gone, I managed to make some yards up the middle of the field, Jerry chipped cleverly ahead and Matt Perry made good ground before colliding with Justin Marshall. The ball was loose and Phil de Glanville was there to pounce and smuggle it over the line. Jonny converted the try to make it 16 points apiece. At that point, it was anyone's match and the tide was with us.

Then Lomu made his entrance.

He had been quiet all game and had hardly touched the ball in the first half. Ten minutes after Phil's try, Christian Cullen sent a long pass out to the left wing and Jonah was away. It was like a re-run of 1995, a horrible sequel, and I could scarcely believe my eyes as it unfolded before me. He brushed off Jeremy Guscott, swatted aside Austin Healey and powered on to the line from 40 yards out, despite Dan Luger and Matt Dawson also doing their best to halt him. No other winger in the world could have come close to scoring that try, in my opinion.

From then on, the psychological balance had tilted totally back to them and they added a third try through the second string fly-half, Byron Kelleher, late on. We failed to add to our 16 points and I watched the last nine minutes from the bench after being substituted.

Where did it all go wrong?

Clearly we had underestimated them. For a start, Lomu was every bit as hard to bring down as he had been four years earlier and that, with Mehrtens' cool, corner-flag conversion, was worth seven of their points.

Before the game I had looked at their likely XV and convinced myself that they were pretty weak defensively, compared to teams like South Africa and Australia. I was wrong. On the day, I found their defence was outstanding.

On the other hand, we missed our man in one-on-one situations too often. Jonah Lomu was, of course, a case in point. The technique has to be perfect with him. You must get close in and keep your legs driving hard, forcing him off-balance. In this match, I think people were guilty of hitting the contact area but being flat-footed and not continuing to drive the legs. When you do that he's going to break tackles. But, like I say, it's easy to say that now. It is always easier in theory.

Conversely, their effective, aggressive tackling disrupted key areas of our game and their pace in attack also often left us struggling for position. Faced with this black wall, we had reverted to kicking out of hand, instead of keeping the ball and relying on our ability to retain and recycle possession. It was baffling, considering we had shown great continuity in all the other games.

The overall pressure which was created led to some unforced errors, notably in the line-out and with our place-kicking. Cocker sent a throw or two astray. And Jonny Wilkinson, for the first and, so far, only time, had a poor day with the boot. He missed four kickable penalties, penalties he would normally pot in his sleep, which might have made the difference. On a couple of occasions, too, the wrong decisions were made. Tries were on out wide for us but the killer pass was never made.

Maybe you have to look back to before the World Cup and the schedule of warm-up games which was arranged for us. Certainly, those fixtures were of a far lower intensity and pressure and perhaps that left us unprepared to cope with the level of scrutiny which the New Zealanders put us under.

But it was not all about our mistakes. You have to hand it to them. They played superbly and fully deserved their victory. Mehrtens, in particular, was magnificent with his kicking out of hand and with his place-kicking too. I think he missed just one scoring kick all day. Josh Kronfeld had a stormer, too. But hardly an All Black had anything even approaching a bad game. They were just too good on the day.

CHAPTER 11

The Long Road to Disappointment

AFTER THE All Black defeat, we retired to the Petersham to lick our wounds – I had eight stitches in a boot gash on the front of my head and two to another stud-wound on the back – we tried to take away some positives with us. New Zealand had been the form team coming into competition and there was no doubt we had been in that game.

The more we thought about it, the more our mood became surprisingly upbeat.

Effectively, we were into the knock-out stages of the tournament early. Tonga, the other side in our group, beat Italy that evening, though it was a close-run thing, only 28–25. That gave added importance to our fixture against the Islanders a few days later. If we did not win that game we were out of the competition before the quarter-finals – a thought just too dreadful to contemplate. Surely, though, we would be too strong for the Tongans, for all their beef and aggression and flair. Victory would see us take the long road to the final: a 'best-loser' play-off, probably against Fiji or France, before the knock-out stages proper, in which we would probably face all three Southern Hemisphere sides *en route* to the final. Having watched South Africa and Australia play their games, I certainly thought we could beat both of them. And, given another crack at the All Blacks in the final, maybe things would be different. Analysis of the New Zealand match had suggested areas where we might profit if we met up with them again. Tactically, it looked as though we had missed a trick when it came to taking advantage of their defensive patterns. Watching the video, it was clear that they were always keen to get their full back up, which meant they left a gaping hole in behind one of the wings. Kicking in behind the full back, or over to the undefended side of the field, would turn them and would create attacking options for us. It was a shame we had not spotted it on the day.

I mulled over the video and looked at the statistics which the team back-up guys had produced for us. They showed that I had played fairly well. I didn't miss a tackle. I carried the ball up. And only once in the game did I lose possession and that was right at the death. At that time the gash had been opened on the top of my head and there was blood everywhere. I'm not making excuses. I lost the ball because I went in with poor technique and not because of the blood. Other than that I was very pleased with my game and I felt I contributed as well as I could. I was very confident that I would take my form into the next games. Other guys had played well too and this was even more evident on watching the re-run. Phil de Glanville was outstanding. Johnno, Hilly and Lol had also had good games.

The stats for the match as a whole made astonishing, even bizarre reading. We had 65 per cent of the possession, won 85 rucks and mauls against 38 and were awarded 19 penalties and free kicks compared with the All Black's 11. We won 80 balls in open play. They won 24. The line-out was about even. We didn't lose any of our own scrums. And yet we lost. It proved the point, perhaps more vividly than in any other game in which I have played, that it is what you do with your possession that really counts at this level.

No one individual deserved blame for the defeat. Collectively we made mistakes in what was an intense and mentally taxing game but individually everyone played their hearts out and you can ask no more. And in some ways, I felt the defeat – coming at a time when we still had the opportunity to put things right – might actually have been a blessing in disguise. Easy group games would not have prepared us for the knock-out stages. At least now we were all aware of the pressure and the intensity we would need to perform under. I felt that was our rusty game for the competition out of the way.

The following day we had a team debrief. We identified our errors and talked about ways of avoiding them in future. Clive, though clearly agonising over the defeat, was excellent. He gave us a really constructive, balanced talk. The gist was that we had been unlucky to have a bad day against an on-song side. They would probably not play that well again and we would not play that badly.

Again I was allowed home on the Sunday. It was great to get away from rugby, to get away from the World Cup, the hype, the media. Some of Ali's folks came to the house, and it made a nice diversion.

On the Tuesday, Clive held a press conference. He was asked what he thought of our performance and, like the honest guy he is, he was fairly critical. We had kicked away too much possession he said, apparently adding: 'If we'd gone out of the competition by playing like that I'd never have spoken to the players again.' But the main purpose of the conference was to announce the team for Tonga, three days later. The winner would be group runner-up, since there was little doubt that New Zealand would beat Italy.

I was rested. The management, with one eye on the play-off which would follow, took the view that the 10 stitches in my head made me too much of a risk. I was on the bench in case I was needed. Amazingly, I was not too disappointed about being left out. There is something I never expected to write! The rest was important, mentally and physically, and the cuts were a problem. It was unlikely I would have been able to play in both games and the quarter final without re-opening the wounds. And certainly, I was glad to be on the bench rather than not be involved at all. Clive made clear to me that he would bring me on if necessary, which made me feel that he still valued me highly. Just in case I got the nod, I had a word with Kevin Murphy and Terry Crystal, the team physio and doctor, and discussed ways of protecting the worst of the two cuts. It was in an awkward position, right above my eyes. They came up with a dressing which offered maximum protection and came as close as possible to ensuring it wouldn't split, or split too badly, if I had to go on.

Positionally, Richard Hill was switching to openside, and Joe Worsley would wear No 6. I knew Hilly would do an excellent job and I felt Joe was probably the right sort of back row to play against Tonga, who are always a very physical team. I hoped he would have an outstanding game and would follow on from how he had performed in the warm ups. He deserved full credit for his first start in Test rugby. He had worked very hard over the last year or so, learning a lot from his Wasps team-mate Lawrence Dallaglio, and had changed from a young boy to a man who was well capable of Test rugby. As soon as the side was announced I shook his hand and congratulated him on his selection.

There were a few other changes to the side. Richard Cockerill was rested, Phil Greening taking his place. That was an interesting one. Each had their strengths. At that time, I think I would have said that Richard was the better man to have around at first phase scrum and lineout. He is a strong, heavy individual with plenty of aggression and presence. I saw Phil as a more mobile player, quick and with good hands, who would really punish a tiring opposition in the later stages. I thought the best way to use the hookers was to play Cocker for the first hour and then to bring Phil on as an impact man for the final twenty minutes. As I write this – post-South Africa 2000 – I have a different view. Phil is now a formidable scrummager without losing any of his pace around the park. Then, though, I wasn't so sure.

Will Greenwood, recovered from his hammy, took over from Jerry, who did not even get onto the bench, in the centre and

Paul Grayson replaced Jonny at fly-half. Danny Grewcock and Jason Leonard were also rested, which meant Graham Rowntree got a start on the loose head and Garath Archer in the second row. I was pleased for Wiggy, in particular.

That night we went out for our out-of-hotel meal – a Mexican for a change, organised by Austin Healey. It was fantastic food, the service was great and we had a relaxing time with little inkling of the troubles ahead.

They came the following day, when the press blew up in our faces. Clive's team changes were distorted by a media which seemed to be trying to find scapegoats for the New Zealand defeat. He had tried to make clear that he was putting out the strongest side he could against Tonga. Only injuries and the need to rest key players had got in the way. But some reports read as though their authors had not been in the press conference. Jonny had been dropped for Paul Grayson, they said, and Jerry Guscott had been kicked out of the side for good. Jason Leonard's future was also highly in doubt, if you listened to some commentators.

As the week wore on, a few pressmen tried to read more into Clive's remarks about never speaking to us again, too. Will Carling was one. Under the heading 'Woodward putting morale at risk' in the *Mail on Sunday*, the ex-skipper claimed he was 'staggered' by Clive's remarks and his man-management skills. The coach should not be criticising his players in public like that, suggested Carling.

The fact is that Clive has never said anything outside the changing room that he was not prepared to say inside. He was right. We had played poorly. And poor man-management skills? From a man who saw at first hand the way the England set-up used to be run? Come on. As for his comments about never speaking to us again, no-one in the team took any personal offence at those remarks to the best of my knowledge. Clive is just like that. He is passionate and emotional, he wears his heart on his sleeve and he speaks his mind. The whole tone of Will's piece was critical and sensationalist and I wasn't the only one to find it in bad taste and a little disappointing. That kind of talk – and the speculation about players' futures – cannot help their morale. Some of the guys who were being rested had had a tough enough 24 hours as it was and, much as you try not to take any notice of negative press, it can get to you. Any way you look at it, it was not pleasant.

In the end, Clive felt the need to call the squad together and reiterate that no-one had been dropped and that the changes really were forced. He was careful to stress that he had retained all eight of the pack who played against New Zealand in the 22 and that even though four of us were on the bench he still saw us as the starting pack. He was giving the other, younger guys an opportunity to show what they could do. But, if it hit the fan, he would still have his first choice guys to come on. As it happened, a few journalists were made to eat their words almost immediately, when Jerry was recalled to the side. It was hard on de Glanville, who had sustained bruised ribs against the All Blacks and hard, too, on Mike Catt, who had been on the bench. But no-one could deny that Guscott, if he was at his best, was a weapon we could not ignore.

Training went well during the week. The focus was strong. We knew our task and we knew we were equal to it. I found it frustrating knowing I was going to be a replacement. It was the first time I'd been on the England bench for well over a year and I was slightly unsure of my role in training. I took a bit of a back seat and tried to give Joe Worsley all the support that I could. He was naturally very nervous but I had no doubts about him. Defensively, Joe is an excellent player and he carries the ball up well. My only fear was that the new back row would function so well together that there would be no need to bring me back!

*

Like all South Sea Islanders, the Tongans are big, explosive and aggressive. The day before our match, Samoa had turned over the Welsh, beating them by 38 points to 31 and crossing the Wales line five times as against just once by Graham Henry's men, though they were also awarded two penalty tries.

Going into that crucial encounter, our team talk was all about being physical, being brave and being hard. Fighting fire with fire, in other words. We felt that the way to win well was by pushing the Tongans on to the back foot. And we managed that comfortably, handing the red-shirted Polynesians a 101 points to 10 drubbing.

It was satisfying and fitting that we rubbed their faces in the dirt because the game saw some of the dirtiest play I have ever seen on an international rugby pitch. The worst incident was a horrific spear tackle on Matt Perry by the lunatic Tongan replacement Isi Tapueluelu. Tapueluelu caught him in mid-air and dumped him straight down to the ground on his head. It was the sort of incident which can leave players paralysed and Matt later told us he had thought for a few seconds that that was what had happened to him. Phil Vickery, furious at what had happened, launched himself at Tapueluelu, more to push him out of the way than anything, and that sparked a mêlée, in which another nutter, the prop Ngalu Taufo'ou, smashed Richard Hill in the face from behind with an unprovoked punch. Order was quickly restored, with Taufo'ou sent off and Vickery and Tapueluelu receiving yellow cards. I though Tapueluelu should have followed his team-mate. His challenge on Matt was horrific and should not be seen on a rugby pitch. It brought back memories of Max Brito. Max, a young Ivory Coast winger, had been paralysed in a 1995 World Cup group match, also against Tonga. The circumstances were different – Brito was trapped in a ruck – but the potential consequences of this latest incident were identical. I was one of a number of England players who had visited Brito at his home after the '95 tournament and I never want to see that happen to another player.

In terms of our play, the match went superbly. The back row functioned well and when Lawrence came off with 10 minutes to go, Phil Greening was switched to the flank to save my head and Cocker went on as hooker. Paul Grayson had an excellent game, too, scoring 36 points off the boot. That broke the England record set an unlucky 13 days ago by Jonny Wilkinson.

Downsides? Jerry scored a brace – including a glorious, gliding 90 metre run-in reminiscent of his best years – but his groin niggle returned. Surgery looked certainty post-World Cup. Matt Dawson also injured his chest.

I was not required. It was tough to watch 13 tries scored and not be able to get among the action but the right decision had been made. The head wound had really healed and I had the stitches out late that evening. I'd be fine for the playoff, against Fiji, unlucky 29–19 losers against France, at Twickenham the following Wednesday. Fiji would be the best and most physical team we'd played, other than New Zealand, so we were not getting too carried away by the result over Tonga. The Fijian defence was outstanding and it was only a dubious try which France scored late on that stole the game. My own feeling, though, was that Fiji had played above themselves against the French and that we would have no real trouble against them.

A relaxing weekend was capped by another visit home, this time for both the Saturday and the Sunday. There were a few tears from Ali on my departure because a win against the Fijians would see the England camp relocate to France for the quarter-final against the defending champions.

Selection was announced on the Monday morning. It had a slightly 'make do and mend' look about it, but that was under-standable under the circumstances. A number of players were being rested in anticipation of the South Africa game just four days later. Jonny Wilkinson was back at fly-half. Daz Garforth replaced Phil Vickery at tighthead. Phil Greening and Garath Archer retained their places. Danny Grewcock was rested completely, giving Tim Rodber a slot on the bench. In the back row, I returned in place of Richard Hill. Catty was in at centre with Will Greenwood – another new combination at 12 and 13. Austin Healey would start at scrum-half for only the second time in his international career. I knew he would not let us down. Nick Beal would take his place on the wing. The bench was packed with seasoned internationals.

It was a strong a side as we could muster and one I felt could do a job on Fiji. But there was no doubt they would not be the walkover that Italy and Tonga had been. Their backs, weaned on Sevens, were among the most dangerous in the tournament. But their concentration on the shorter form of the game had compromised the development of their forwards for the XV-a-side version over the years. Lately, with the ex-All Black forward Brad Johnstone in charge, that had changed and they now had line-out and scrummage play in their armoury too. They had frightened France, stealing at least 10 balls from them in the line-out. We needed to make sure we weren't caught napping and the pack put in two long sessions.

In the event, however, it was easier than we had feared. We beat Fiji 45 points to 24. I scored with a practice field move. The idea is that Jonny sends a deep kick from one side of the field to the other, a winger runs on, catches it and crashes over. I happened to be out wide where the wingers would normally be and the move worked a dream. It was pleasing, especially to the coaches, to see an off-the-wall move that we train for come off on the pitch. Full marks to Jonny for a pinpoint kick.

The game was actually won after 20 minutes, when we were 20–3 up. We relaxed slightly, trying to save ourselves for South Africa, and leaked three soft tries in consequence. That did not concern us. The injury list did. Dan Luger, who beat three Fijian backs to score a dazzling individual try, his 11th in 14 Tests, went off before half time with a hamstring strain. Austin hurt his back and didn't come out for the second half, Daws coming off the bench and getting through the remainder of the game despite his injured chest. Near the end, Jonny Wilkinson took a swinging arm in the face and had to be helped off, while Matt Perry damaged his shoulder right at the death. Even those who stayed the course were battered and bruised and virtually the whole squad spent the evening on the massage table or in and out of ice baths, saunas and Jacuzzis, rehydrating, taking on pills and protein shakes to aid recovery.

For one guy, though, it was all too late for that. Jerry Guscott's groin was worse than we had feared. He announced he was quitting international football. They called him the Prince of Centres and, when you consider he played most of his rugby in a forward-dominated side, I think that's about right. It was a very sad occasion and there were tears in a few people's eyes when he told us. His record spoke for itself: 65 England caps, in which he scored 30 tries and two drop goals, plus another eight British Lions caps. Jerry was an outstanding player, even though he had not been at his best during the tournament, and a well-liked member of the squad. He left a big hole but would stay with the group for the remainder of the competition. Mark Tindall, a young Bath centre, came in to replace Jerry. He had showed some outstanding form in the warm-up games and a good attitude in training, so I had no problems with him joining us.

*

South Africa in the quarter-final of the World Cup. The defending champions. Games don't come much bigger than that. We were battered, bruised and tired but I felt we would lift our minds and bodies for this challenge. Thursday morning, we had an early breakfast before travelling to France aboard the Eurostar. It was my first trip under the Channel and I was looking forward to the new experience. It was something of a let down. Twenty minutes of darkness and then we were in France. And I didn't really think much of the 'first class' accommodation. The meal was a bit ropey too. At least the journey went quickly. The train set off at 10.35am and we were in Paris by two-ish. Getting to the hotel was another matter, though. Paris was even worse than London for traffic. We spent ages at a standstill. When we finally checked in, I took the opportunity to grab a massage, and had a swim and a Jacuzzi for a bit of recovery. That evening I took a sleeping tablet, something I very rarely do, because I wanted to get off to sleep as soon as I could. I was gone by 9pm.

Next day, Friday, saw us do a little light training – a team run. We needed to conserve our energy. Dan Luger didn't train at all, which was a worry. He was perhaps our most potent attacker. When Clive announced the side that day, though, he was in. I thought his inclusion was vital if we were to beat the World Champions.

There were a few other changes. Paul Grayson replaced Jonny Wilkinson and Nick Beal had Austin's place on the wing. Phil Vickery was back in at tighthead, Phil Greening retained his place as starting hooker and Hilly was back on the blindside in place of Joe Worsley. Sadly for Joe, he didn't even get a place on the bench – Clive preferred the greater experience of Martin Corry, a more experienced back row who also covered the second row. Archer was out for Danny Grewcock.

Grays for Jonny was an interesting decision. Grays was clearly the more mature player and was probably better tactically, at that stage, with his kicking. He had far more experience. It was significant too that he was paired at club level with Matt Dawson. Their understanding would naturally be better than Matt's with Jonny and that could make all the difference. There was a possibility of rain and if it was wet Cocker would start ahead of Greening. A wet ball would lead us to try to play it a bit tighter, where it was felt that Cocker's more powerful scrummaging would be an advantage.

We had a trip to the Stade de France, where the game would be played. I had a couple more massages and another good night's sleep.

On the morning of the match, feeling good, I spent some time just sitting and visualising all the hard work I had put in in recent months, with Steve Redgrave's remarks about the opposition in mind. The training sessions had been absolutely gruelling. I had come in to the house on one or two occasions and Ali had thought I was dying because I was in so much pain. It would all be worth it if we beat South Africa and went on to win the competition. The Springboks had been playing the game down, as we were, but they were due to hit some form. They had also had eight days' break since their last game. But we were in good shape, too. Our mood was brilliant, and we were ready.

*

The magic boot of Jannie De Beer denied us victory.

I felt he was the difference between the teams. When a guy has a freak day – and that's what it was – there is not a lot you can do about it. De Beer would not even have been playing if Henry Honiball's hamstring had cleared up and all most people knew about him was that he had had an average season with London Scottish. We had looked at him, of course, and we knew he was a fine kicker. But five drop goals in half an hour. No-one saw that coming.

I certainly don't think the final score of 44–21 reflected the difference between the sides. The first half was very tense, with Grays and De Beer swapping penalties. They only went in front with a suspect try by Van Der Westhuizen, in which he hit the corner flag before touching down. Even then, we closed back to within four points at 25–21 before the drop kicks, and a late try by Pieter Rossouw, took the game away from us.

A lot of people questioned the presence of the drop goal in modern international football after that match. It was an anachronism, they suggested, and should be done away with.

England have been on the receiving end and we have dished it out too – most notably when Rob Andrew's kick sent Australia out of the 1995 tournament which was, of course, won by a Joel Stransky drop-kick. While it was still a rarity, it had spectator appeal. Following De Beer's Test it seemed people were popping them over in almost every game and I think that devalued the currency. I tend to think that the drop goal still has a place in the sport but that maybe only one or two points should be awarded, rather than three. Ultimately, we want to see games won by tries and not drop goals.

After the match, the feeling was one of emptiness, of flatness. A few of us made it out into Paris to drown our sorrows in a beer or two. Lots of fans were out and about and most of them, as usual, were brilliant. There is always one idiot, though. Lol, Jerry and I met ours in a bar. We were standing chatting when three England supporters came up to us. They commiserated at first, but one of them starting winding us up. Eventually, he said: 'The problem is, Backy, you guys didn't play with any heart today.'

I was fuming. I put my drink down and said: 'Do you want to say that again, mate?'

Grinning, he shot back: 'You didn't play with any heart.'

A short-arm right-cross wiped the smile straight off his ugly mug. It was like a cartoon knock-out. His eyes went first, then his legs started to wobble. I even had time to reach over and take his pint out of his hand before he hit the deck, out cold.

Lawrence and Jerry hooted and shook my hand. Sometimes, you have just had enough.

Was he right, though? Was it a question of heart? The short answer is no. In all the games we played – New Zealand and South Africa included – England had 65 to 70 per cent of the territory and possession. The forwards did their job, were on top and were never outplayed. So what went wrong?

You might say that, as a unit, our backs lacked a cutting edge. For heart, for guts, for hard-work and effort, not a single one of the guys could be faulted. They were prepared to die for their shirts. But they found it tough against Southern Hemisphere defences.

The centre was our biggest problem area. Jerry Guscott was coming to the end of a fabulous career. At his best, he would have made a big difference. Phil de Glanville had a good World Cup and he certainly had the greatest respect from all the boys, both for his attitude and ability and for the way he bounced back after losing the captaincy to Lawrence. But while he is certainly an extremely good international player, who does what he does very well, I don't think he is world class. He lacks that tiny extra bit of pace and variety for modern Test rugby. Will Greenwood didn't have the greatest of competitions. He has masses of ability and is a world-beater on his day but, for some reason, it didn't go right for him.

Playing in the centre in modern international rugby demands pace, vision, power and great defensive ability. It's rare to find all four in English players. If you look at the top sides, their midfields all had a very explosive, powerful runner. With the Wallabies, it was Herbert. The Springboks had Muller. New Zealand have people like Ieremia and Gibson. And they all have quick, skilful guys playing outside them – like Tune and Roff, Wilson and Cullen. We lacked a centre partnership that will get us across the gain line. In his heyday, Jerry Guscott was a fabulous talent, the sort of player who could pick his way through defences almost at will, but inside that position nowadays it helps to have a powerful, route one player to suck in defences and punch the necessary holes, to smash over the gain line and give you a target in front of your forwards. We didn't achieve that against South Africa. In that game, tactically we made a bad choice in kicking possession at them from deep, which gave them plenty of time to attack us in numbers. If we had had a fit Austin on his wing, if Jonny had started and played well, if Dan had been at really full fitness . . .

The whole tournament was a massive disappointment for Northern Hemisphere rugby, apart from that one blindingly brilliant performance by the French against the All Blacks in the semi-final. That is the only time I have been cheering for *les Bleus* I can assure you.

Despite all the negatives, I think we are arriving at a point where we can live with the Southern Hemisphere teams in most areas. Our pack certainly bears up. If you look at our half-backs individually, they compete. We had no problems on the left wing and at full back. Matt Perry was one of our players of the tournament, with Bealer providing excellent back-up, and Dan Luger has developed really well and is a deadly finisher. On the right wing, Austin Healey is now a world class player but he was still growing into the role when the World Cup came along.

After the tournament, too, our centre situation looked to be improving. Mike Catt had a great Six Nations at 12 and Mike Tindall had also come in to add firepower. Leon Lloyd and a host of other young guys are now knocking on the door but they were not ready in time.

Will we ever win it? I think we can. We have a coach now who backs his judgment on young players and an ethos which prizes try-scoring and strong defence. The England team which went to South Africa would have whupped the side we put out in the World Cup – and it was basically the same guys. We have just improved.

I heard people saying that a team with England's pack and the Wallaby backs would have beaten anyone anywhere. I don't know how fair that is. I actually rate the Aussie pack very highly. It doesn't have any real superstars, John Eales apart, but collectively, they do what's required of them. They win their own ball at lineout and scrum. They compete for every inch of pitch. And defensively they are superb – the whole team is. They only conceded one try all tournament and that was a freak score by the USA. Their backs are, undoubtedly, superb – led by Tim Horan. He is an absolutely world class player: quick, clever and strong. The Player of the Tournament, and rightly named in my view.

I thought the Aussies deserved their win.

CHAPTER 12

The Tigers

I LOVE Leicester Tigers. We may not have the really big name foreign stars of a side like Saracens or a multi-millionaire money man behind us like Gloucester. We may not have the glamour of Harlequins or Bath. But what we do have is a superb set of supporters, a great team spirit and a sheer, bloody-minded will to win.

How much does all that mean to me?

Well, I turned down a pair of offers, each of which would have made me a millionaire, to stay at Welford Road.

The first one was an approach to my agents from a rugby league agent who said he could place me with one of the clubs up north. The figures being bandied around were substantial but my heart was not in a change of code. I enjoy watching league and I think I would fit in to its frenetic, stop-start style as well as any union player. We have taken plenty from it in the last few years, particularly defensive techniques and tactics. There is a history of players crossing the divide, too – Jonathan Davies, Alan Tait, John Bentley and more.

But I prefer the game I am in and I decided to stay where I was.

The second approach gave me much more food for thought. Bristol made me an offer which would have seen me become the highest-paid player in English rugby.

It was shortly after Bob Dwyer moved to Bristol. He called me to ask whether I was interested in following him West. He had big plans for his new club and wanted me to be a part of them. I was surprised and very flattered and said I would think about it. But I told Bob the offer would have to be really special.

'How special?' he asked.

Almost off the cuff, I replied: 'A million pounds.'

Dwyer didn't hesitate. 'I think we can do it' he said.

The offer he eventually tabled was exactly that: a £200,000 signing-on fee and £200,000 a year for four years.

I was 29 and had recently got married. Ali and I had bought a house and, after living with my parents for most of my twenties, I was getting used to the financial realities of life. We wanted to have children. A million pounds over four years would see me almost to the end of my playing career and would set us up for life as a family.

It was a hard decision. The salary I was earning with the Tigers was nowhere near what Bob was offering. I had sleepless nights, weighing in my mind my loyalty to Leicester – after all, they had given me my big break in rugby – and my responsibility to Ali. My agent, the former Tigers centre Tim Buttimore of Leamington Spa-based SCG, talked to Leicester. Dean Richards and Peter Wheeler were understanding: they did not want to lose me but the best they could offer was an increase, still nothing like what Bob was promising, and an extended contract. There was no sugar daddy behind the club, it was run on a strict plc basis and they had no spare money to throw around. Ali and I discussed it and I consulted Tim. He was happy to negotiate the move for me but made the point that some things in life are more important than money. Ali took the same view. I turned Bob down and I pledged my future to Welford Road in a package which will see me through until at least 2003.

So what is it that is so special about the Tigers?

The fans are a big plus. We consistently achieve the biggest crowds in English rugby and our great old ground is often packed to the rafters. They are a noisy, partisan and knowledgeable bunch who expect hard graft, guts and determination from their players. I am always conscious, every time I run out on to the pitch, that every person there has parted with hard-earned money to see us play. I do my best to entertain them and to pay them back for their support. They have been good to me over the years: I have had thousands of letters in the past decade from Tigers fans either commiserating with me on my non-selection for England or congratulating me on it since. I always feel that part of my England shirt is theirs because that encouragement was invaluable during the Cooke and Rowell years.

The team ethos is another factor. Tigers sides have traditionally been built on teamwork, not stars. We have had major foreign names, like Joel Stransky, occasionally in the past. We have big England names at the moment. But we have always been reluctant to buy players just for their names. If you look at our recent overseas players, Dave Lougheed and Fritz van Heerden were certainly not glamour purchases. What they were was talented, hard-working, hard-nosed individuals who fitted into our side like locals. And that is another point: Leicester has always been a local club which happens to have an internationally famous name. A lot of our players are home grown lads: from Martin Johnson down, a good proportion of the team has come from junior clubs within a 30 mile radius of Leicester. Our team spirit is great in training, it is fantastic in matches and it's strong away from the sport, too. We socialise together a lot, which is important.

And I like the way we play. Critics have claimed for years that we are a stick-it-up-your-jumper side who like to win by starting a rolling maul on the half-way line and walking it over the try line. That's garbage. A lot is said about our forwards. What about our backs? Few Premiership One sides could boast a back line containing the likes of Austin Healey, Pat Howard, Leon Lloyd, Tim Stimpson, Dave Lougheed and Geordan Murphy. Few teams could afford to let Will Greenwood go. The fact is we score plenty of tries: some are catch-and-drives and some are run in from half way. Variety is the spice of life, someone once said.

We play to win and yes, at times, we infringe. BSkyB's Stuart Barnes is a big one for talking about us killing the ball. But we are by no means alone in this. Occasionally, penalties are awarded in our favour you know.

Sometimes, maybe, we get over-competitive defending our goal line and as a result kill the ball. The All Blacks have been doing it for years. It is not up to the players to police the game, it is up to the referees. Our fans want to see us win; they don't want to see us come fifth but top the fair play league and be lauded as jolly good sportsmen. No-one wants to see the game wrecked by cheating. But everyone should accept that professional sport is played right to the edge and, sometimes, in the heat of the moment, even over the edge. If the ref sees what is going on, he punishes you – and you take your punishment.

*

The 1999/2000 season started on a financial high-note when the club announced a seven-figure, three-year sponsorship deal with the car manufacturers, Vauxhall. That would bring in much-needed revenue and would help to stabilise the Tigers. In these early days of professionalism, many clubs are still struggling to get onto a sound financial footing and support from sponsors like Vauxhall – and our other commercial partners such as Next, Alliance and Leicester and Cotton Traders – is vital. Leicester is a successful club but we had still lost £1.5 million in the previous year. With the new sponsorship, some cost-cutting and fundraising and a return of the European Cup, Peter Wheeler was eventually able announce an end-of-year profit.

Our deal with Vauxhall included a £50,000 bonus if we retained the Allied Dunbar Premiership or won the Tetley's Bitter Cup. To a soccer club, this would be small change. To us it provided a real incentive.

The change of sponsor meant a new logo on our shirts and the decision was made to re-vamp our kit. The colours had altered slightly over time, but our world-famous broad-band stripes had not changed since 1909. The new-style strip featured narrower stripes and different, darker shades. Some of the supporters accused the club of trying to milk them for money. I didn't think that was particularly fair; it was not as though we were doing a Manchester United and bringing out half a dozen new strips a season.

The real interest, though, centred on what would happen on the pitch. A combination of hard work, total commitment and ability had seen Leicester grab the Allied Dunbar Premiership One title for 1998/1999. I was very proud to be awarded the Unisys Top Try Scorer of the Year award for touching down 16 League tries (with another three in the Cup) and Johnno deservedly was voted RFU Player of the Year. At the start of the next season, we faced uncharted territory. No team had retained the League championship since the game turned professional. Could we be the first?

The critics said not: we were ageing, we didn't have the passion any more, the game had changed and we could not adapt. Predictions of our demise spilled out wherever you looked and I have to admit we had our own doubts, too. One of the penalties of being a good side is that you tend to have a lot of internationals among your ranks and we were set to haemorrhage players to the 1999 World Cup in early season. Ten would be out. Eight, including myself and a major chunk of the pack, were with the England squad, Dave Lougheed was with Canada and Fritz van Heerden was with South Africa.

Into our places stepped a bunch of young guys in their late teens or early twenties. How would the likes of Lewis Moody, Ben Kay, Paul Gustard, Adam Balding, James Grindal and Andy Goode fare in the absence of the more senior players? I hoped they would see it as an opportunity and would seize their spots, even if Lewis and Guzzy would be hoping to take the No 7 shirt. One bright spot was a rule allowing three points for post-

World Cup wins, as opposed for the normal two. This might help redress the balance.

The Tigers' opening game against Northampton appeared to confirm all our fears. It was a disaster, the young lads going down 46-24 at Franklins Gardens. During the game, they had been taunted by laughing Saints players saying: 'You're not going to win the league this year, boys.' We would see about that. Dean Richards told the *Leicester Mercury*: 'I don't think a lot of the new young boys coming into the side realise what a Northampton-Leicester game is all about. We tried to instil it into them all week but to go out and do it on a Saturday is another thing. It's been an eye-opener for them.' Away with England, we discussed whether we would be able to make up the lost ground if we came back to find ourselves 10 points adrift of the lead.

Then things went from bad to worse. One of the remaining old heads quit: Matt Poole called it a day after 11 years with persistent ankle and pelvic injuries and Leon Lloyd was called up by Clive Woodward after David Rees withdrew from the World Cup squad. Twelve players down, now.

Our fans must have been fearing the worst when, towards the end of September, the depleted Tigers played host to a Sale Sharks side roaring with confidence after their defeat of Wasps on the opening day of the season. Even though Sale had beaten Tigers only once, and never at Welford Road, and had off-loaded nine players to make budget cuts, the odds were with the Northerners. Our predicament was worsened by problems at tight head prop. We had signed a South African called Ken Fourie from West Hartlepool as cover for Darren Garforth during the World Cup. Ken looked the part but he was essentially unfit, too soft and was not cutting the mustard. Derek Jelley, normally a loose head cover for Graham Rowntree, had been forced to move to the other side of the scrum. We were also having trouble in the second row with Martin and Fritz away and injuries affecting their stand-ins. Despite that, the cubs turned in a good performance, beating Sale 18–3 in a downpour.

Shortly afterwards, John Welborn, an Australian international with six caps to his name, was signed to bolster the second row.

One win and one loss from two games. It could have been worse.

The next fixture was away at Gloucester. 'Glaws' had produced some interesting statistics which suggested that it was harder for a visiting side to win at Kingsholm than at any other sporting arena in the world. They won 77% per cent of their home fixtures. Coached by Philippe Saint André, they looked a good side. Before the match, John Wells predicted the younger guys would struggle to cope with the physical and mental pressure of a tough game in front of the notorious 'Shed', and he was right, with the Tigers demolished by 34 points to six. Clearly, the inexperienced hands were struggling to crew the ship and, in the World Cup camp, we were starting to fear the title might be lost.

For the next fixture, against London Irish at The Stoop, the England contingent arranged to visit so we could support the youngsters. The Irish were topping the table but a stunning game, orchestrated by Pat Howard and Tim Stimpson, saw us run out 31–30 victors. James Grindal, making his debut, had an impressive game as the lads overturned a 17 point half-time deficit to win with the last kick of the game, Stimmo converting Paul Gustard's injury time try to cap a superb comeback. The England players rushed onto the pitch to mob the team, delighted for them and the travelling fans.

Towards the end of October, Dave Lougheed was the first international to arrive back, after Canada's group round exit from the World Cup. Bristol, now top of the table and coached by Bob Dwyer, visited Welford Road. In an inspired performance, the Tigers blew away Bristol 36–19. According to reports, the game was won by Leicester's fighting spirit. One of the Bristol players later said: 'We did not appreciate the respect and tradition that goes into this club and how they play, regardless of who is playing. They had more enthusiasm for the game, they were quicker to the breakdown, they looked fitter and were willing to play with the ball.'

The same day, England lost to South Africa in the quarter-final of the World Cup. I knew Dean and others at the club had been torn between pride in seeing so many Tigers away on England duty and the desire to see them back in harness for Leicester. Now we were returning and the general feeling among us and at the club was that our young players had done us all proud. Five games and three wins, and just one point behind Bath and Bristol. There was no mountain to climb and one or two of us might even struggle to win our places back!

*

On our return from international duty, our first game was at home to Bedford. Martin Corry, Leon Lloyd and Austin Healey were the only England guys to play. Myself, Graham Rowntree, Richard Cockerill and Darren Garforth were on the bench. Will Greenwood was rested with a shoulder injury. Ominously, Johnno was rested too. He had played throughout the World Cup with an Achilles injury. It was caused by a piece of bone rubbing away at the tendon and it was the sort of problem which can cure itself. Equally, if it is played on, it can require surgery. Surgery to an Achilles can be career-ending and is to be avoided wherever possible. Rest seemed to be the best option for the skipper. Achilles injuries can appear to heal during the winter if the ground is wet and soft, only to return later in the year when the pitches harden up again. If he took the weight off his feet for a while, the injury could heal and we would avoid losing him later in the season. The word was that he would be out for a few weeks. In his absence, Ben Kay had been doing an excellent job at lock and he or Martin's brother Will would partner Fritz when he returned from an injury he had picked up too.

I was glad not to be thrown straight back into the fray. I was shattered, physically and mentally, and disappointed, too by our

World Cup performance. But Bedford was not a bad game for Austin and the other boys to make their reappearance. The Southern side were playing their first Premiership match since a supporters' buy-out. Their backs were to the wall but we expected to beat them comfortably and a 61–12 scoreline tells the story. The ABC Club of Rowntree, Cockerill and Garforth were introduced at the start of the second half to a rapturous welcome from a crowd which had clearly missed them. Immediately, the bolstered pack punched the Bedford eight backwards and three scrums later we had rubbed out a first half pushover by Bedford. The boys chalked up 43 points unanswered in the second half, in what was the club's 100th league game.

A night trip to Newcastle followed, for my first appearance since the World Cup. A dour 12-all draw followed, in the worst conditions I have ever played in. We had warmed up in shorts and t-shirts in the sunshine. It started raining when we went in to change and by the time we had come out it was pouring. The wind got up and we gradually got colder and colder. By the end of the game, the backs were literally running up and down, off the ball, to keep warm and Pat Howard, used to warmer temperatures, had gone visibly blue. Leon Lloyd was shaking uncontrollably and lamenting the fact that he had none of Nobby West's plentiful body fat. When the whistle went, everybody raced straight off without handshakes, desperate to get in. Guys went straight into the showers in their kit and rehydrated with hot tea! The result hardly mattered. Significantly, Garf hurt his neck in a tackle but picked himself up and carried on playing, appearing to shake off the injury.

News broke that Jonah Lomu had been offered to the Tigers by his agent Kingsley Jones at a rate well above what the Tigers could afford to pay. Among the players, we chatted about whether Jonah be a good buy for the Tigers. Let's say his salary was £250,000 a year. He would struggle to repay that money by putting extra bums on seats. He might do so at a club like Wasps, with current crowds of six or eight thousand in a venue which can hold 20,000 or more people. At Welford Road, we are close to sold out a lot of the time anyway, although Lomu would probably ensure more sell-outs. Would he help us win more prize money? Well, he would help any English side to win games, as long as he had the heart for those sleeting night games at Sale or Newcastle. The club would also expect to make money on Lomu merchandising. And you might find that a sponsor would be willing to help fund his signing. As rugby's only world superstar, his arrival would generate massive interest in the media. As it was, none of that mattered because the NZRFU offered him a package good enough to keep him.

Mid-November brought a home clash against Wasps and my first try of the domestic campaign in a game we won by 28 points to 9. We were there or thereabouts in the table and I felt that we were becoming the team to beat.

A few days after the Wasps encounter, it was time for us to open our European Cup campaign. That match – against Leinster at Donnybrook – heralded the hardest 10 weeks in my time at the Tigers. Between late November and the end of January the next year, we would play 12 matches in the Allied Dunbar Premiership, the European Cup and the Tetley's Bitter Cup, a schedule which would test us to our limits. And injuries were starting to become a major concern. Johnno's rested Achilles was showing no signs of recovery. Darren Garforth had joined him on the sidelines after his neck injury worsened against Wasps. He later admitted he should never have played against Wasps. The pain he had felt had left him frightened for the first time on a rugby field. He needed a scan and a visit to a specialist at Stoke Mandeville and, although it was muscle damage rather than anything more serious, a neck injury is always bad news for a tight head prop. Garf was ruled out for the foreseeable future. Leon Lloyd had a knee injury which meant he, too, was unavailable.

We did not start that 10-week run well. The trip to Leinster was a disaster. We never seem to play well in Ireland and this was no exception. Their small ground was jammed to the rafters and I glanced into the home dressing room as I walked by to see dozens of big posters saying 'Leicester Tigers – No Respect!' to psyche themselves up for the battle. Obviously, they and their fans were up for this one. They scored 27 points to our 20, with their fly-half playing exceptionally well, kicking all their points as they turned around a 17–12 half time deficit. Glance casually at the match statistics and it looks like our discipline let us down: we simply gave away too many penalties.

The fact is, the referee, a Frenchman called Jeanne Christoff Gastou went a long way towards costing us the game. His performance was scandalous. He appeared to speak hardly any English – a handicap when you are trying to run a game involving 30 English speakers. At two points during the match we were ordered to retreat 10 yards for dissent. In fact, we were not dissenting at all: we were simply trying to establish what we had been penalised for so we could avoid doing it again. In the second half, a perfectly good try by Dave Lougheed was disallowed and an eminently kickable penalty was reversed when I was yellow-carded. The ref accused me of violence when in fact I was covering up while my head was being used as a punch ball. It was perhaps the most surreal experience of my life. We contributed to our own downfall, though. At one point, we had an attacking scrum right on the Leinster line after a scintillating break by James Grindal which was hacked on by Andy Goode. Incredibly, we were pushed off our own ball. That was a shock for a Leicester pack. We did have the satisfaction of scoring the only try, through Pat Howard after I slipped him a pass from a line out in the sixth minute. But that was scant consolation for losing a game the bookies had us 5–2 on to win.

The following Saturday, we had another European Cup game, this time at home to Stade Français. The first bit of good news was that Clayton Thomas, the Welsh referee – who speaks English, after a fashion – would be in charge. The second bit of good news was that our European campaign was back on the rails. In a niggly game characterised by the odd sneaky punch and a bit of stamping, we overcame the French by 30 points to 25. Importantly, we survived a scare when Stade Français came back from being 24–9 down five minutes after the break, slotting three penalties and scoring a converted try to move to within one point of us. The 13,000-strong crowd was hushed and tense but Tim Stimpson stayed ice cool, kicking two late penalties, and the pack staved off a last-gasp surge near our line to win. As they left the pitch, the French came over all mouthy and their No 8 started saying things like 'We'll get you in Paris', which reflected the spirit in which the game had been played!

I later read that three and a half million people had watched the match on BBC television, which was excellent, twice the normal average for Sunday Grandstand. Similar numbers tuned in in France and others watched on BSkyB's EuroSport, BBC Wales and BBC Northern Ireland. That had to be good for the game.

A week later, we faced a Saracens side which was attempting to stop the rot after three successive defeats. It was a Sunday night game, staged at 6.30pm at Vicarage Road. This was crazy timing but the Allied Dunbar Premiership rules stated that it was up to the home side as to when to play a game, as long as it took place any time between Friday and Sunday. You had to question how much leverage BSkyB had in the matter. The timing may have been good for the armchair viewer but did not suit our travelling army of fans. The company's coverage of rugby has been great, in some senses. As with cricket and soccer, it has introduced innovative camera angles and gimmicks, plus much more use of statistics, to make the game more entertaining and accessible. It has also employed ex-players who know rugby inside out as commentators. More fixtures have also been covered since we moved to satellite. The gripes I have are that not everyone has BSkyB – so we are missing a massive potential audience – and also maybe that TV has become too powerful. On the other hand, BSkyB pumps around £5 million a year into the sport, with each Premiership One club receiving £250,000 of that. You cannot have your cake and eat it, I suppose.

We had won only one game in eight in the previous two years under lights. Thierry Lacroix had obviously read his history books and extended that losing streak with an excellent display of kicking. We were all square in tries but his boot made the difference.

Early in December, the injury gloom surrounding our two senior forwards deepened. No good news on Johnno, and now Garf would be out until the New Year – at least. Richard Cockerill was also sidelined and we had a big game coming up against Glasgow Caledonians in the European Cup. The sides in our Pool – A – were all square, played two and won one, and we were second on points difference. A win could see us go top. But we lost by 30 points to 17, turning in a poor performance in Perth. Our handling was bad and the Scots played with more passion, pace and strength.

Almost immediately, though, we had the chance to make amends, when they visited Welford Road. Some days you're the dog, some days you're the lamppost. Today we were the dogs, turning them over 34–21, with Austin Healey playing brilliantly on a frosty day. I scored, and Dave Lougheed and Austin scored too. But the match was perhaps most notable for another achievement by Oz. With Joel Stransky having to retire through injury, we had struggled to find anyone to fill in at fly-half. Andy Goode had given it a good shot, and was clearly a great prospect, but his inexperience was telling in the pressure games. Dean had even tried Geordan Murphy and Pat Howard at stand-off. Eventually, he and Joel decided to give Healey a go. It was a brave decision, even with a footballer of his ability. But in Stranners, he had found the best possible coach. The pair of them worked hard together in the few days before the game, Joel giving Austin a crash course in No 10 play. Come the game, he struggled in the new position at first but after a half time chat, in which Joel reinforced the need to keep it simple, he played a blinder.

As Christmas approached, Johnno's injury was still showing no signs of improving and the verdict from the physio room was that he would miss the first two Six Nations games, plus seven club fixtures. Privately, Dean was saying he didn't think Martin would even make the summer tour to South Africa. I know he felt very low about it but there was nothing he could do. Mark Geeson is one of the top physios in Britain and he was trying everything he knew.

John Akurangi, a 29-year-old Maori tighthead, was signed up and flew in on Christmas Eve. The shaven-headed, battle-scarred, 5ft 11in and 17st 'Axe' was a typical Maori – tattooed all over his body with the traditional designs and proudly bearing a triangular design reading 'Made in New Zealand' on his forearm.

Amazingly, given his long flight, he came straight in for the game against Bath on Boxing Day at the Rec and immediately looked the part. We knew he would do a job until Garf was back. We won 13–3 in appalling conditions. The next obstacle in our way was our final game of the millennium – the December 29 meeting with Quins. We beat them, 29–17, with Fritz van Heerden, recovered from injury, making his seasonal debut for the Tigers.

CHAPTER 13

Digging Deep

TO MARK the start of the new millennium, the squad posed in shiny, silvery suits and shades, courtesy of one of our major sponsors, Next. They put a lot of money into the club and their clothes are generally first-class but I wouldn't advise anyone to part with their hard-earned bunce on those particular outfits. The boys looked like exceptionally cheesy game show hosts. Still, the pictures got us publicity!

As far as matters on the field went, we knew we had to dig deep if we were to retain our championship. As a squad, we had sat down together prior to that Boxing Day game at Bath and laid out what we wanted to achieve that season. Northampton and Bath were our biggest rivals and both sides looked likely to challenge for our title. Looking at the way the table stood, I made the point that we could not afford to lose a single game. We pledged to win every one. That pledge had held with the Bath match.

I had a bruised hip and had not played since we had beaten Harlequins. This was unfortunate because, early in January, we had a trip to Paris and a crucial Heineken Cup clash with Stade Français. I would not make the 25-man squad – neither would Johnno or Garf – but at least Leon Lloyd's knee injury had cleared up sufficiently for him to be named in our party. Sadly, despite scoring a try which Stimmo converted, Leon could do

158

nothing to prevent a defeat. The Tigers lost 38–16 in front of a thousand travelling fans.

A key area for concern during the match was our pack. We had failed to sign a class tighthead prop at the start of the season as cover for Garforth. Ken Fourie, a South African signed from West Hartlepool, was currently on loan to Rugby and had not made the grade. When we finally brought in John Akurangi from New Zealand at Christmas it was too late because the deadline for European pool games had passed. Wiggy was standing in at tighthead but that is a tall order – especially against a French scrum – even for a guy as hard, skilled and committed as he is. Graham had a tough game as he himself admitted, later telling the *Leicester Mercury*: 'They found a weakness, which was me, and they just kept coming for me.' No-one at the club blamed him. In fact, we were proud of his attitude and bottle, which summed up the Leicester spirit. At the end of the season he was to win an Outstanding Service Award at our presentation evening in recognition of his efforts above and beyond the call of duty.

Before the game, Deano and Brace had tried to get an exemption from the cup organisers to allow Akurangi to play. Garf was injured, Perry Freshwater was out with flu and Graham Rowntree's wife was pregnant and overdue. Dean argued that where circumstances truly conspired against a side and where the position involved was a specialist one there ought to be some latitude. This seemed fair, especially where the position involved was tighthead prop. It is genuinely dangerous to play people out of position there. We were pretty angry about their decision. What if Wig had been injured too? What would they have suggested? Play Austin at tighthead? I know he's played just about everywhere else but . . .

The only way we could now go through to the quarter finals was if Glasgow beat Stade Français and we took Leinster apart. Early calculations were that we would have to score a minimum of nine tries to qualify for the quarters. There was confusion later when the organisers told us that the deciding factor was points difference and not points scored. Behind the scenes, the club tried to clear up the confusion before the game but were unable to do so. To a certain extent, however, it was irrelevant. Whatever the winning margin required, it was going to be significant. And whatever it was, we still felt it could be done. Anything was possible at Fortress Welford in front of the faithful.

When the game came, it was one of the most disappointing I have ever known in my Tigers career. We were playing for a place in the knock-out stages of the European Cup. Fixtures don't come much more important. But we surrendered, fairly meekly in front of a disappointed crowd of over 12,000, Leinster beating us by 32 points to 10. Ezulike and Lloyd were on the score sheet for us, with Tim Stimpson failing to convert. Leinster crossed our line twice, converted both scores and added five penalties and a cheeky drop goal. We were not helped with injuries – my hip had recovered but I had picked up flu at an England session, Garf was still out, despite having played for the Extras in mid-week, and so was Johnno. Even so, it was very disappointing. Quite apart from anything else, our early cup exit cost the club a lot of money. If we had reached the quarter finals, a 15,000 crowd paying £10 a ticket would have produced £150,000. After costs we would have realised £40–£50,000. That is serious income for a rugby club.

We still had the domestic Tetley's Bitter Cup to consider and the league championship to defend. We needed to bounce back against Saracens the following weekend. And our young Irish winger Geordan Murphy had something to celebrate, too, when he was called up to Ireland's Six Nations training camp as one of 16 uncapped players in their 45-man squad. The 21-year-old Dubliner, who had been skinning wings all season in the Allied Dunbar Premiership, fully deserved his call up. Geordy is far and away the quickest, most agile and most skilful footballer at the Tigers. Off the pitch, he likes to entertain people by performing the sort of tricks with a rugby ball that Pelé used to do with a soccer ball. Some people think that he is a little light for international rugby. I think he's got the pace and skill to make up for any shortfall but he is always trying to put on weight and eats like a horse, much to the envy of most of us who have to be careful what we eat. He is a quiet lad, who tends to hang around with the younger guys like Lewis and Leon, but he has a tremendous attitude to training and to matches and it was a major plus when we managed to hang onto him in the face of the Irish Union's entreaties that he return home. The only thing I would say is that he is labouring under the misapprehension that he looks like one of the guys in the teenybopper pop group Westlife ... wake up and smell the coffee, Geordy!

Johnno, meanwhile, was still a familiar sight on the treatment tables in our cramped physiotherapy room at the Oval Park training ground. Our physio, Mark Geeson, was trying everything to get him right but these injuries can take forever to heal. I was starting to wonder whether he would make any of the Six Nations games.

It was a cruel way to lose your England place and the captaincy and obviously he was very disappointed. He was still a key member of the England camp, though, and stayed involved by spending time negotiating on the players' behalf with the squad's commercial agents.

*

During the week, Stuart Potter announced his retirement. Potts had been a great servant of the club, joining in 1992 and winning an England cap in Australia in 1998. Injuries and travelling had taken their toll and he was returning to his family insurance business in Tamworth. He is known as 'Pernod Potts' after his favourite tipple – and when he tipples, he really goes for it. One or two is never enough – he goes ballistic. He is a top lad who used to brighten up our journeys to and from games with a spot of karaoke at the front of the bus. Two favourite items from his repertoire were 'The Lichfield RFC', his junior club song, and an infamous bingo-calling act. Both are far too obscene to repeat here but stop me if you see me and I'll be happy to regale you.

Matt 'Ponty' Poole's testimonial season was in full flow and he was working a damned sight harder on that than he ever did on the field. The latest money-making venture was a ladies-only dinner at Leicester's Grand Hotel. About 20 of the players were roped in as wine waiters. The idea was that we would smile politely and circulate, picking up drinks orders for the guests as they enjoyed a pleasant evening out, away from the husband and kids. In fact, it was Bedlam. Our first inkling that things might get out of control came as we waited backstage and watched 300 cackling, squealing 'ladies' take their seats at their dinner tables. Every last one of them was bevvied up to the hilt and they were soon piling into more champagne, cocktails and wine. Ponty is renowned for sweating when he is nervous; tonight, he looked like he'd been hosed down. He had some notes for a speech in his hand but he had to throw them away because they became too soggy to read.

We were all in a small room off the main ballroom and we watched through a crack in the door with horrified fascination as these women got rowdier and rowdier. My wife Ali – the only partner there, apart from Matt's wife Emma – had bought a table and I could see they were more out of control than most! Eventually, like a point man in the Vietnam War, Pooley crept out, to a massive roar. Somehow, with women tearing frantically at his dinner jacket, he made it to the stage. After a few brief remarks, he peered out into the room where we were supposed to be to see . . . nothing. Panic! Wild-eyed, he ran back in to find all 20 of us huddled in a cupboard under a staircase wetting ourselves laughing at his expense. Then it was time to face the music as Pooley introduced us one by one. Pat Howard, dressed in his silver Next suit, was first out, flouncing in with a tray carried high. The place went absolutely mad – Pat was being fondled and grabbed as he fought through a sea of hands to his table. I looked around the rest of the boys. No-one was laughing now. We had a big game against Saracens coming up in a couple of days' time and we were all stone cold sober. There were 19 very pale, bug-eyed players looking more nervous than I have ever seen them. I was 19th to be called in and I honestly almost bottled it and went home. Once inside, I was poked, prodded and groped all night – it verged on sexual harassment! A typical ploy went something like this: 'Neil, will you give my friend a kiss, it's her 40th birthday.' Nervously, you'd say okay but the minute you went anywhere near you'd be pounced on.

Dave Lougheed, Craig Joiner and myself were all wearing Tigers shirts to be auctioned, which we had to peel off as they bidded in a frenzy of screaming and whistling. Axe and Perry Freshwater stripped to the waist and performed the *haka*, which also went down well. Poor old Stimmo was the waiter for Ali's table. Apparently, he started off trying to be smooth, thinking that would keep them under control. By the end, his bow tie and half his shirt had been ripped off and he was struggling to keep them at bay. Ali had a great time – I later found out she had bought five bottles of champagne on our credit card – and at the end of the evening, I was sitting with a woman on each knee having a photo taken when she waltzed up, saying 'Mr Back, Mr Back! Can I have your autograph?' Then she leaned over and grabbed a kiss. These girls on my knees thought this was hilarious – they didn't know she was my wife! Our game a few days later against Saracens would be a cake-walk in comparison.

The ABC club was almost reunited as we faced Sarries. Garf had recovered and would partner Graham Rowntree – now the proud father of Lily-Rose – in the front row. Former policeman Dorian West would squeeze between them instead of Cocker, though. Westy had just become a father for the second time and Garf had young kids too. It was hilarious listening to these gnarled front-rows swapping tips on nappy changing and furrowing their brows as they explained to Wig all about feeding techniques and habits.

The Old Dads were up against two promising England prospects, David Flatman and Julian White, and we knew that no prisoners would be taken there.

In Johnno's absence, I captained the side in a pulsating but ill-tempered game, which saw Garforth and Akurangi sin-binned for foul play at the line out and dissent respectively. Despite that, we won 48–20. Austin Healey was the star. It was only his fifth game at stand-off but he was growing in stature match by match and completely outplayed Lacroix. He made the opening try for Murphy and scored one of his own, a blistering, 50 metre solo effort at the start of the second half. He also played a part in two of our other three tries. Sarries had looked capable of winning and actually led 20–17 after half an hour but we blew them away, scoring 31 points without reply, including two monster penalties from Tim Stimpson who kicked beautifully for his 23 points. I managed to get onto the score sheet with a try at the end.

It was good to bounce back after our European Cup disappointments. And now people were starting to talk about Austin as England's fly-half. Joel Stransky was one of them. He reckoned that the only thing keeping Jonny Wilkinson in the side was his goal-kicking and thought Clive ought to move Jonny to inside centre and play Austin at No 10. He told the *Mercury*: 'Clive should pick him because he is exciting and breaks defences down. Austin's success has not surprised me because he has got all the talent, all the skills. He is one of the most talented footballers I have ever seen. He understands the game, he is a thinker, which gave him a huge head start when we moved him to play at fly-half. He has also played a lot at scrum-half and in many ways the two positions are quite similar. He has also played at wing. So he understands the game from an inside back's point of view and from an outside back's point of view.'

I did not agree with Joel about Jonny and I think subsequent events have proved Wilko is the better fly-half. However, I agreed with all he said about Austin's many talents.

Austin – also known as 'Oz', 'Naus' and 'Dwarf', depending on how irritating he is being – is so quick, both in his feet and his head. The only problem is that whenever there's a lull in the conversation he finds it necessary to remind us all of this. He loves to be the centre of attention and if he was not surrounded by level-headed guys he would have gone into brilliant self-destruct by now.

He is his own worst enemy at times. By his own admission, he's got a big mouth at times and he also rises easily to the bait. That makes him an easy target for the mickey-take. The Team England management decided a year or so ago to revamp the home changing room at Twickenham. The experts from the TV programme *Changing Rooms* were called came in. One of the things they did was to put little name tags above all our pegs. The idea was nice but the tags were a bit cheap and cheerful and Clive thought we could do a bit better. He had them replaced with solid wooden plaques, apparently made out of English oak, with our names embossed on them in gold next to the English rose. They cost around £150 each and the idea is that after your last cap you will be presented with your plaque as a nice memento of your career. Almost immediately, one of them went missing – Austin's. There was a big hoo-ha, with the stadium security people called in to find the thief. Clive didn't need their help. With half an eye on a leg-pull, he said, straight away: 'I know who's taken it. It must be Austin himself – any sane thief would have taken Jerry's or Johnno's. Austin's wouldn't be worth much.' He sent a letter out saying as much to every squad member and adding that Healey was dropped and he was being fined £1,000. Austin came on the blower to Clive, crying about being dropped, begging for mercy, swearing it wasn't him. Eventually, some of the other Leicester lads in the squad – who had actually removed it – sent it back, but Austin had fallen for the wind-up hook, line and sinker.

But when he is on form he is a top lad. Before Lawrence took over the captaincy from Blouse, there was a lot of speculation in the press as to who would get the job. Austin sidled up to Clive and said: 'I've got a proposition for you. Do you know what the odds are for captain?'

Clive didn't have a clue so Austin ran through them – Martin Johnson, 7–1, Lawrence Dallaglio, 7–1, Rodber, 10–1, Jason

Leonard at whatever, and so on, down to Austin Healey – 150–1. Then he said: 'Look Clive, I've got twenty grand, you've got twenty grand – we'll put it on at Ladbrokes, you name me as captain and we'll get out of here.'

Clive just stared at him and said: 'I wouldn't make you captain if you were the last person on earth.'

Lately Oz has become obsessed about his receding hair line. At one point recently, he was talking about having his agent put him up for the Graham Gooch hair treatment – of which more later – and he has won another nick-name . . . 'Ray Reardon'.

*

Almost immediately, we faced Wasps at Loftus Road. This was the sort of game which would show whether we had the character and strength of mind and body to retain our title. Three days to recover and a game against a side with footballers like Lawrence Dallaglio and Joe Worsley. It was certainly a test for me.

We won the game with a bizarre effort two or three minutes from time. Trailing by 20 points to 19, Austin tried a drop goal which was diverted onto a post via someone's hand in an attempted charge-down. As the ball fell to the ground, Geordan Murphy scooped it up and dived over the line. A great poaching score by a player with great awareness, it was only our second win under lights in the last dozen matches. I had a hand in the easiest try Dorian West will ever score. Geordan Murphy rounded Kenny Logan, the ball went out to Healey who passed it to me. I shot through a hole in their cover defence and almost literally handed the ball to Westie. Half an hour after the whistle, of course, Dorian was blithely insisting he had scorched home from 20 metres!

Our defence, in the face of some vigorous Wasps attacking, was excellent – Martin Corry put in one monster tackle on Trevor Leota, for instance – although Worsley managed to batter his way over after a scrum. Tim Stimpson's goal-kicking, once again, was superb, while Kenny Logan had an off-day.

More importantly, the win lifted us one place to second behind Gloucester, whose own run of eight straight wins had come to an end at Saracens.

Meanwhile, Will Greenwood was getting twitchy. From being the find of the 1997 Lions Tour, injury had lent a stop-start air to Will's career and he had failed to make our starting line-up for the last seven games. Although he had been playing well for our Extras, he was hardly being kept out by a nobody – the guy in his place was Pat Howard, and it is not easy to elbow your way past a man who has played Super 12 rugby and has around 20 caps for Australia.

I like Will as a bloke and I rate him as a player, too. I don't think he has ever really recovered his confidence from the incident in South Africa during the Lions tour, when he effectively died on the pitch. Will – 'Celery', after his legs, or 'Shaggy' after the Scooby-doo character to whom he bears a striking resemblance – was desperate to regain his Tigers and England spots. Maybe he will be back for his country now he has rejoined Quins: on his day, he is an absolutely superb player which a gift for unlocking the tightest defence.

The following Saturday, we faced London Irish at The Stoop in a Tetley's Bitter Cup 5th round clash. It was our third hard match in a week, which was absolute lunacy and made me question whether the people who drew up the fixture list had ever watched a game of rugby, let alone played in one.

Our backs were depleted, with Leon Lloyd and Geordan Murphy both missing. Leon had tweaked his cartilage and needed an operation which would keep him out for two to three weeks; amazingly, his op was being delayed because of a shortage of beds in local hospitals. Geordan, meanwhile, had damaged a shoulder when he crashed into some advertising hoardings in scoring the winning try at Loftus Road and it looked as though he would be sidelined for a similar length of time.

London Irish then kicked us out of the Tetley's Bitter Cup in a 47 points to seven drubbing. It was humiliating, but the defeat was not entirely our fault. Our guys were virtually dead on their feet after the Wasps and Sarries games. I had been suffering the after-effects of my England camp flu – I'd actually spent six days in the last fortnight in bed – and really struggled to get myself going. It was like I had run out of petrol – my foot was to the floor but there was simply nothing happening. In the end, on the half-hour, I admitted defeat and asked Dean to substitute me. It was something I had never done before and I hope never to have to do again.

We got no sympathy from the Paddies, of course. By the final ten minutes, the London Irish fans were chanting for 50 points and catcalls and cackles of glee rang out around the ground.

The match raised important questions about the organisation of modern English rugby – questions which, to my knowledge, have yet to be answered. Chief among them was 'Is less actually more?' I think it is. Professional players, expected to perform to a high standard in front of expectant crowds who have paid handsomely for the privilege, should not be asked to take the field more than once a week – maybe with the odd midweek game thrown in. This is the rule, for instance, for Super League's sides. They understand that fewer games *does* actually mean more entertainment for the fans. Reduce the number of games and you will see a faster, more skilful battle. Increase the number and you will see mismatches full of dead feet and fumbling hands.

Dick Best, the London Irish coach and an England selector, had benefited from our tiredness. But even he made the point after the game, saying: 'When guys like Neil Back ask to be substituted, it is obvious there is a serious problem. Back was dead on his feet today – you cannot play three games in seven days the way he plays.' Chris Goddard in the *Leicester Mercury* summed it up perfectly, saying we had performed 'like thorough-breds twice in the previous eight days but now looked more like candidates for a glue factory'.

*

Back at Leicester, tired legs were rested the following day. The England side for the opening Six Nations fixture against Ireland had been announced and Clive Woodward had decided against playing Healey at fly-half. Cocker had no place in Clive's set-up but Rowntree, Stimpson, Lewis Moody and Ben Kay, who had played just nine league games for the Tigers, had been called up to the A team. Johnno was still injured.

In his regular column in the local paper, Peter Wheeler had some interesting comments to make about Clive. He wrote: 'Clive has changed a lot of things for the better and increased the professionalism of the administration around the team. But I'm not sure he has brought any clarity to selection or the style of play. He dismantled the old England style that many countries were successful with in the World Cup and persevered with the new one. But I'm not sure whether he knows he has got the right players to be able to play the style he wants.'

Typically forthright stuff from Brace, a man with a massive knowledge of rugby and strong opinions on the game and its future. For myself, I agreed with Clive's selection of Jonny and also with the new style of English play. I was also delighted to be selected for the national squad once again.

In the column, Peter Wheeler also raised points about our fitness and the playing schedules, saying Clive would have to perform miracles to get the England team fresh physically and mentally. The fixture list was mad. No-one at the Tigers disagreed with those sentiments. On the same page, five Leicester 'experts' predicted the outcome of the Six Nations. Peter Wheeler, Joel Stransky and Dean Richards all fancied France, which raised some eyebrows with the England contingent at the club. Chris Goddard went for Scotland while only Les Cusworth, the ex-Tigers and England fly-half, believed England would triumph. Dean even thought Ireland would turn us over in the first match. He knows his rugby, alright!

As we entered February, smashing the Irish despite the expert opinion of Mr Richards, strong rumours were starting to circulate that Johnno was to make a welcome return against

Newcastle. Those hopes were dashed when he was concussed and put into Leicester's Nuffield Hospital during a training-ground accident with, of all people, 'Jocky' Joiner. Craig, at 5ft 10in tall and around the 14st mark, was one of the smallest guys in the squad and – although, as a former gymnast he was immensely strong for his size – if you had been asked to bet on who would knock Martin out he would not have been the man on whom your money rested. Jocky was renamed 'Rocky', the joke being that he was about to be called up by Ian McGeechan, since he was the only Scotsman who'd taken out an opponent that year. Johnno, meanwhile, was ruled out for another three weeks – the mandatory recovery time for concussion. He was spitting nails because he was desperate to get back in the Tigers and England sides. I actually reckoned his enforced lay-off could be a godsend for him. He's so committed that I knew he would be tempted to come back before the Achilles was properly mended. He'd play while it was 90 per cent right, getting by with adrenaline and guts for the other 10 per cent.

The three week limit certainly ruled him out of an England recall in the second Six Nations game against France, since he was pencilled in to return in our second team game against Bath just a few days beforehand. That would not give him the match fitness to go straight into an international.

While it was bad for England, this was probably better for the Tigers. A frustrated, pent-up Johnno is someone you don't want to play against and we needed to keep our league winning streak going.

Before the France game, the *Mercury*'s pundits were given another chance to show their in-depth knowledge. Once again, Deano backed the opposition. Sadly, his judgment was shown to be hideously flawed a second time, when England beat the French in the Stade de France.

Dean had taken advantage of a few days off during between international matches to fly to New Zealand on a five-day scouting mission. According to reports, he was looking at New Zealanders and, specifically, Islanders. Some people get twitchy and nervous when they hear that the club coach is off looking for new players. My view is that fresh blood is be good for the club and good for the existing squad. As it was, there were obviously one or two positions where we could do with more strength in depth – centre, wing and second row among them.

Johnno finally made his return to the field of play for the Tigers Extras against Bath in early March. He came through that test very well and slotted into the place of Ben Kay – a very promising young player who rejoices in the nickname of 'M'lud' because his father is a judge – in the side for the first team game against Bedford, as we returned to Allied Dunbar Premiership One action after a month's break. Will Greenwood and Richard Cockerill also made notable returns to the team – Cocker for what was only his third start of the season. It was Will's first since the defeat at Glasgow. At that stage, we were second in the Premiership. Gloucester, the leaders, had played 14, won 11 and lost three for a points tally of 28. We were one point behind, with a draw where they had a win.

The Bedford game, at Goldington Road, saw us win 37–22, with Clive Woodward watching from the stands as Johnno made a towering comeback.

On the same day, there was a tragic reminder of the dangers rugby can pose when the England A centre Andy Blyth was seriously hurt in Sale's 56–28 loss at Saracens. Apparently, Andy was tackled heavily early in the game and suffered a spinal injury. He has not been able to walk since – a tragedy for anyone, but even more poignant, when you consider he was just 24 when the incident happened and had a promising sporting career ahead of him. I have never, ever been scared of injury on a rugby pitch but this sort of thing brings home to you the reality of your sport. There, but for the grace of God, go any of us when we step over the white line.

CHAPTER 14

Back on Top

OUR WIN at Bedford and Gloucester's loss against Northampton took us back to the top of the table, with a one point lead over our East Midlands neighbours. People were saying that our forthcoming clash at Welford Road at the end of April could well decide the championship. The Northampton game is always a big one for us and this just added extra spice. Dean and the coaches was playing that down, though, and making the point to us that all the remaining games were tough ones. Each match was a must-win if we were to hold on to our title. We faced London Irish, Gloucester, Northampton and Bath at home and Sale, Harlequins and Bristol away. Arguably, that at least gave us easier fixtures – struggling Quins and Sale – away from Welford Road. If the venues had been reversed our task would have been tougher still. At least Northampton and Bath had similarly hard routes to the finish.

Whispers started circulating concerning our three foreign players. The word was that Pat Howard, Dave Lougheed and Fritz Van Heerden would all be leaving at the end of the season, for different reasons. I hoped they would stay. Dave was certainly considering heading home to Canada, where his wife had a good job as a chiropractor, and Pat was thinking about making a renewed attempt to get back in the Aussie side but Dean was at pains to point out that both guys could have fresh deals if they wanted them. It was true, however, that Fritz had a problem with his knee and that he was thinking of calling it quits and heading back to South Africa.

The Six Nations Italy game came and went. Johnno played in the winning England A game and Austin notched up a hat trick in the senior game. I popped over my drop goal. Despite his apparent fitness, however, Clive did not select Johnno in his 25-man squad for the Scotland game.

In late March, we faced London Irish at Welford Road. No doubt about it, this was a revenge game. No sportsman wants to hear the opposition crowd jeering and chanting for 50 points, as the Irish fans had done during our Tetley's Bitter Cup clash, and we used that to motivate ourselves during training. We watched a video of the match; at the end of the game, the camera flashed to the scoreboard and you could clearly hear the London Irish fans chanting. It really got under our skins and made us very determined to hand out a lesson. From a personal point-of-view, I was fit and well and wanted to make up for my showing in the first encounter, when I had played through flu.

Psyched-up to boiling point, we exploded onto the pitch and attacked from the first moment. We beat them 41–16 and got a bollocking from Deano for easing off in the second half. Besty took the defeat on the chin, admitting his side had been blown away by a backlash they were expecting. But he insisted in the papers that Northampton were the strongest side in the Premiership. More motivation. Thanks, Dick.

That week, Joel had announced that he was leaving the Tigers at the end of the season to go into business. He had been approached to join the internet boom with an e-sports company based in Hong Kong. Stranners told the local paper his decision to quit was very hard, because he and his family had had three great years at Leicester. It was a 'wonderful club with a wonderful bunch of people'. We were sad to see him go. Joel is a great guy and a genuine rugby legend – a man who won the World Cup with a drop goal – and that guaranteed him instant respect from everyone at the club as soon as he joined. But he never took that for granted and, despite his fabulous playing record, there was no trace of arrogance about him. He was the consummate professional and a superb example to aspiring young players: he was always immaculately turned out and always willing to spend extra hours on the training ground practising basic kicking and passing skills.

He was later said to be joining Bristol in a coaching role after having second thoughts about the internet position but that fell through. Whatever he goes on to do, I wish him all the best in the future.

*

After the thrashing of London Irish, the England players in the Tigers squad temporarily put the championship chase behind them in favour of the more rarefied atmosphere of a Grand Slam decider against Scotland. Once more the *Mercury* pundits were wheeled out and, once more, the merchant of doom known as Dean Richards stuck stubbornly to his depressing guns, predicting an England loss and pointing out that if ever the Scots were to raise their game this would be the occasion. This time, sadly, Deano was proved right.

Amid the disappointment of defeat, there was more outrage at Leicester when Clive announced that Matt Dawson would be leading England on the summer tour to South Africa. Speaking to one of the papers, Joel Stransky referred to Martin Johnson's Lion Tour triumph, saying: 'Johnno knows what it takes to win in South Africa and I would have made him captain again.' Peter Wheeler said: 'I think Matt Dawson has done a good job but when the chips are down and strong leadership is needed, Martin is the man.' I think Johnno was just glad to be back in the playing frame, though. History records, of course, that injury later kept Matt out and re-opened the door for Martin. A lot of Tigers fans and players felt this was a just outcome – though it was desperately sad for Matt.

Meanwhile, Dean was being linked with a job in charge of

the England A team. A lot of people misunderstand Deano's role at Leicester. He is strictly a manager – he leaves almost all of the coaching to Wellsy and Pat Howard. He occasionally gets involved in a ruck or maul session – we always know we are in for a tough time when Dean arrives with his boots over his shoulder and his false teeth out. I think he would make an excellent coach, however: his knowledge of the game is second-to-none and he is a great motivator. He would be good for England A in either a coaching or managing role and, ultimately, the senior side. I can't see many Leicester folk wanting to say goodbye to him, though.

Early in April, Dean confirmed that All Black fly-half Carlos Spencer was a target for the club. At 24, Spencer had amassed 156 points in 12 Tests for the All Blacks – not a bad record, considering he was usually second choice to Andrew Mehrtens and considering also that he had suffered a bad knee injury. He would have been an outstanding signing for us, releasing Austin to play at 9 or, if we were satisfied the scrum-half position was sorted, on the wing. Sadly, Carlos eventually opted to stay with the New Zealand RFU.

In April, conscious of the need for players to stay sharp, the Tigers staged a friendly against European Cup quarter-finalists Munster, with reduced admission prices to try and attract a big crowd. This was a good idea, since – with the internationals being played and following our European Cup exit – some of the guys had gone a while without a game. Although I wasn't playing, our plan was to use it as a stepping stone for the next League game against Gloucester. It was also a yardstick by which to judge ourselves in the European context. We had failed in Europe and Munster had been successful so far. And the boys did pull off a terrific victory, beating them 25–17 and scoring three tries to two. The continuity of the match was spoiled somewhat, with Munster using 12 replacements against our six. Ultimately, it was good for 'run-out' purposes but these games rarely serve to demonstrate how the Tigers will play in a truly competitive fixture as our annual pre-season losses demonstrate!

Our clash with Gloucester was not only an important game as regards the championship. It would also see the Tigers make history by becoming the first English club to attract more than one million supporters to home League games. It was the latest in an impressive list of records set and smashed by our fantastic supporters. Since League rugby began in the 1987–1988 season, 999,812 people had watched the Tigers to that point in only 105 League matches. The average gate was 9,522 per game – not up to soccer standards, for sure, but good in rugby circles and twice as high as those mustered by most other clubs in the top division. We had had 47 five figure games and in 1994/95 we had averaged 10,000 per game for the first time. Welford Road had attracted the best English attendance of the weekend on 39 out of a possible 43 occasions since the game went professional in 1986/87. I don't know the other four but I wouldn't mind betting that they involved games where we played away – the loyalty of our travelling crowds is superb, too.

To cater for the already high demand for the games ahead against Gloucester, Northampton and Bath the club was erecting a temporary stand to take our capacity closer to 17,000.

Our problems at tight head had gone some way to being resolved with the signing of Ricky Nebbett. Ricky had been sacked by Harlequins after being jailed for nine months on GBH charges following an incident on the way home from training. Dean had visited him in Wandsworth Prison – where he said he had been like 'a fish out of water' – and, after being released on parole, he had joined the club. He fitted in straight away and was soon christened 'Godber' after the character in the prison sitcom 'Porridge'. He is a quiet bloke, a grafter and technically very sound. Cocker speaks very highly of him and rates him as the long-term successor to Darren Garforth. If he can fill those boots, he'll be doing alright. He is a little smaller than Garf – both are 5ft 10in tall but, at almost 18½st, Darren is over a stone heavier. The Scaffolder's measurements are astounding. He has a 42in waist, a 50in chest and a 29in inside leg and looks like the square Mr Men character Mr Strong. Before each season, our clothing suppliers Next send us all new suits. Dorian West was having trouble with his – the trousers wouldn't seem to pull tight at the front and kept sliding down, no matter how tight his belt. Puzzled, he raised it with a chap from Next. This guy scratched his head and thought long and hard before, suddenly, it came to him.

'Ah,' he said. 'I know what's happened here, Mr West. We seem to have supplied you with trousers made to Mr Garforth's design. He has a special "drop-bellied" cut. I do apologise.'

Naturally enough, this story spread round the squad like wildfire.

We temporarily relinquished our lead when Bath leapfrogged us following their win over Sale. But we were confident, despite the dangerous look of the West Country side's late surge of seven straight wins in the league and ten in all competitions.

The following Tuesday we were proved right when we brushed aside the former leaders Gloucester, winning by 24 points to 13 in filthy, wet, muddy conditions to go back to the top of the table, two points ahead of Bath with a game in hand. Five matches left, and I felt we were odds on to win a fourth title, and our second consecutive championship, despite the tough games ahead. The key to this game had been Healey and Tim Stimpson dropping excellent kicks on to the Cherry & Whites fullback Terry Fanolua. No tries were scored but the game was full of aggression and I was sin-binned, along with Elton Moncrieff.

The win was soured somewhat by the confirmation that Fritz Van Heerden and Dave Lougheed were leaving the club. They were both top guys and both excellent buys. Fritz was a hard, uncompromising second row, athletic and skilled. He was a deeply religious man and very conservative and it took him a while to get into the dressing room chat and humour but by the end of his two years he was talking like a local. Log always kept himself very fit and lean and was well-liked. He is a big-hitting, hard-running wing who made up for his lack of electric pace with determination and a lot of power. He is the only back ever to make it onto the back seat of our team coach. There's an unwritten seating plan on the bus. On the way to a game, everyone's serious, focused and quiet. On the way back, it's a different matter. Mayhem erupts with everyone fighting to take those precious back seats. It's like being on the school bus, except that the lads are really fighting, literally punching and kicking each other to bits. Shirts get ripped off and thrown out of the skylights, noses are broken. There's always blood everywhere, and I've seen it get so seriously physically violent that people have had to step in to pull guys apart. On one occasion, a table got smashed and Dorian 'Nobby' West – known as Deano's lapdog – gashed his leg on it. When we got back to the hotel in Leicester, we couldn't find the doctor. There was a lump of muscle hanging out of Nobby's thigh. Deano just got a pair of scissors and physically snipped the muscle away. Westy still has a nasty scar on his leg but he doesn't miss the flesh. He's got plenty of that.

As I say, Dave is the only back to make it to the back. It is usually the older forwards – Garf, Cocker, Wig, Johnno and myself. Derek Jelley has started drifting down lately, I notice. In fact, maybe it is because I'm getting a bit too old for the aggro, but I have started moving into the middle, getting with the younger lads like Guzzy and Lewis. Ali is not too happy about that: she seems to think these younger lads will lead the old married man astray!

Those bus trips can be great fun, with a tremendous *craic* among the players and staff. The main thing is card schools. The serious one usually has Deano, Joel when he was at the club, Wellsy and Dorian West playing for cash at the front. The young lads have an under-21s school, playing for chocolates I think. Bless them.

After Gloucester came Sale Sharks, also away. That game saw us extend our lead when we beat them 48–13 at Heywood Road. The half time tally of 41–3 was a club League record. Geordan Murphy scored after just 58 seconds, Dave Lougheed bagged two and Austin Healey, Leon Lloyd and Tim Stimpson all touched down as well. There were some excellent passages of play, with great decision making, lovely hands and nice play to link the back and forwards. We were now two points clear of Bath with a game in hand but we had no room for error. Their great run was continuing. On the downside, Dorian West smashed a cheekbone. He is a fairly hard nut and he didn't realise what he had done until training the following Tuesday, when his cheek started to move around. He needed an operation and was expected to miss the rest of the season – and the sell-out clash at home against Northampton. This was a massive match, with Northampton still entertaining hopes in all three competitions. A win, and we would keep Bath at arm's length. A loss, and they would be breathing down our necks.

At the forefront of our minds was the mocking our boys had had to endure in the away game. Those words had provided us with fantastic motivation and we were determined to stuff them back down the Saints players' throats.

The game was a sell out, the 16,800 crowd beating the previous high of 15,499 against Quins in December. On a dazzlingly sunny spring day and a firm pitch, we outscored them three tries to nil in a scrappy game that ended 26–21. But we found it hard to deliver the knock-out punch. Tim Stimpson had a rare off day, although he still scored 16 points, including a try, and now needed just four to break former full-back John Liley's club record of 272 League points in a season.

The outstanding moment of the game was a brilliant 40-yard dash by Martin Corry, who reached the line with people literally hanging off him. I can't speak highly enough of Cozza either as a person or as a player. He always gives 100 per cent and is utterly dedicated to his training and his diet. He has been unlucky so far not to be an England regular – he and Joe Worsley have both been pushing the current back row hard – and there is no doubt in my mind that he will become a key player for the national side, either at No 8 or, dare I say it, in the second row, before too long.

We had the points but it was not a great win against an exhausted Northampton side who still had interests in the Tetley's Bitter Cup and the Heineken European Cup. They were without Pat Lam, a very talented guy with great power and good hands who is involved in everything that's good about Northampton. Gary Pagel, Budge Pountney and Nick Beal were also missing.

Before the game, the crowd was told that the former club groundsman Derek Limmage had died. Derek lived for Leicester and was loved by the players and everyone at the club. He always had the kettle on and I often slipped into his room for a cuppa and a chat. There was a minute's silence, scrupulously observed, and the players wore black armbands during the 80 minutes. He and his cheery 'Alright me duck?' will be sorely missed. We were playing the game for him and that steeled us, giving us an extra incentive because he was in our thoughts. Without that, and had we been facing a Northampton at full-strength, we might have suffered a reverse. We could not afford a slip-up like that. The pressure was on us. We needed to win every game.

On the squad front, there was good news for the following year. Pat Howard had decided to put his international comeback on hold to take over from Joel Stransky as the backs coach. Pat had been involved in coaching with ACT Brumbies in Australia and we knew that his ideas and communication skills were excellent. Another great team player, off the field Pat is a typical Aussie. He can make the most expensive suit look scruffy and his favourite thing, usually during Six Nations weeks when we have no game, is to take himself off round Europe on a mini-backpacking break. Recently he was arrested and spent eight hours in a Prague jail for allegedly being drunk and disorderly, though he swears the police were just trying to extort money from him.

There was also talk that the club was in the market for a big name scrum-half. The Cardiff, Wales and British Lions player Rob Howley had been in talks with us and had actually visited

Welford Road. I know Rob fairly well from the 1997 Lions tour and from Barbarians games and I have no hesitation is saying he would have been a brilliant buy for Leicester – more so, even, than Carlos Spencer. I understand that the club made him a good offer to leave Cardiff, where he was temporarily struggling to keep his place. We would have given him a new lease of life and the chance to regain his form. Class like his does not desert you for long. Unfortunately, eventually he decided against the move. His arrival would have taken some of the pressure off Jamie Hamilton and young James Grindal. Jamie has a winger's pace and a great pass and his vision and decision-making are outstanding. All he needs to become the complete scrum-half is a bit more 'attitude', a bit more bossiness, but I'm always happy to play alongside him and he is a great squad member.

On May 6, with Bath still keeping pace and still being spoken of as potential champions, we faced a Quins side who had shipped 127 points in their previous two games. They were demoralised and we thrashed them 54–5 in front of a crowd of almost 6,000, grinding them into the dust on Ricky Nebbett's first visit back since his sacking by the Londoners. Their fans had been expecting it. On a toilet wall in the ground, someone had apparently written the following: 'Our only chance of a win today is if Leicester end up with nine in the sin bin. And even then I wouldn't take odds on it.' I was named Man of the Match on BSkyB – Barnesy must have received the case of red wine I sent him, because I don't remember playing outstandingly well. We didn't need to to beat Quins. They are a funny side. Traditionally, they have lacked fight and guts and even the great Zinzan Brooke was unable to turn them around after he came in. His end-of-career decision to go to The Stoop was obviously money-oriented, which is fair enough I suppose. He was one of the truly outstanding international forwards but was unable to show this at Harlequins because most of the guys surrounding him – Jason Leonard being one of the exceptions – were fairly uninterested. The fact that, even after quitting playing, he was still a huge talent was shown when he played for the Ba-Bas against Leicester at Twickenham at the end of the season. Surrounded by quality players he was able to perform like the old Zinzan.

The win at Harlequins meant we could win the title the following weekend against Bristol, a match oozing added spice, given the identity of their coach. When 'Barbed Wire', also, predictably, known as 'Rolf Harris', joined Leicester, I felt it was a bold move by the club and a breath of fresh air. We had a top international coach, a man who had tasted success at the highest level with the Wallabies, a guy with years of experience and the perfect attributes to take Leicester into the professional era. His name alone drew exciting international talent from around the world, guys like Joel Stransky and Waisale Serevi. Serevi may not have been an outstanding success but his signing demonstrated to the fans and the players that the club could attract top names. Bob and Duncan Hall, his assistant, did a great job at Leicester. The only criticism I would have is that he loved to get it absolutely right. That meant that if things weren't going well we would be out on the training field for three-and-a-half hours. This was not particularly professional. It left us weary and heavy-legged and was perhaps a relic of the old-school to which Bob really belonged.

I remember one time when Johnno was injured. While the rest of us were training, Martin was by the side of the pitch beating hell out of a tackle bag. He put so much into it that by the end of our session he had collapsed and was sprawling on the grass. Bob walked past and said out of the side of his mouth: 'Not bad Johnno. But hit the bag a bit harder next time.'

If anyone complained of being tired his answer was: 'If you're tired, train harder. If you're still tired, retire'. He had some other gems, too. One was 'If the ball's there, pretend it's a grenade, it's about to kill your family and jump on it! It's that important. Well, maybe not that important, but it's pretty damn close!' My favourite was: 'If you're struggling for pace during a match, pretend you're being chased by a tiger. If you can't imagine a tiger, try a man with a knife!' We got the message.

He was so passionate. I remember one occasion in particular, when we were playing away at Toulouse and the French crowd were really lifting the home side. Bob was sitting on the bench with our replacements and reserves. Suddenly, he stood up in front of them and shouted: 'Come on you blokes, after me! One, two, three . . .' Then he turned to the pitch, started waving his arms and chanting: 'Tigers, Tigers, Tigers!' He was deadly serious about it.

The beginning of the end for Bob came when he dropped Deano for Eric Miller – another class player he brought to the club, although, again, a guy who didn't turn out quite as well as we had hoped. Bob underestimated what Dean Richards means to Leicester fans and to the club as a whole. At Welford Road, Deano is almost a god, having been one of Leicester's and England's most faithful servants and perhaps the world's best No 8 in his day. Politically, benching him was a mistake. But in playing terms, I thought Bob's decision brave, at the time, right. The game had moved on and I felt it had become too quick for Dean at that point. He was still a fabulous player but he had simply got older: it happens to us all. It was always great to have him around, because of his experience and knowledge, and there was a place for him in the set-up. But I think anyone would find it difficult, having been at the top as long as Deano had, to be dropped for a young lad. It would be very hard to remain motivated and to play off the bench. I know I won't be able to do it.

Bob also fell out with one or two players. The day before he left the club, I was told that either he or Austin was going. Will Greenwood also didn't see eye-to-eye with him. In the end, they stayed and Dwyer went, acrimoniously. I was disappointed but if you look at Dean Richards' record since it seems the right decision was made.

The knowledge that Bob would be desperate for his new club to stop our title charge was bubbling under the surface as we headed for the Memorial Ground in sauna-like heat. We knew Bristol were a dangerous side who would not be looking to do their West Country rivals Bath any favours. Bob's side were pushing for a European place themselves. Dean Ryan was a very physical forward, a great leader and a guy I respected for his no-nonsense attitude. He had been crucial to Newcastle's championship season during his time up north and we knew he would have wound up their pack, which included Andrew Sheridan, the new young lock everyone was talking about as a future England star. Sheridan is tremendously strong. His power-lifting is just below the Olympic threshhold. But he needs to work on his basic skills, like handling in contact, if he is to really make it in the big time. The Argentinian fly-half Agustin Pichot was crucial to their back line.

In the event, we played superbly to win 30–23, with Lewis Moody swan-diving over for a fantastic try which graced the sports pages the following day. Tim Stimpson scored 15 points to take him past 300 for the season and on to a new club record. Steve Lander sin-binned me killing the ball but I wasn't disappointed – for reasons I'll come to shortly. We were battered, bruised and utterly exhausted after what Johnno later told the press was his toughest game since returning from injury. We had lost 11 players to the World Cup and then suffered an injury crisis which robbed us of key men like Martin Johnson and Darren Garforth for much of the season. We had been written off at the beginning and then told that Bath would catch us at the end. But 10 months of sheer hard graft had paid off. Proving everyone wrong and winning, away but in front of a huge band of travelling supporters, was immensely satisfying.

Deano was soaked with the ritual bucket of water. A lap of honour, media interviews, and several beers followed. Stuart Barnes, Leicester's favourite BSkyB TV commentator, got more than he bargained for when he popped his head around the dressing room door to proffer his congratulations. Dean hauled him in and the players drenched him with champagne and beer. He spent the next half an hour trying to wring his fancy designer tie out. It's a good job he lives a mile from Bristol's ground! But he made a speech which was spot on, complimenting us on our great team spirit and conceding we were no longer just a forward-dominated side. We had deserved to win the championship, he admitted. That buried the hatchet as far as we were concerned.

People said afterwards that it seemed that Bob Dwyer was having difficulty controlling his emotions towards the end of the game but he was magnanimous in defeat. He said: 'They're deserved champions, absolutely no doubt, the two best teams in the competition are first and second, fair enough. They are a very good team all round the park. The one thing you know when you're playing Leicester that's different to the other teams is you can't just stop them in one or two phases of play and come out on top. You have to stop them all round the park and for 80 minutes. A couple of lapses and there's tries.' Ironically, Bob had introduced three of our scorers, Leon Lloyd, Lewis Moody and Geordan Murphy, to the team. On the way back to Leicester, the team bus stopped off at a pub for a few beers.

Sadly, I couldn't enjoy myself. Again, I'll come to the reason soon.

*

Unless you have been there, it is probably impossible to comprehend the build-up of pressure and tension associated with an eight month campaign to retain a League title. You spend all that time without a drink, watching your diet, making sure you get enough sleep. You train like a demon and play like every game is your last, for fear that everything you have worked for will be snatched away. Almost every waking hour, you are controlling yourself, trying to ensure you peak for exactly the right 80 minutes.

Once you have succeeded, you can go a bit bananas. I know we did.

On the Tuesday, we had a big squad barbecue at our Oval Park training ground. Matt Poole sponsored the day, as a thank-you for our support during his testimonial, and laid on stacks of meat and beer. Garf and Wig were the chefs. Things started quite soberly. In the morning, we had a clay pigeon shoot. The organiser asked us to sign a ball but when we started to run out of clays, I nicked it back and kicked it up and six of the lads filled it full of holes. The chap was gutted at first – until he realised how unique it was. Then we all had to have our pictures taken with him and this shredded bit of leather. Later in the morning, we had a game of 5-a-side soccer – well, we had to do some 'training' – before things started to get a little out of hand. Log was going home to Canada so he kindly donated his Nissan Cherry car for a spot of fun. After a couple of hours of time-trial slaloming, handbrake turns and being driven around in circles while the boys batted golf balls at it, the vehicle was completely written off. Jocky Joiner was getting married and the day was a kind of stag-do for him, so we nailed him into a wooden crate. Unfortunately, Craig is a powerful guy and he kicked his way out after a short incarceration. Lots of beers were drunk and steaks eaten and, in the evening, the younger guys went off into town for a bit more of the same.

It was a great way for the squad to let off steam and forget, for a few hours, about rugby.

That was back on the agenda the following day, however.

We may have had the championship in the bag but we still faced Bath at the weekend. It was a home game, it was sold out and we were determined not to let our fans down. And we didn't. Maybe Bath thought our minds would not be on the match but we showed them they were wrong, showing a totally professional attitude to beat them 43–25 in the scorching sunshine at Welford Road. Sporting a shaven-head haircut described as looking like it was sponsored by Flymo, I scored a hat trick of tries, all from pack moves close in. The 43 points was our highest total against Bath and marked our 13th straight win in a game which saw us beat the West Countrymen's First Division record run of 30 unbeaten home matches. We also became the first side to complete a League double since professionalism, finishing eight points clear at the top of the table. Our 17,109 supporters had a great time, reserving most of their affection for Johnno, Deano and the outgoing Joel Stransky, Dave Lockheed, Fritz Van Heerden and Stuart Potter. Later, Johnno was named England captain for the summer tour to South Africa after Daws had to pull out with his shoulder injury. Uncapped centre Leon Lloyd was also included together with Austin Healey, Tim Stimpson, myself, Martin Cory and Darren Garforth. Graham Rowntree was omitted, which many at the club thought was a shame. The feeling was that he had been by far the best loose head prop in the Premiership for the last six months.

Austin Healey was named Allied Dunbar Premiership One Player of the Season, very well deserved we thought, given his outstanding performances in a new position. We hadn't lost a game after Dean Richards moved him to fly-half. In an uncharacteristically modest speech, he said: 'I'm very flattered, but it's a team game and awards like this are for 15 guys, not one.' His comments back at the club were a little less restrained.

Ahead of us were the Ba-Bas and, for a lucky few, South Africa.

*

So, why was I pleased to be sin-binned against Bristol and what stopped me enjoying myself when we celebrated after the game? And why the savage 'Flymo' haircut I sported for the Bath game?

The three are horribly connected.

When I started playing for Leicester, I had long, blond hair cut into a sort of bob shape. It became my trademark, almost, and I kept it that way for years. Eventually, however, the ravages of time catch up with us all and I started losing my locks. I'm thinning a little on top these days and receding at the sides a bit too. Listen, I'm nowhere near as bad as Austin 'Ray Reardon' Healey – or Lawrence 'Patchy' Dallaglio, for that matter.

Nowadays, I have it cut short and most people don't even notice the thinning. But I can see it.

So, on one unfortunate evening at my house, did one of my agents. Almost for a joke, he said he would contact Advanced Hair Studio, the company which was behind Graham Gooch's amazing and seemingly overnight transformation from embarrassingly bald to astonishingly hirsute and which regularly advertises in the sports pages. These were the guys Austin had been talking about approaching. The thought of getting one over on little Nause was too good to miss.

When my agent made the call, suggesting I might be a suitable spokesperson for them, they were immediately interested. They had cricket covered – via Goochy and a few Australian players – and John Hartson was a footballing client. In rugby, they had no-one. We travelled to London to meet up with their experts and we were very impressed with their operation. It seemed to be run along very professional lines and the 'before' and 'after' photographs they showed us demonstrated amazing results. They explained how they would be using an exclusive system to replace the lost hair. I have to admit I was impressed and, when they made a substantial financial offer, after a little thought and discussion with Ali, I agreed to go for it.

A week or two later, I duly showed up at the company's Birmingham salon where the 'treatment' was due to take place. I expected some sort of amazing and revolutionary technique would be employed, but in the end – in layman's terms – they shaved the top of my head and glued a wig to the skin. Still, I thought, it did look amazing. You literally could not tell where my hair ended and the false stuff began. Even my brother, a hairdresser for 20 years, could not tell how it had been done despite examining me closely.

Feeling a little self-conscious, I turned up to training a few days before the Bristol game. Would the lads notice anything? No-one said a word. I trained hard, sweated buckets and the hair stayed in place. I even went swimming and, again, there were no problems.

Match day came and I had almost forgotten I had had anything done. Come kick-off, I was just concentrating on the game and the championship which awaited us. And for the first 40 or 50 minutes, everything was fine.

Until I went into a big tackle on Dean Ryan. And felt my 'scalp' give. Horrified, I put my hand on to the top of my head and realised the false hair had started to come away.

Imagine my predicament. A close-fought, must-win game, televised live, and Backy's wig comes off. I would never, ever live it down. Everyone would assume I'd been a secret syrup wearer for years. But what could I do? We had used all our forward subs so I couldn't go off. I had to play on and hope things didn't get any worse.

They did.

A few minutes later, the hair was a third off. If the situation deteriorated, I was going to end up looking like the snooker player Willie Thorne.

Luckily – and I swear I didn't do it on purpose – I was binned a few minutes later for killing the ball. It is the one and only time I have been glad to leave the field of play. As I headed for the dug-out, Deano and the boys must have thought my red face was down to my exertions. Thank God they were watching the game and didn't have time to notice that my barnet was skew-whiff.

I straightened it as best I could, praising the Lord for those 10 minutes of contact-free grace.

All too soon, it was time to re-enter the fray. Not long left. Watch the video and you will see that I spent the rest of the game running bizarre defensive lines as I basically tried to avoid the ball.

Obviously, if we had been losing I would have had to swallow my pride but – tears of thanks in my eyes – it never came to that.

When the final whistle went the boys started hugging each other, bouncing up and down and singing. The odd tousled head was being ruffled by a joyous team-mate and I knew buckets of water would soon be employed as the celebrations took hold. Desperate to avoid further embarrassment, I scurried into the dressing room and found a baseball cap. With that securely jammed down over my head, I ventured timidly outside. Look at post-match pictures. You will see a load of grinning, shouting, singing players – all with their own hair – and one grim-faced, tight-lipped fellow in a hat. I was quiet on the bus back and quiet in the pub too. I didn't want to draw attention to myself – and my cap – because that would invite horseplay, and I wanted to stay sober so I could scarper if anything started. In the end, mercifully, no-one noticed me amid the drunken hullabaloo.

The following day, my brother shaved my head – giving me that 'Flymo' cut. And on the Tuesday I was finally able to, er, let my hair down.

To this day, I've kept quiet about the whole thing. A few of the lads later found out I'd had the treatment done but I just told them, I hadn't liked it.

That wasn't strictly true. The hair was fantastic and I would recommend it to anyone. Anyone, that is, who doesn't have to stop Dean Ryan with his head for a living.

To this day, Graham 'Wig' Rowntree has no idea how close he came to losing a nickname.

CHAPTER 15

Then There Were Six

IF I DO not end my career with at least a Grand Slam – and I'm still hoping for a World Cup – I will consider I have failed.

I've proved myself as a player. I'm a British Lion. I've represented my country in two World Cups. Since I made my debut, England have won the Triple Crown and Calcutta Cups galore, drawn with the All Blacks and beaten the Springboks and Australia on a number of occasions. But I have never won either of the ultimate prizes in an England shirt. The World Cup is the hardest of all and only comes around every four years. We'll have to wait and see about that one. But a Grand Slam is up for grabs every year. Somehow, we have failed to grab it. We had come close in the 1999 Five Nations, only to see Scott Gibbs race away in the final minute of our last game to dash our hopes of that ultimate Northern Hemisphere prize.

That had been a savage blow to me and to the whole team.

Depression. Despair. Agony. Ten minutes before Snake – named, for some obscure reason, after the Kurt Russell character Snake Pliskin in *Escape From New York* – grabbed the ball and set off on his horrible, charging run, we had one hand on the trophy. Half an hour later, we sat in our dressing room, heads bowed, in silence.

We couldn't let that happen again. Despite the French

performance against the All Blacks, I felt we shaded them as the strongest side in our half of the world. As the new millennium dawned, I was desperate for us to prove that.

*

I may have had less opportunities in Five Nations rugby than I would have liked but I can at least say that I've played in every one of England's Six Nations matches!

The great old competition welcomed the Italians into the fold for the first time in the year 2000. I feared for them. In European club rugby I had played against Italian sides and they were quite a way below the standard of clubs from the other nations. To add to that, their international side had been on the end of two horrendous thrashings during the World Cup. They had some talented individual players and played with a lot of heart but I feared they lacked the nous and the strength in depth to compete in the Northern Hemisphere's toughest competition. It looked like they were in for a bruising and deflating time.

Our campaign opened at home against Ireland. We needed to get off to a good start after our own World Cup disappointments but were missing some key players.

In the forwards, Martin Johnson and Danny Grewcock, our first choice pairing in the second row, were missing with injury. Garath Archer and Simon Shaw would be our locks. That meant we'd lost an inspirational captain in Johnno. He was to be replaced by Matt Dawson. It was a choker for Martin, who had himself come by the captaincy in unfortunate circumstances when Lawrence was forced to step down after his infamous run-in with the *News of the World*. In his short time at the helm, the players felt he had proved himself an excellent captain, if one with a different style to Lol. Johnno leads very much by example. He has a great work ethic, is a good trainer, and always gives of his best. He is not particularly talkative – something which is often, wrongly, seen as sullenness. He is just reserved: he would rather take a back seat and let others say what they think needs saying. Martin has the final say and that's how he likes it. Lol is every bit as committed but is far more vocal and always says what he means. Daws was more like Lawrence, very chirpy and chatty, and always keen to talk tactics.

The backs had a different look about them, too. Jerry Guscott had retired. Phil de Glanville was out through injury, as was Dan Luger. Dan's replacement was the Northampton youngster Ben Cohen. He's pacey, 6ft 3in tall and weighs over 15st, more like a Southern Hemisphere back than a traditional English player. We knew he would cause problems if we were able to get the ball out to him. The Bath centre Mike Tindall was also gaining his first cap, playing outside a recalled Mike Catt in the centre.

The Irish side had good performers like Keith Wood and we knew that the youngster Brian O'Driscoll was very sharp in the centre. Their own World Cup had been less than ideal and we thought they'd come out aggressively but that our superior fitness would tell in the second half.

There had been a lot of calls for Clive Woodward to be sacked after the World Cup. It was a typical British reaction. As a nation, we expect instant success and if it doesn't arrive we start agitating for change. The revolution Clive had been trying to bring about wasn't going to happen overnight and the players had faith in him. We backed him 100 per cent and we desperately wanted to put on a good first performance for Clive and to exorcise the memories of Jannie de Beer.

Our start to the campaign could not have been much better than England 50 – Ireland 18. I touched down for my 12th try in 28 tests, contributing to our highest total against the Irish. In doing so, I became the leading try-scoring forward for England, which made me feel very proud. I wonder what Geoff Cooke and Jack Rowell were thinking as they watched? Mike Catt had a stormer, being named Man of the Match in his 40th game for England. I was really pleased for Catty. He hadn't whinged or moaned during the World Cup when he wasn't being selected but had just buckled down in training like the team player he is. He was like a rock in defence and showed excellent acceleration to leave the Irish floundering at several points. His best moment was a lovely dummy to put Austin Healey clear for one of his pair of tries. It was nice to hear the applause from a Twickenham crowd which has been harsh to Catty in the past. Inside centre looked his most natural spot after a career spent of playing almost everywhere for his country. Daws, too, had a great game, running lots of tap penalties at the opposition who scattered before him for fear of the sin bin. Ben Cohen had a dream debut, scoring a brace of tries in the absence of Dan Luger to stake his claim for the No 11 shirt on a permanent basis. His finger-wagging try celebrations were on most of the back pages the following day.

Mike Tindall also scored on his debut, swallow-diving into the corner and, from looking a little thin during the World Cup, it suddenly seemed as though England had an embarrassment of riches in terms of good young backs. At fly-half, meanwhile, Jonny Wilkinson had kicked four penalties and four conversions in a good performance which suggested he had put the World Cup firmly behind him.

It was exactly the Six Nations start we needed, despite the fact that we'd let the Irish back into it after half-time, when they scored two tries.

The Irish coach Warren Gatland summed up the afternoon's work when he said: 'It was probably the best I've seen England play. For a number of our players it was a big lesson.' Poor old Keith Wood, winless in 10 Tests as Ireland captain, put it differently: 'We were slaughtered ... I looked up at the scoreboard when we got our first three points and it was already 28 minutes on the clock. England played really, really well.'

Despite all the fireworks, though, the Twickenham crowd was rather muted, reserving the biggest cheer of the afternoon for the Tannoy announcement bringing the astonishing news from Rome: Italy had beaten Scotland by 34 points to 20. Like most Englishmen, I'll cheer anyone who beats Scotland, from the Northern Hemisphere, at least, but for this young rugby nation to make such a start in the tournament was excellent. It was a shot in the arm for the inaugural Six Nations. No-one wants to see the underdogs being repeatedly stuffed out of sight. Later I had the opportunity to watch the game on video – all England and Leicester matches are supplied to me by the broadcasters – and it became apparent that their players had moulded together well since the previous October. Troncon and Dominguez were highly talented half-backs, Luca Martin and Cristian Stoica were quick and solid in the centre and the young openside Mauro Bergamasco looked tremendous. By the end of the competition, most of the press were naming him the best 7 of the Six Nations. He was good, but not that good.

In the other game, Wales folded to France 3–36 in Cardiff. Another openside, Olivier Magne, also had a storming game and it confirmed what I already knew: they were the side we'd have to beat to win the championship. That game lurked a fortnight over the horizon: we would face *Les Bleus* at the new Stade de France, the ground where Jannie De Beer had drop-kicked us out of the World Cup. I hoped that was not a bad omen.

*

Nine days later, at our training camp in rural Chantilly, north of Paris, Clive was able to announce an unchanged England side. It was a luxury not afforded to Bernard Laporte. Lamaison was out and the former Saracen Alain Penaud was named instead at fly-half. Later, their plans would be thrown into further disarray when he, too, would go out with injury.

The build-up to the game was intense. The rivalry between France and England, not just on the rugby pitch, is massive, and the media were stoking the fires for all they were worth. The French players didn't disappoint them. Richard Dourthe told one paper: 'The English don't like the French and the French don't like the English.'

The skipper Fabian Pelous was equally unequivocal: 'The rivalry between France and England has existed since Joan of Arc and it's not about to end now,' he said.

The coach Laporte also forecast fireworks, saying: 'This game will be a real boxing match.'

The boxing metaphor certainly held true when you looked at their heavyweight pack. Guys like Christian Califano, Marc Dal Maso and Franck Tournaire don't back down easily. Benazzi, winning his 72nd cap, had the ability to breach the gain line and Magne had proved in the World Cup what a superb openside he was. Talking up the battle of the scrums, Benazzi said it would be 'trench warfare' and predicted 'a clash of Titans'. 'The priority is for a good set play,' he added.

They were massive but, as Clive Woodward pointed out, our forwards weren't exactly small – with one notable exception. We would not be intimidated. The battle up front would be hard and physical and it would be the defining part of the game but it held no fears for us.

We were still missing Martin Johnson and Danny Grewcock but we had faith in Garath Archer and Simon Shaw. Arch – never a man to take a backward step – summed it all up in a comment to one of the papers: 'On their own patch, France can be a monstrous challenge. But anyone can stomp around like an angry bee in front of a home crowd. You've got to show you can be as physical and rough as them. It's not for the tame-hearted to play France in Paris. It can be aggressive and intimidating. But you must not be afraid to assert yourself in front of all those nutters.'

I knew what he meant. The French crowd are a noisy, hostile bunch but they will also turn on the home team if things aren't going their way. It was our job to make that happen.

As well as asserting ourselves, we knew we had to retain possession. If the French backs get the ball they can cut you to shreds as the All Blacks had found in the World Cup semi-final. If we kept the ball, held our patience and sucked in their defenders, the gaps would open up. Penaud correctly identified this aspect of our game, saying: 'The most frightening thing about England is their patience. They will wait and wait, recycle and recycle, before they strike.'

Above Running rugby with the Barbarians. I love their attacking style and it suits me down to the ground. If only England had been so adventurous.
PICTURE WWW.RUGBY-HEROES.CO.UK.

Above The Leicester fans express their feelings at my omission from the England side during a game against Brive, adapting Will Carling's infamous phrase. *Below* My big mistake – I'm about to push over referee Steve Lander, as the Bath players celebrate, and earn myself a six-month ban from the game.

Above What a difference a year makes – back in the England fold and tackling the awesome Jonah Lomu in a Test against the All-Blacks in 1997. If you look closely, you'll see two of my team mates helping out! PICTURE BY EMPICS.

Above A proud moment – receiving the 1998 Player of the Season Award from then-RFU President Peter Brook. PICTURE COURTESY OF THE RFU. *Below* The 1999 Player of the Season, Leicester and England's Martin Johnson. Johnno stands head and shoulders above most people – in all senses of the phrase – and would be my choice to skipper the Lions in Australia.

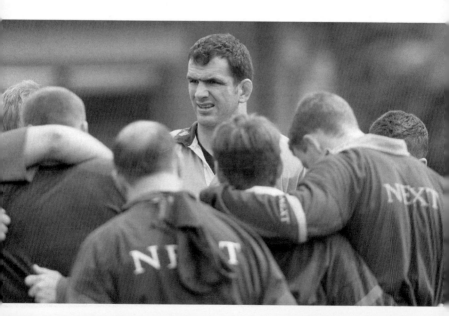

Above With a few of the boys at the Royal Marines training camp prior to the 1999 World Cup. *Right* Training for the 21st Century – running with a parachute to improve speed and strength. *Below* About to touch down against Ireland in the inaugural Lloyds TSB Six Nations Championship in February 2000 as Justin Bishop hangs on. PICTURE BY EMPICS.

Reasons to be cheerful: *Above* Pushing through the Bristol defence on the day we retained our title in the 1999/2000 Season – but watch that hair! *Left* Leicester legend Dean Richards enjoys our end-of-season defeat of arch-rivals Bath. *Top right* Celebrating Leicester's title defence with our magnificent supporters. My head is shaven following the Bristol nightmare. *Bottom right* The back row boys – a triumphant moment with my England colleagues Richard Hill and Lawrence Dallaglio after beating South Africa in the second Test in Bloemfontein in June 2000. PICTURE BY DAVID ROGERS/ ALLSPORT.

The proud father: an Athena poster pose with my beautiful daughter Olivia.
PICTURE BY JASON TILLEY.

As we made our way to the new stadium in the unattractive, industrial St Denis suburb of the city, the tension was high. We had not won in Paris since 1994 and this was a must-win game. In the dressing room, there was a palpable sense of pressure. Our customary dance tunes blared out on the team stereo but noise from the crowd above us still filtered down and made the hairs on the back of my neck stand up. You have to use that tension and pressure in your favour by allowing it to build up your adrenaline and energy levels and then using them. I couldn't wait to get out onto the pitch and sing the national anthem. Once that happened, I couldn't wait for the whistle to go.

In the end, though, it wasn't a pretty game. The rain muddied the pitch and hampered both sides' desires to run the game wide.

Our defence was awesome, with Jonny Wilkinson – pound-for-pound, one of the best tacklers in world rugby – putting in one particularly outstanding tackle on Emile Ntamack just before half-time. He took the Frenchman and smashed him over and backwards, dumping him five metres back the way he'd come. It was the sort of tackle that forwards love to see backs make, the sort which can really lift a whole team.

No tries were scored although a controversial decision did lead to the French having one disallowed. About 25 minutes in, Christophe Dominici made a break and passed to Thomas Lombard who made it over our line. But it was ruled out by the Australian referee, who decided Dominici's pass had gone forward. Although I agreed that it was forward, it was a close call. But we've had plenty of those go against us and you just have to forget about it and get on with the game. Somehow, though, the French seemed to let it play on their minds. Jonny had an excellent game, out-kicking Thomas Castaignède and Richard Dourthe by five to three, missing just one penalty, and becoming the youngest player ever to pass 200 Test points. Dourthe was even mocked by his own crowd when he slipped and banged his head as he ran up to attempt a fourth penalty, which would have brought them up to 15–12, and the sound of

Frenchmen climbing onto the backs of their team was music to our ears.

Perhaps most importantly, we ran the much-vaunted French pack ragged. Despite all the dire warnings, we proved we were stronger and far fitter. They were bent double trying to get their breath back half an hour into the game.

Having said all that, the French could have won the match right at the death. Three minutes into injury time, they were camped less than 10 metres from our try line. Simon Shaw had already been sin-binned for killing the ball and Lawrence Dallaglio blatantly and deliberately put himself offside to stop a score by diving into a ruck on the wrong side to kill the ball. No-one would have blamed Lol if he'd been sent off and a penalty try had been awarded – it was the only option he had to prevent the try. Amazingly, the touch judge instead pointed out that Austin had also infringed slightly earlier by holding onto the ball to slow the game down. It was a professional foul, again committed to keep our line intact. On the advice of his assistant, the referee decided to bin Austin instead of Lol. We didn't want to lose anyone but at that stage of the game we were far happier to say goodbye to a winger than a No 8 and I breathed a silent prayer of thanks.

Still, we were down to 13 men, missing a lock and the French had a penalty five metres out. The score was 15–9. The crowd were howling for them to take the scrum but, unbelievably, Pelous opted to run it.

At that moment I knew we'd won the game. The passion and commitment from the England players as they came at us was something I'll never forget. We were screaming at each other to hold them, to knock them back, and I knew they would never get through. They won another penalty and came again and this time we turned the ball over and Mike Catt banged it into the top row to end the game.

Afterwards, the dressing room was jubilant. Clive told us it was his proudest moment as a player or coach. And the French were magnanimous in defeat. Ntamack said: 'No excuses. They were stronger, physically. Simple as that.' Dominici admitted: 'People say that England are the best Northern Hemisphere side. They are right.' Pieter de Villiers said: 'England were very strong, physically, which wore us down. If you run into a brick wall all the time you are going to get tired.'

It was certainly one of the greatest team performances I have ever been involved in. It needed to be, with two men binned in those crucial last few minutes.

After France, we faced our 1999 nemesis, Wales. We had a score to settle.

*

Pre-match, all the talk was of avoiding complacency. No-one wanted a repeat of the previous year's game at Wembley when Scott Gibbs had taken the Grand Slam and the Championship from under our noses with his injury time score. Daws, who was proving himself a good captain, made a point of going round all the new caps – Ben Cohen, Mike Tindall, Iain Balshaw – during the week, asking them to talk to the guys who had played that match 12 months previously. To a man, they'd been gutted. None of them wanted to experience that feeling again.

We knew Wales had a strong spine to their team: Garin Jenkins at hooker, Scott Quinell at No 8, Rob Howley and Neil Jenkins in the half-back positions and Shane Howarth – not exactly a Welshman, as it turned out – at full back. Everyone was well aware of the need to avoid giving away penalties anywhere within Jenkins' range. He misses very few kicks and he can really punish you.

Wales had not won at Twickenham in a dozen years. So far in the tournament, they had lost to France and beaten Italy at home. Their fans reckoned they were going to stuff England on the back of that. Graham Henry was more cautious, saying his side would need to improve 'astronomically' to have any chance against us.

I felt he was right. We were fitter, sharper and better focused than we had been the previous year. Before the game, we ran through their key players. Quinnell could be dangerous blasting off from the base of the scrum – at 18 stone, he is hard to stop if he gets any momentum going. The key is to close him down. Shane Williams looked quick on the wing but we felt our cover defence would contain him. Above all, we knew they'd come out hard. Like everyone, they always want to beat the English.

As it was, they were woeful and we destroyed them.

Jenks kept them in touch early on with penalties and a drop goal but every time he potted one, Jonny pinged one back, eventually ending with 21 points to his name. Meanwhile, we were the only ones who looked like scoring tries. Greening's effort was outstanding, helping him win a deserved Man of the Match award, and propelling him onto the front pages of some of the Sunday papers. The favourite picture seemed to be Phil doing his best Brian Glover impersonation while hugging a grinning Ben Cohen.

I was pleased that the back row each contributed a try on our 20th appearance together, even though Hilly's was just about as blatantly off-side as you can get. He just snuck in the back door and stole the milk, peeling off a maul and running unopposed to dot down under the posts. Lol scored a magnificent try, a surging rampage, with Welshmen hanging on for dear life, after picking up from the base of the scrum around 15 metres out. My 13th test try, out wide on the right in the 53rd minute, was a good execution of a well-designed team move with Tindall cutting through to Catty after Arch won line-out ball.

Ben Cohen managed to spare the backs' blushes with a lovely score after a great pass by Austin just over the halfway line. This was Ben's third score after just three internationals. His outstanding contribution to the tournament meant we weren't too damaged by the loss of Luger, himself a tremendous winger.

In the end, the Welsh just couldn't compete with us in terms of fitness, skill and desire. In the dressing room at half time, we weren't even blowing but as the Welsh boys trooped off they were knackered. They never came anywhere near our line, looked bereft of ideas and missed too many tackles. They gave away penalties, were crooked in their lineouts and were generally poor.

To me, the Quinnell brothers epitomise what's wrong with Welsh rugby. It's trading on its past glories and the players don't want to buckle down and work. The Quinnells are both talented players but they're too unfit for the modern, professional game. They know they're good, the media have built them up over the years and, following that string of wins including the victory over South Africa, they started to believe their own publicity. When it comes to a match against a fit, fast side like us, they're too heavy and too slow and they react by fouling. Scott Quinnell was binned and Craig should have been, each guilty of nasty high tackles. Garin Jenkins was binned too, adding to the general appearance of ill-discipline.

To my mind, the Quinnells let themselves, their team-mates and their country down.

They should take a long look at Phil Greening. In a post-match press interview, Phil told the assembled media: 'You all know what I was like when I first started. Overweight, not really doing anything. Then I met John Mitchell and Dave Reddin and they inspired me.' Phil had worked phenomenally hard at his fitness and his try in the Wales game showed just how far he's come. He may have been wearing No 2 but he played centre, wing and back row as well during that game.

After the match, the Welsh were suitably shame-faced. Graham Henry gave an interview in which he called us 'outstanding' and added: 'We needed 24 players, not 14,' referring to the sin-binnings. I reckon we might have beaten 24 of them. Their fitness coach Steve Black said: 'England are definitely the best team we have faced, both physically and psychologically, since I have been with Wales.' He included Australia, who knocked Wales out of the World Cup. Steve later quit following criticisms of the Welsh fitness. He blamed the length of time he had with the players – a perennial problem in the club versus country debate.

The result had equalled the record 34-point margin which had separated the sides two years previously and the press were generally kind to us, too. In *The Guardian*, Robert Kitson described it as 'a savage birching'. Former England fly-half Stuart Barnes said in *The Daily Telegraph*: 'All the little England inhibitions have been blown away. Years of being told "You can't play that attacking type of rugby at international level, you must soften them up until the final 20 minutes" has been exposed.' He said it had been 'rugby heresy' to criticise the Carling/Rowell era – but went on to do so.

He wasn't the only one. Daws made a strong attack on the old England set-up in his *Daily Telegraph* column the Monday after the match. He made the point that the new faces in the Six Nations squad were all being given the opportunity to express themselves, to be creative. He said: 'That hasn't always been the case with England. I remember when I first played for England five years ago I was expected to do as I was told. Jack Rowell and Les Cusworth, the coaches, didn't want me to do anything except pass, kick and organise the forwards. I did as I was told. That's not the case these days. It's criminal not to use the talents of everyone, to let them make a contribution. Everyone has to feel comfortable.'

I couldn't agree more. You'll always have the on-field decision-makers – 8, 9 and 10 call the play as it happens and whoever is skippering decides on kicks and so on. But it is crucial that new players are made to feel involved and that their opinions are heard. Under Clive, that's the way it is. We are a really close-knit bunch but we make newcomers welcome and everyone chips in at team talks. For all Rowell's supposed 'interactive rugby' style of play, can you imagine a hooker sprinting 40 metres to a score? Can you see Jase Leonard selling dummies, or Phil Vickery taking quick tap penalties?

At the press conference, Clive played down our performance. He told the media he felt we deserved 10 out of 10 for ambition and six out of 10 for execution. This wasn't a criticism: it was the ambition he was looking for. This was totally against the

Rowell and Cooke ethos of setting a limited game plan and sticking to it as tightly as possible and we were heading in the right direction by at least trying to play attacking, flowing rugby, even if we fluffed the occasional pass.

Our points difference was now 96–30 and everyone outside the squad was talking about the Grand Slam. We kept our feet on the ground. We still had Italy and Scotland ahead of us.

Scotland – our final opponents – were hard to gauge. They were having a nightmare Six Nations, having just gone down to the French 28–16, making it four losses in a row since they beat Western Samoa in the World Cup. However, against the Auld Enemy, we knew they could raise their game and we simply would not allow ourselves to get carried away.

Before that, though, we had a trip to the Stadio Flaminio.

*

Heading for Rome, we knew in our heart of hearts that we were going to beat the Italians. It's often said that to have such an attitude is dangerous but, realistically, we couldn't lose. They had peaked against Scotland and then subsided to big defeats against Wales and Ireland. They would be up for the confrontation but ultimately, unless we were extremely poor, we would come out on top.

And so it proved. In a small, intimate stadium filled with as many Englishmen as home supporters, they started the match fired up and full of aggression and their tackling verged on the illegal. We struggled to assert ourselves for the first 20 minutes or so and they drew first blood through a Luca Martin try which gave them a 7–6 lead. But once we managed to get control and stretch the play they weren't even at the races. Austin Healey scored a hat-trick, Cohen and Dawson grabbed a brace each and I became the first English forward ever to drop a goal. Half-an-hour into the game, I was about 10 metres out, the ball came to me and I just popped it over without really thinking. It was a great feeling although I wasn't aware at the time that I was making history! The final score, 12–59, meant that, after four games, we'd smashed the old Five Nations points aggregate, scoring 170 against the previous record, 146.

Fair play to Italy, they fought hard and crossed our line twice. Beating Scotland and, with a superb performance against France still to come, it was a good Six Nations for them. I enjoyed the trip to Rome, too. We didn't get much time for sightseeing but it is a fantastic city and, by all accounts, it has already become the must-go-to destination for England fans in future tournaments.

Despite the win, we weren't pleased with our performance. In particular, our passing and positioning were poor at times and, while the ambition was there, at times we weren't able to execute it. Still, we were on course for the Grand Slam with only Scotland to beat.

That game would mark a milestone for myself, Richard Hill and Lawrence Dallaglio: it would be the 22nd time we had played together as an international back-row, equalling the record set half a century before by the French trio of Jean Matheu, Jean Prat and Guy Basquet. We wanted desperately to celebrate with a win.

*

As I say, I have never won a Grand Slam with England. My career goal is to be around long enough to play in the next World Cup but, with guys like Martin Corry, who I rate tremendously highly, and Joe Worsley knocking on the door, I realise it will be tough. A Grand Slam, therefore, is very important to me because it might be the biggest piece of silverware I win with my country.

In the build-up to the Scotland game it looked as though I would never have a better chance. The Scots were a side in disarray. Stuffed by Italy, Ireland, France and Wales, they looked a team without ideas, self-belief or flair. From being champions the year before, the Wooden Spoon now apparently had their names carved all over it. In 1999, they had scored 120 points and conceded just 79 in their four matches; those figures were almost reversed in their four fixtures thus far in 2000, with 76 scored against 132. They had slipped to eighth in the world rankings and the media and supporters certainly seemed to think an England win was a foregone conclusion. We did not. We were desperate to avoid a repeat of the climax to the previous season. There was more history, too. In 1990, the Scots had defied all the odds to stop another English steamroller as it headed towards a Grand Slam.

Before the game, we trained hard and spent hours going through video of the Scots side. We were determined not to underestimate them: something you should never do with a side coached by Ian McGeechan. So we tried to forget all about our trouncing of the other four sides we had played and treat this as though it was the first game of the championship. We were keen to avoid giving off any hint of swagger or arrogance, which Geech could leap on and use to gee up his men. Matt Dawson knew him well from Northampton and others, myself included, had gained first-hand experience of how he added a masterful use of psychology to his technical and tactical brilliance.

Our tactical talks centred on doing the simple things well: winning the forward battle, getting the ball out wide and putting in good defensive hits. We were sure our fitness and strength were better than theirs and I felt the game would be won in the final 20 minutes. Player-for-player, we were clearly the better side. But they had some class performers. My opposite number, Budge Pountney, was a guy I had encountered often in Leicester-Northampton clashes and someone I rated very highly. I needed to be first to any loose ball or breakdown and I knew Budge would push me all the way. Above all, our mantra was: focus and concentrate. If we managed to play ourselves into a winning position, we didn't want Craig Moir or Gregor Townsend doing a Scott Gibbs on us at the death.

We hoped for a clear day. Our back line had more pace in it than theirs and on a firm pitch with a dry ball the odds would be stacked further in our favour. And as we left the hotel it was dry, although a severe weather warning had been issued. Two hours later, the sleet and rain bucketed down and turned Murrayfield into a rice paddy and our Grand Slam hopes had been sunk.

The game started well, as we kept the Scots pinned back in their half. On the half-hour or so, Mike Catt chipped the ball through and we won a scrum five yards out from their line. Lawrence picked up and drove through unopposed, sliding almost to the advertising hoardings with his fist clenched in triumph. Jonny Wilkinson converted and then knocked a penalty over and we had a good lead. But Duncan Hodge replied with three penalties and, at half-time, it was 10–9. In the dressing room, there was no panic. The general feeling was that things were going okay, and that Scotland would flag as the game wore on. But as the rain soaked the pitch, forming puddles on our goal-line, we failed to adapt our tactics. Scotland pinned us back in our 22 and let us keep the ball, obviously reasoning that we would make mistakes with it. And we did. Passes went astray or were knocked-on as guys were still trying to run it out, despite the conditions. We should have kicked deep or tried to maul the ball up field. Added to that, we lost vital possession at the line-out and were poor in the scrum. Five minutes from the end, we wilted under a Scottish drive and Hodge was over for a 19–13 win.

I can't explain the feeling of disbelief as the final whistle went. It had been our year, of that I had been sure. Once again, the Slam had been there and snatched away at the last minute. Around me, guys sank to the sodden turf as the Scots began to celebrate with a huge crowd of their fans who had invaded the field.

Back in the dressing room, the atmosphere was glum as we concentrated on warming down and cleaning up. Not a word was said. It was a sad end to John Mitchell's coaching career with England and I felt for him. He was not an Englishman but he had put in as much as anyone else and a Slam would have been a nice parting gift to take back to New Zealand.

That night, we hit Edinburgh's bars, sinking a few pints of 80 shilling to put the disappointment behind us. Again, we were very quiet. The girls had come up to join us, hoping to celebrate a Grand Slam, and most people got fairly early nights. Amazingly, there was no gloating from our Northern cousins – instead, commiserations at the defeat and compliments for our performances throughout the tournament. Like the Irish, the Scots who follow rugby are a knowledgeable and fair bunch.

*

What went wrong at Murrayfield? I've outlined most of the problems. Failure to adapt. Bad weather. Poor line-out. Martin Johnson and Danny Grewcock were available but Clive, not surprisingly, decided not to change a winning side. Would they have made the difference? We will never know.

You can't take it away from the Scots. They played better and, roared on by a desperate crowd, they out-fought us too.

Should Italy have taken the Wooden Spoon, though? I don't think so. They almost beat the French and did beat Scotland and for that they deserved to finish above the Jocks.

Words of consolation for England. The Scotland game apart, it was a good Six Nations for us. In patches we'd shown every attribute that a top side needs to display. Flair against Ireland and Wales, winning big when not playing so well against Italy, guts and resolve under massive pressure in Paris. The present side is a young one. As the 2000 Six Nations got underway, Jonny Wilkinson, Mike Tindall, Matt Perry and Ben Cohen were all aged 20 or 21. A lot of the other guys were in their mid-20s. They will win Grand Slams, no doubt, and they'll have two or three more opportunities to try for the World Cup. Even the old hands like myself have time.

Once again, we had failed at the crucial moment. The big question remained: Were we bottlers?

We would find out in South Africa.

CHAPTER 16

The Fittest Man in Rugby?

I NEVER claimed to be the fittest man in rugby.

That tag – hung on me by the sportswriters – caused me loads of grief with a lot of other players who thought, I'm sure correctly, their fitness levels were as high as mine and assumed I'd gone around bragging to the newspapers about my own exercise regime.

In fact, the papers gave me the title based on some RFU fitness tests a lot of the players did in which I just happened to come top. On another day, someone else might have pipped me at the post. Who knows?

But once a person has an idea in his head about you it can be very hard to change his mind and journalists are no different in this respect than anyone else. They also like to find a few words to sum you up, to help build a mental picture for the readers.

So someone, somewhere saw those test results and the decision was made: 'Neil Back . . . fittest man in rugby.'

Look back through the papers from the early 1990s and you'll find lots of references to this. *The Daily Star* – never particularly noted for its rugby coverage – said on New Year's Eve, 1991: 'Neil Back is officially the fittest player in English rugby union. The wing forward from Leicester gained the highest marks in the stringent physical tests undertaken by all the top stars.' Well, it's always nice to hear yourself described as a 'top star'! Around that time, John Reason in *The Sunday Telegraph* wrote: 'Back has set the highest standard of fitness ever achieved by a player in any of the England squads.' And in 1992, Tony Bodley in *The Daily Express* was routinely describing me as 'Neil Back, the fittest man in English rugby union . . .' One *Express* headline even christened me 'Mr Fitness'.

Nice words, and very flattering, but I'm sure they got up the noses of a few of the senior guys. You can imagine Jerry Guscott or Rory Underwood reading those sorts of comments and wondering 'Who the hell does this guy think he is?'

However, there's no doubt that I was *one of* the fittest men in the sport. Fitness has always been very important to me and my style of play. In an international match, I will cover 6–7km, make at least 20 tackles and spend at least 30% of the game at a heart rate above 185 beats per minute – about 90% of my maximum. You have to work hard to be able to operate at that level. I'd like to think respected observers like John Reason based their estimations on watching me play, and not just on a bunch of bleep test results.

The 'fittest man' tag sprang up in the 1990s before professionalism, when most of your fitness work was done in your own time. The club only had you a couple of evenings a week and that was for basic rugby skills and working on tactics. We would do a few warm-ups and then get into passing and tackling and the scrum machine. There was a cramped club gym, full of chipped, dented old free weights in a back room at Welford Road and you could either use that or find another place more convenient to you. Tony Russ, our coach at that time, pretty much left you to your own devices.

It wasn't that the clubs didn't care about fitness. We just didn't go into it in the same depth as we do now, though at Leicester we were better than most. Players who were out of shape were carpeted or dropped and you were expected to take responsibility for keeping yourself fit but there was very little in the way of professional back-up: there were no club fitness advisers or dieticians and no individually-tailored exercise programme to help you.

Another major factor then was that we were all working in jobs outside the sport. I was a senior pensions manager at AXA Equity and Law in Coventry. While it was a demanding job, at least the time was fixed to 35 hours a week. Away from the office, I spent another 30 hours a week on training, playing and travelling. I was effectively doing two full-time jobs. Most nights I didn't get home until well past 10pm. If I wasn't at the gym I would be working out in my mum's attic, where I had set up a little exercise area with dumbbells and barbells.

There were other guys, self-employed blokes or those with employers who demanded more of their time, working a 50 or 60 hour week in their regular jobs. It's a big ask to expect players with that commitment to come home and then go out to the gym. Most of them still did but it was bound to have an effect on their ability to train hard. You cannot burn the physical candle at both ends.

That's why picking out any one person and naming him as the fittest was silly. There was no level playing field.

Another advantage I had was a guy called Rex Hazeldine, then the Head of Physical Education at Loughborough University. Given the lack of available club help, at junior level, Nottingham or Leicester, I went to see Rex throughout the late 1980s and early 1990s, starting when I first played for England under-21s. We spent hours together during Rex's free time and I am tremendously grateful for his help. In those early days it was his enthusiasm and motivation which provided me with the foundation to go on and achieve what I have. He drew up detailed, day-to-day fitness programmes, divided into four or six week blocks, and I followed them to the letter. Looking back, some of it we wouldn't do now but, for the time, Rex's programmes were state-of-the-art and a great inspiration to me.

However, I have no hesitation in naming Darren Grewcock as the biggest single influence on my career from a fitness point of view. Grewy has put his life and soul into helping me to play for England. He was the fitness supervisor to Coventry City FC, where he worked with the likes of Mustapha Hadji, Robbie Keane and Gary McAllister. These are multi-million pound assets and they don't entrust you with the fitness of people like that unless you really know what you're about. He later went to Leicester City and was a consultant to adidas and, through that, he's also worked with athletes like Daley Thompson – plus people in rugby like myself and Martin Johnson. He is also the fitness editor on *Rugby World* magazine.

When I first met him he was a scrum-half at the Leicester Tigers. A local guy, he'd been around at the club for years, joining the youth team in 1979. Before my time there he had been known as a good club player but he had let himself go, getting up to 17st, and by the late 1980s he was meandering towards the close of his playing career. Around then, he took himself off to Australia, hoping to play a bit of rugby and see another part of the world like a lot of guys were doing then – I half regret not doing so myself. While he was out there, Grewy had his eyes opened by the Australians, who were streets ahead of us in terms of their preparation. He was exposed to the science of fitness, of how your performance on the field could be altered dramatically by putting more time and thought into your off-field training. He got himself into shape and took a number of courses at Sydney University. He came back to Leicester not long after I joined from Nottingham and shocked the people who'd known him before with the change in his appearance. He'd lost three and a half stones and shaved his head. Even his mum didn't recognise him and thought he was seriously ill!

We met during a training session at Welford Road. Matt Poole introduced us as 'one mad fitness head to another'. We did not hit it off immediately. I had only been there a few weeks and was keeping myself to myself. Grewy interpreted this as me being arrogant and stand-offish (where have I heard that before?) and to this day his nickname for me is 'Jack' as in 'I'm alright Jack'. He thought that summed up my attitude.

After a few months, though, we found we had more in common than similar height and the same blond bob hairstyle and got chatting about fitness and training routines. It was widely known that he was a qualified fitness coach and I found he had a fascinating store of information inside his head, together with the ability to convey it in simple terms.

He was aware of my early disappointments as regards non-selection by England and began to take an interest in seeing what he could do to help me further my career. We started training together, either at the club or at any one of several local gyms.

His approach was certainly more scientific than anything available to me before that point. He swept aside a lot of what was then the prevailing wisdom. One thing we had set a lot of store by was bleep tests. Darren showed me that while scoring high on these tests was excellent for recognition in rugby circles it wasn't necessarily particularly good for rugby fitness. Bleep tests involve running back and forth between two points 20 metres apart, in time to bleeps. These bleeps start at Level One – slow enough for you to jog between them – and go up to a quicker level after every eight shuttles of 20 metres. They carry on up to the point where no-one could cover the distance in the time available. It's murder. I got up over 17 when, admittedly, most people didn't get much above 15. That was one of the things my 'fittest man in rugby' tag was based on. The bleep test in the early '90s had an almost mythical status to it when really it is just a sub-maximal VO^2 test – a way of measuring the volume of oxygen a player can use throughout aerobic activity and, thus, a provider of one indicator of fitness. But, as with most such things, it really only tests your fitness for bleep tests. It doesn't test your ability to play rugby at a high pace – where you need to get down and up quickly, to change direction at pace, to physically stop another person, and to keep doing all this over 80 or more minutes. Grewy changed the emphasis of my training so that I could perform repeated, explosive power movements throughout 360 degrees for a sustained period, rather that run at an ever-increasing rate between two markers 20 metres apart. My bleep test results declined a little but my rugby fitness improved.

Another basic concept I learned from Grewy was fluid intake. As I have said earlier, in those early days fluid was not a big issue. Anyone who was caught drinking during training was slaughtered – until around 1992, it was regarded as a serious weakness. Darren was one of the first people who actually explained the reasons behind why it was important to rehydrate yourself during training or games. Dehydration affects the body's ability to work and it slows recovery. Thirst is a very poor indicator of dehydration – by the time you feel thirsty, your body is screaming out for liquid. Ideally, you should be taking on little amounts of fluid fairly often to keep yourself hydrated. That does not mean you don't rehydrate at the end of the activity. Even if you drink throughout, you will certainly become dehydrated to some extent. It's easy to find out how much liquid you've lost. Weigh yourself – without clothes – before and after exercise. Every kilogramme in weight which you have lost after the exercise is equal to a litre of fluid and that is fluid you need to replace. But this is only a rough idea. Don't forget that you'll probably continue to lose weight through sweating and urinating for some time after the game. If your weight test shows you lost two litres, it may be more like three. Water or isotonic drinks – containing a little sodium, which helps your body to absorb and retain the fluids for longer, and carbohydrates to boost your energy levels – are the sort of thing to take.

In 1993, Darren and a business partner opened a gym in Hinckley. They gave me free membership and in return I'd help out with bits of PR where it was needed. We'd be there most evenings and at weekends. He pushed me incredibly hard. Contrary to popular belief, I have never enjoyed training but I knew it was a means to an end and, with Darren cajoling, supporting and occasionally shouting, I kept the necessary focus and commitment, existing on what seemed at times like a diet of Metrex protein shakes, egg-whites and Myoplex energy bars. We were taking creatine too. Creatine has had a bad press. The French aren't allowed to use it, for instance, and have hinted darkly that our superior strength and fitness is as a result of some sort of chemical 'cheating', when actually it's all down to harder, better training. If taken incorrectly, in the wrong amounts and with insufficient water, creatine can be damaging and I would not advise any player to take it without supervision. But it's like any supplement. Bananas are good for you. But fifty bananas a day for six weeks is bad for you. If used properly, in the right amounts and as part of the right exercise programme, creatine is a major aid to building muscle strength, enabling you to go to your anaerobic threshhold more often. You can 'max-out' on your strength work more efficiently and more regularly. A lot of Premiership soccer players use it and, as I say, these guys are huge assets to their clubs. If there was any serious problem with creatine they wouldn't be allowed to use it.

Grewy and I worked together all through my pre-professionalism wilderness years. It was always very structured, with exactly what I was doing and when I'd be doing it mapped out weeks in advance. We even trained on Christmas Day one year, simply because my schedule demanded it. Our relatives thought we were mad but even when we were inside this quiet gym it didn't feel strange to us. It was Thursday, and Thursday was a cardio-vascular day. Simple!

His commitment was every bit as strong as mine. We were out in South Africa together once on a Leicester tour and decided, with an hour to go before our bus left the hotel to take us to the airport, that we'd go for a hard CV run. We sprinted for half an hour through the streets which ran alongside the beach. Then we turned round and, almost as we did, the wind changed and started whipping all the sand off the beach and straight into our faces. On your own, or with a lesser training partner, you might have decided to walk back but we spurred each other on and ended up sprinting back in the teeth of this sandstorm, hardly able to see where we were going. That sort of support is invaluable . . . and, when you think about it, mad! (We caught the bus, by the way).

Perhaps his biggest input came before I won my first two caps, in the 1994 Five Nations. It had become clear to me that I was fighting an uphill battle for selection because of this nonsense about my size. So I turned to Darren. I couldn't grow any taller but if I put on a stone in weight – and told everyone about it – maybe that would be enough. The plan was hatched. He worked out a revolting, carbohydrate-loaded cocktail called a 'smoothie' for me to drink: one pint of milk, two scoops of ice-cream, one tablespoon of honey, two teaspoons of sugar, one tablespoon of malt, one banana, two eggs – and a 'secret ingredient'. We told a few reporters about how I was building myself up to play for England and hinted at this magic, secret ingredient. They were fascinated and a few papers carried pieces on my fight for selection. In reality, the ingredient was just protein powder! In four months I increased my weight by about 12lbs with this high-carbohydrate diet and a core strength regime. It's impossible to develop 12lbs of lean muscle tissue in so short a time and over half of what I put on was fat, although it was good quality fat. By that I mean it was in the right places – over muscle – and it gave me a bit of extra protection and mass, both of which help in contact. The downside was that, although I became bigger, my power-to-weight ratio and body speed did drop back a little. Because the goal was a long-term one – selection for England – I wasn't aiming to peak on Saturdays and my performances actually dipped slightly below my own standards for Leicester. But we soon turned that lean muscle mass into an explosive commodity by changing the emphasis of my gym work.

Eventually, we were able to unveil a bigger Neil Back with more strength and no loss of power and history records that the plan worked because I did actually break through into the senior side in 1994, albeit for a short time.

By the mid-1990s, when rugby turned professional, Leicester had cottoned on to the need for a serious approach to fitness.

Access to facilities and assistance via the club became easier. The biggest difference was that I was able to leave my job in assurance and go full-time. That meant I had all day to train and recover, and it also meant that the Tigers wanted, and were able, to keep an eye on what the players were doing. Since most of my work was, therefore, now at the club, my reliance on Darren naturally faded slightly, though he was always on hand for advice and help and we still trained together a lot.

In 1996, for instance, I spent the summer with him while I was banned from the game following my shove on Steve Lander. It didn't start well. It was the day England played Scotland in Euro '96 and there was a large group of players, wives, kids and friends round at Johnno's house for a barbecue. I was really down about my ban and Grewy just caught me at the wrong moment when he made some personal crack – or what I thought was a crack – aimed at me. His sense of humour can be a bit dry and obscure and we'd spent a lot of time together over the last few years. Maybe we had just subconsciously got on each other's nerves. I don't know. Anyway, I went out of the room, stewed for a moment or two, then came back in, walked up to him and chinned him. He fell back onto the sofa, a bit stunned. There was a bit of a flare up and I think someone pulled me away and told me to cool down. Which I did. Later that week, I rang him up and asked him if he would spend a few weeks with me, getting me right in time for my return. He readily accepted so clearly there were no hard feelings. The work we did together that year helped me kick off the following season well and probably played a major part in my Lions' selection.

The biggest endorsement came in May 1998, when I was voted RFU Player of the Year for my performances with the Tigers. At last I felt I had nailed the size debate. But there was to be no let-up, and – even though I was due to marry Ali – I again turned to Darren Grewcock for a summer's work, pre-season.

That was the year Australia slaughtered our under-strength side. I missed the tour because of an injury. I felt I needed to work hard on building my strength and fine-tuning and I asked permission from the club to spend a couple of months training on my own. I engaged Grewy, paying him £2,000 of my own money to spend nine weeks with me. Like most of his programmes, it was designed first to stimulate muscle activity, then looked at building up core strength – lean muscle tissue – for three weeks and finally worked on converting that core strength into explosive power, speed and agility.

And there was no let-up. On the day before my wedding he had me on a workout designed to increase my midsection power – so I was working on, among other things, power squats, vertical and horizontal plyometrics and deadlifts of up to 190kg. For warm-up purposes I did 10 minutes of cross-aerobics and five minutes of stretching. I got my wedding day and the day after off but he had me working throughout my honeymoon, three days on and one day off, which meant we had to find a hotel with a good gym!

A typical core strength day would see me bench pressing perhaps 90kg and 120kg – the weights changed regularly – for a specified number of slow repetitions. I'd also do bench dips and inclined and upright presses. Another would have me bent over rowing with weights of around 180kg, upright and seated rowing with lower weights and doing lat pulldowns and raises. Midsection power saw me doing similar movements – plus other things like arm curls and wide chin pull-ups – but with lower weights and more speed.

Recovery was very important – he prescribed a 10 minute quick walk on a flat treadmill, followed by 20 minutes on a Life Cycle with a maximum heart rate of 125. Then I was to stretch my hamstrings, quads, adductors, glutes and calves before taking a sauna – maximum seven minutes – and finally a stretch in the pool, again working to relax my hamstrings, quads and glutes.

That summer really helped me prepare for the 1998/99 season and gave me a headstart over a lot of other guys.

Despite his own addiction to fitness, he's quite capable of letting his hair down. On one occasion, we were both out in Dublin – he'd been playing for Leicester and I was out there with England A, I think – and having played our games we decided to go out on the town. By 11.30pm we've run out of cash and are just resigning ourselves to the walk back to the hotel when this colossally pissed Irishman, squinting out of one eye and struggling to keep upright, spots us and lurches over.

'Backy!' he shouts. 'Backy! To be sure, you should be playing for England now. 'Tis a disgrace them not picking ye, a disgrace. Ye're the best flanker in all the world!'

Which was nice. Except that he was looking Grewy straight – at least, as straight as he could – in the eye. Like I said, similar height, similar hair. Grewy's grinning and nodding, standing there in his Leicester blazer and tie, and this Irish fellow's completely ignoring me and the big red rose on my blazer.

'Backy,' he says. 'Backy, I'll buy anything off you as a souvenir. *Anything*. Can I buy something from ye?'

So Grewy proceeded to sell him his socks. Filthy, rotten, black M&S socks. For £20. As a bonus, he even signed the guy's shirt. On the back. It read 'Best wishes, Darren Grewcock.'

Then we piled back into the Guinness courtesy of this old geezer's twenty quid. If he reads this, I owe him a proper signed shirt!

They are lovely people over there, and they love their rugby. It's hard to imagine an English fan making such a fuss of an Irish openside in London. Or, for that matter, getting completely the wrong bloke and paying £20 for his socks. Later that same night, I was treated to a horse and carriage ride around the city by another set of Irish fans who plied me with champagne while poor old Grewy walked home to the hotel.

There's no doubt that the old attitude is long gone now, at Leicester and everywhere else. Everyone has an understanding of the basics of fitness and all the clubs have good, professional advice on hand if needed. Perhaps the biggest change has been in the international set-up since Clive came in. It's another element in the all-new professional England which he has created.

The Fittest Man in Rugby?

Our diet and exercise regimes are watched very carefully. In charge of exercise is Dave Reddin. Dave is a top guy who really knows his stuff and I feel we are in very safe hands with him. He has two good sayings. The first is: 'Everyone has a will to win; very few have the will to *prepare* to win.' The second is: 'Every morning in Africa, a gazelle wakes up. It knows that it must run faster than the fastest lion or it will be killed. Every morning a lion wakes up. It knows it must outrun the slowest gazelle or it will starve to death. It doesn't matter if you are a lion or a gazelle. When the sun comes up, you'd better be running.' I feel they encapsulate what should be the professional athlete's attitude. It is not about wanting to win. It is about doing the hard work, on cold, muddy, sleeting afternoons in January when you'd rather be watching TV, so you put yourself in the position where you can win. It is also about recognising that, if sport is your livelihood, you have to be able to outperform the other guy to survive. One of the first things Dave did was ditch the old bleep tests as a fitness indicator. In its place, he instituted a 3k run to test aerobic endurance. This gives a better idea of where individuals are but it is still not specific enough and Dave is currently developing an interval test which more closely replicates the demands of the game. Anaerobic endurance is assessed with repeated shuttle runs. Strength is measured with back squats, bench presses, bicep curls and seated rowing. Speed is tested with standing five, 10 and 30 metre sprints and flying sprints over 10 and 30 metres. In pre-season, we spend a lot of time developing basic endurance fitness levels to support the high intensity work we will do later on. It is important to develop the aerobic metabolic pathways in the muscle. They are correlated strongly with aerobic endurance capacity and also play a big role in accelerating recovery from bouts of high intensity exercise, which most of my game revolves around. Also during pre-season we work hard on increasing muscle size and endurance, targeted towards developing areas which are prone to injury, like shoulders, knees and ankles. And we spend time developing core stability – the control of the spine and the muscular system of the trunk. This also plays a big role in preventing overuse injuries, which often result from poor posture and muscle balance. In pursuit of this, Dave ditched the murderous, old-style timed sit-up tests, where players had to be up and down in time to a 50bpm bleep on a tape. This was carried out to measure the endurance of the abdominal muscles but it actually tests the wrong muscles – those which move the trunk, rather than those which stabilise it. Instead, we now place emphasis on developing abdominal control and stability. This allows us to use our upper body strength much more effectively by ensuring we are operating from a stable base. One of the ways we measure this is by balancing standing up on a 65cm rubber ball. The better and longer you can do this the better your core stability.

During the season we have different objectives at different times and Dave tailors each player's programme to meet his needs at that time. My programmes tend to be 16 weeks in length – targeted, say, towards the Autumn internationals – and to change every four weeks to match different objectives. For basic strength we will work with weights. For high intensity endurance levels, we use interval and hill work. Other sessions will focus on injury prevention.

Dave also has me working on specific movements and drills targeted towards my playing position. For instance, I'll be timed while I go through a series of movements involving me hitting the ground, getting up and sprinting away.

The volume and intensity of the training decreases towards the weekend and the game. We also have specific 'unload' weeks, where training is reduced right down to let the body recover and 'supercompensate'. As we move towards the peak of each programme, training volumes come right down and this helps in the recovery process.

One of the best things about Dave is that he has closely examined rugby and adapted his methods to suit. For instance, he recognised the need for neck strength. The modern game is so much faster and players so much bigger that there is potential for whiplash-type injuries. Before, it was very unusual for players to do any neck work at all. Now, all the players are on a neck strengthening programme, developing both static and dynamic neck strength using things which look like torture harnesses.

*

Of course, all the clever training techniques in the world won't bring about a top performance if you aren't fuelling your body correctly. Eating properly is vital.

A recent – but equally vital – influence has been Roz Kadir. Roz is the Senior Nutritionist at the Centre for Nutritional Medicine in London's famous Harley Street and is one of the UK's leading authorities in her field. She has a particular knowledge of how protein can be used to increase lean body mass and, with her colleague Dr Adam Carey, the centre's director, looks after the whole England squad – plus a large number of other athletes.

I first met Roz in May 1999, as we sought ways to improve our bodies in the build-up to the World Cup. I was immediately impressed with her and the whole set-up. I filled out a detailed, eight-page questionnaire to give them the most basic information they required. Then I had a medical check with a doctor based at the centre. The detail they went into was astonishing. For instance, they saw that I had six mercury amalgam fillings in my teeth so they ran tests to see if any mercury was leaking into my system. Apparently, heavy metal toxicity can be a problem, stressing the body, and is something which would have to be addressed with dietary treatments to remove the excess. Fortunately, I was within safe limits. They also noticed that the left ventricle in my heart was enlarged. This was something I already knew, it having been discovered when I was investigated for possible asthma in 1994. Luckily, I didn't have asthma – though my brother is a sufferer – and the ventricle actually is nothing to worry about.

All my measurements were taken. I weighed 90.7 kg and had 12 per cent body fat. Surprisingly, Roz thought that was too high and suggested I could get that down to 10 per cent. To do that, she needed to assess my diet. She made an appointment to see me a week later. In the meantime, she said, I was to weigh all the food I ate and keep all wrappers from any packet foods I had eaten. That information, together with the details on my questionnaire, would help her decide the way forward. On my return to London, she analysed my food intake and found that over 50 per cent of my diet was carbohydrate – and that much of it was refined carbs like white rice and bread instead of the wholegrain varieties. Around 22 per cent was made up of fats, with too much saturated fat, and only 21 per cent protein. Roz felt these proportions were wrong. Reducing fat and upping protein would increase my muscle bulk – allowing me to produce more power – while lowering 'dead' weight from fat. My average daily meal plan then was something like the following: (Breakfast) Cereal and skimmed milk with toast and Marmite to follow. (Lunch) White pasta with chicken and vegetables followed by a banana and an orange. (Dinner) Green salad with ham or chicken, bread rolls and a pot of sweetened rice or a yoghurt to finish. I was also eating fruit bars and taking on carbohydrate replenishment drinks during the day. That doesn't sound too bad but Roz felt I could make improvements. All refined carbs were out – and I was to eat fewer of them. Protein was increased. My new daily routine became more like this: (Breakfast) Egg-white omelette – five whites, one yolk – with grilled vegetables, or rye toast with low sugar beans. (Lunch) 30–40 grammes of protein from chicken breast or fish with a big salad. Lots of vegetables and a little brown rice to provide my necessary carbohydrates. (Dinner) More protein and different vegetables. Further protein was provided by taking the Centre's own '2XL' range of products. Additionally, I was prescribed a programme of nutritional micronutrients, including multivitamins and minerals, antioxidants to prevent cell damage and reduce my susceptibility to coughs and colds and extra essential oils as my requirements were likely to exceed my daily intake. Finally, I was to cut down a little on fruit – too much sugar – and eat fish as often as I could.

It was not easy following some of these instructions. I love fruit and, at first, I didn't much care for brown pasta. But the results spoke for themselves. by October I weighed in at 90.2 kg and my body fat was down to 10 per cent. That meant I'd put on almost two kg of muscle at the expense of a little flab. Since then, Roz and I have met on a number of occasions and she has tweaked things here and there to help me get to where I want to be.

It's not just about what you put in. When you put it in is important, too. You'll restore your fuel supplies much quicker if you take on carbohydrate within half-an-hour of the end of a game or training session. Tests have shown that, under those circumstances, the body converts the food into glycogen three times as quickly as it does if you wait two hours before eating.

England team guidelines are that alcohol is to be avoided, certainly within two hours of the end of a game, but we are not banned from taking it.

This might sound like heresy to a club player but there are good reasons why it is the case. Firstly, alcohol is a diuretic which means it increases your need to urinate. This is obviously the most dramatic way in which you can lose fluid. Secondly, it is also a vasodilator, which means that it causes the blood vessels to widen, increasing the blood flow around the body. This can slow recovery from certain types of injury and we are always told not to touch booze if we've been injured that day. It's not a problem for me – I regularly go months without touching a drop anyway. In World Cup 1999 year, for instance, I had about three alcoholic drinks.

But dealing with injury is not just about things you don't do. Getting the right amounts of vitamins and minerals is extremely important if you are to recover properly. The best way to take these on board is via a balanced diet full of fresh fish, fruit and vegetables. But supplements can also help fill in any gaps left by your diet. Vitamins C and E are particularly important because they are antioxidants. Antioxidants have a major role in helping to repair damaged tissue. The advice I've had is that taking higher doses of Vitamin C can help reduce muscle soreness and inflammation and that you need to take supplements to get this effect, since the dosages needed are far higher than you'll get from drinking a pint or two of orange juice. I have a one gramme tablet with a sports drink at about 10pm on the day the injury is caused. The next couple of days I would take a 500mg tablet four times a day. Then I stop. That's the crucial period when the vitamin is working. Vitamin E is also good for body repair but, additionally, it is believed to help restock your muscle glycogen stores after you've finished exercising. The advice is that you might take a 400mg supplement on the Friday before a game, and on the Saturday and Sunday after it. As with all supplements, though, it's not a good idea to take them continuously. Injuries, naturally, are taken extremely seriously. In a sport like rugby they occur fairly frequently, although I've been lucky in my international career. The golden rule for England players while on international duty is to report any problems as soon as possible to one of the medical team such as Terry Crystal or Kevin Murphy. Playing on an injury only worsens it and you should always avoid putting off treatment if at all possible.

Two acronyms spell out how most muscle or ligament strains and bruising should be dealt with: ICE and HARM. ICE is short for ice, compression and elevation. You apply ice to the affected area – hoping it's not the groin! You apply pressure to it and, where possible, you elevate the area to help the blood to flow away. Repeated twice for 15 minutes, this is a simple but effective way to prevent a small injury turning into a big one.

HARM stands for things you should avoid: heat, such as long, soaking baths, alcohol, rubbing and movement, particularly weights or vigorous exercise. It's funny to think that most people might assume these are the very things which will help you.

The other form of recovery – recovery after training – is vital. The mantra is always the same: You don't get fit when you train, you get fit when you recover. You need to take minutes to recover between reps, sets and drills during training. Afterwards, you need to warm down too. Low-intensity workout activity immediately helps to increase the blood flow which in turn pushes waste products out of the body. Studies have shown that lactic acid is flushed out of the system three times more quickly if you go through a gentle routine after every training session or game than it is if you don't. It also prevents muscle shortening and soreness and it is something all players, at whatever level, should take on board. I'm not talking about anything dramatic. We are told to do just five to 10 minutes of light aerobic work followed by 10 to 15 minutes of long-hold stretching of the major muscle groups. Long-hold stretching means around 15 to 30 seconds. That's not too much to ask of anyone and the benefits reaped, in terms of fewer injuries and less general post-match discomfort, make it well worth while.

The England set-up gives us access to the best possible facilities, of course. The Jacuzzi and sauna are important tools for us nowadays. Sitting in a warm Jacuzzi increases blood flow and, therefore, encourages the process. We are prescribed four or five sessions of this a week for between 10 and 15 minutes at a time.

The sauna has similar effects, though it is something we only use a couple of times a week. The first thing to do is take a warm shower, keeping your hair dry. Then you sit on the low level of the sauna for two or three minutes. After that, you lie down on the top level for another six or seven minutes, before taking alternate cool and warm showers of about 30-40 seconds' duration for the next four to five minutes. The whole sequence is repeated four or five times. Because the heat has a dehydrating effect, it is important to drink plenty of fluid before, during and after using the sauna. It can leave you feeling slightly weak too so it is not something we use the night before a game.

A further way to reduce post-game soreness is the cold plunge. It is agony. You sit in a warm bath for a minute and then move immediately into a iced bath for a further minute or two. This, again, is repeated four or five times.

Another important point is sleep. It's an individual thing, but most people need around seven hours a night. As our England players' handbook points out, alcohol disturbs sleep and, while sex before training or matches is not a bad thing, staying up all night trying to get it is!

CHAPTER 17

Controversy in South Africa

I DON'T much care for South African rugby players. Some of them are great people, of course. My old Leicester team-mates Joel Stransky and Fritz van Heerden, for instance, are tremendous guys. I also like and admire the flanker André Venter. Despite being a great talent, he is a fairly humble fellow with a good sense of humour. But on the whole I have found they are an arrogant and unpleasant bunch. The likes of Joost van der Westhuizen and James Small epitomise this trait, caused by being put on a pedestal by the citizens of this rugby-mad nation. When it comes to the ordinary South Africans, though, you have to admire them. Their passion for rugby and their knowledge of the game is second to none.

Playing away to any international side is a challenge. The crowd always makes a big difference. Scotland at Murrayfield, France in the old Parc des Princes, Wales at the old Arms Park – the home supporters make so much noise and throw out so much emotion that it can almost be like playing against an extra man or two. In New Zealand, you are facing the All Blacks and they just expect to win, certainly at home. The Wallabies are similar. It is a kind of confidence and swagger which some players find daunting and which you have to overcome to give yourselves any hope of succeeding.

In South Africa, though, it's different again.

As I had discovered during the 1997 Lions tour, their crowds are so aggressive, so fanatical and so partisan that it's more like war than a game of rugby. And the players themselves feed off and reflect this fervour.

The Afrikaaners have a unique history. Colonising a distant land, struggling to survive in the heat and the dust, constantly battling the wildlife and the indigenous warrior clans, warring with the British . . . these things combined to create a hard breed with a cussed, stubborn attitude to life and little time for losers. Their international isolation in the apartheid years helped to bond them closer still and the religious beliefs they outwardly espouse – Christian values rooted in the 18th century – add a touch of self-righteousness and self-belief. Arguably, these are the perfect ingredients for an international rugby side. And their teams *are* hard, closely bonded and confident to the point of arrogance. That combination – with plenty of additional skill and talent in a land where rugby and cricket are the only real sports – has helped make them a hellishly tough side to beat at home for many years.

Our record against them in the 1990s wasn't too bad. We'd won at Loftus Versfeld in 1994 – our most recent victory over there – and we had ended their record-equalling winning streak of 17 matches at Twickenham in December 1998, beating them 13–7. But they had beaten England, home and away, three times in 1995, 1997 and 1998. Of course, more recently, we had been drop-kicked out of the World Cup by Jannie de Beer on that infamous quarter-final day in Paris. While I didn't feel that we had lost to a better side then, we certainly wanted to set the record straight.

If we could rub a few faces in the dirt as we did so, so much the better.

The pressure on us as we jetted out to Johannesburg in early summer 2000 was enormous. We stood accused of being bottlers who couldn't win the games that mattered. We were fancy Dans, said the critics, able to shred weaker sides with a fast-flowing and attractive style of rugby but destined to be found wanting in the real pressure situations. As evidence, they pointed to the de Beer Test and those awful Five and Six Nations defeats to Wales and Scotland. I honestly felt that if we didn't finally put down a marker in the Southern Hemisphere on this tour there would be major changes to the team and, possibly, the management.

The tour didn't start well for me. A few days before we were due to leave I was injured while playing for Leicester in the English Champions versus Barbarians fixture at Twickenham. We were slaughtered in the match. Perhaps this was not surprising, given that most of the Tigers squad had been out on the lash virtually non-stop since winning the title. Then, immediately before the Ba-Bas game, most of the boys had been out in Benidorm on a group stag week for Martin and Will Johnson, Craig Joiner and Pat Howard. Although I decided to stay at home with Ali and Olivia, just imagining what went on makes me feel the worse for wear! The Leicester public turned out in great numbers to support us against what was the strongest Barbarians side for some years. We hadn't trained properly for the fixture and our collective mental attitude was certainly not 100 per cent right. Speaking for myself, I wanted to win the game because I always want to win but I have to admit that even I was not as psyched-up as I might have been. The Tigers fans are the finest and most loyal in the world, no question, and, to a certain extent, I suppose we let them down. I hope, however, they will understand the pressure we had been under during the season proper. We had had a tremendous battle to retain our title. It meant months of hard training and no drinking and we had to let off steam once the job was done. I'm sure they would have preferred us to win the Premiership One title rather than defeat the Barbarians.

At least we were winning when I went off! Four minutes into the game I went to ground in contact and felt a sharp pain in my right knee, akin to the feeling you have if you rip off a large scab. As the sensation died away it was replaced by a dull ache and I knew at once I had strained my medial ligament. There was no way I could go on so I left the field and immediately iced and elevated the leg to keep down any swelling. After the match I had words with Mark Geeson, the Leicester physio, and then spoke also to Kevin Murphy, his England counterpart. Both were of the opinion that the injury would take at least a week to 10 days to heal. That was if I was lucky. If not, I could forget the tour. They would know more in the morning, they told me, so I spent a fitful night hoping that the prognosis would be a good one the following day. It was. The strain was minor and the 10 day recovery forecast ought to hold good, Murph informed me. The leg was strapped but I could walk on it and was ordered to rest it as much as possible.

That meant missing out during another pre-tour trip to the Royal Marines, where the other guys were put through their paces once again. It also meant missing training for the first few sessions once we arrived in South Africa. Knee injuries can end your career and they must be taken seriously. Rest is usually the best option. You don't have injections in the knee just to enable you to play or train. In a shoulder, for instance, you might take a jab to kill the pain or reduce swelling. The only way I ever would have an injection in a knee is if it was a question of that or missing the World Cup final.

Sitting back watching the guys train was no hardship. Our hotel was stunning. Rather than a block-type building, it was a series of small apartments and villas dotted along a road which wound slowly up a tree-covered hill above Johannesburg. The on-site facilities were superb – although we went out into the city to use a gym – and the food first class. In my bedroom I had a TV which rose out of nowhere at the touch of a button and a view over a small game reserve with elephants and giraffes strolling by in the distance. The South Africans had wanted us to move around the country to different hotels but our management had decided that, in a tour of less than four weeks, that wasn't a good idea. I was glad they had stuck to their guns.

By the third contact session I was back into the thick of it and I knew that, barring any dreadful misfortune, I'd be fine to play.

The midweek team won well and by the time the first Test came around we were raring to go.

So were the South Africans. As well as their traditional heart and pride, they had an added incentive to do well. The whole of the country was in shock at the time, with Hansie Cronje on the stand at the King Commission in Cape Town giving testimony about his cricket match-fixing. It had shocked the proud Afrikaaners that one of their own would stoop so low and it was clear that they expected their boys to speak up for their country on the rugby pitch. I watched some of his evidence on my elevating TV and I have to admit I was gutted. Here was a guy I'd previously respected for his cricketing ability and what seemed like his unflinching determination to do well for his country. He was the last man I would have expected to be involved in throwing games – not least because he was already wealthy from his sport. It was sheer greed and I found it sickening.

People have asked me if I've ever been involved in, or even heard of, match-fixing in rugby. The answer to both questions is a resounding No. I could actually have made a few quid out of gambling on games, too. A couple of years ago one of the big bookmakers got involved with a betting promotion at Leicester. They offered odds on all sorts of things. One was who would score the first try in each match. It was the season I finished top scorer in the league, with 16, and it came at the point where we had perfected the line-out catch-and-drive. Five metres out, it was lethal and we turned a lot of sides over with it. Early on, the bookies had no real idea and they were offering odds of something like 14 to one on me being first to score, while wingers like Dave Lougheed and Austin Healey were at much lower odds. Clever punters in the Leicester crowd saw straight away that, actually, the catch-and-drive made me a likely candidate and backed their judgment quite heavily. And I provided them with a handsome return, touching down first on quite a few occasions. For weeks, until the bookmaker cottoned on and cut my odds, people were coming up to me with wide grins on their faces and fistfuls of notes, offering to buy me drinks. The point of the story is not, however, that I didn't back myself.

The point is that as I went over the line in these drives, Garf and Cocker – whose odds were more like 50 to one – were right next to me. I could have got my brother to stick £250 on Garf and just handed him the ball in the melee. Twelve-and-a-half-grand is a powerful incentive! But it never crossed my mind. I've never had a penny on myself or my team and I never will. The victory itself is enough for me.

There is a postscript to this story, though. Ali was down in London for one of the internationals and she was watching the game with my best man Dai and some of his friends. Ali was lamenting the fact that she hadn't had time to place a bet on who would be first scorer. One of these guys, a stockbroker, turned and said: 'I'll open a book for you. Who do you want?' She obviously nominated me and this chap, apparently from the same school as the odds-makers at Welford Road, offered her 15 to one. Two minutes later I went over for the first try and a minute after that Ali had three £50 notes in her hand!

*

The first Test was in the Afrikaaner heartland city of Pretoria and, to my mind, we won it. It was an controversial and epic match and probably, at 105 minutes, the longest Test in history. The record books say the Springboks took the game 18–13 but the South African video referee robbed us of a deserved try at a vital time and the home side also played fast and loose with the laws on blood replacements. To add to that, we were without Jonny Wilkinson, struck down with sickness and diarrhoea. It turned out he'd fallen ill on the Wednesday before the game. It was all kept very quiet and even the players didn't know he was in bed. Pre-match training was light and the hotel was sprawling so there was nothing suspicious about not seeing him around. Three hours before the game, we were told he was touch and go. I took one look at him, pale and taking on lots of fluid, and

I knew he was out for sure. But his willpower and inner strength would probably have forced him on to the field if it hadn't been for Kyran Bracken, who actually talked him out of playing. In 1995, Kyran had played in a Test against South Africa while himself feeling ill – he turned out to have glandular fever – and put in a below-par performance. He reckoned that had been a mistake and he told Jonny that. Jonny was not the only sufferer, of course. Other players also had stomach upsets and one of them, Martin Johnson, had to go off towards the end of the game.

The most important thing to come out of the match was our defence, which was awesome. We kept the Springboks away from our line and you could actually see their attitude change throughout the game – from confidence to puzzlement to panic – as we knocked them back all over the pitch. We limited them to the six penalty goals which Braam van Straten slotted over, the thin, high veldt air helping him get tremendous distance on his kicks. At the end of the game, we left them to reflect on their first tryless Test at home in three years.

The Springboks were full of talk before the match that they would be running the ball out wide and putting on a feast of running rugby. Although they have produced high quality backs – Chester Williams being the most recent example – the running game has not been their historical forté. Instead, they have relied very much on forward power, traditionally producing big, heavy, aggressive packs who would grind the opposition into the hard dirt of the veldt. This announcement amounted almost to a rugby revolution over there and some of their fans and media were not too happy about it. They take the attitude that rugby is a man's game and that men play in the pack. The others look pretty and provide a bit of a distraction but they don't really count.

In fact, what they were attempting was actually quite similar to the changes Clive had brought about in the English game – we were another country with a reputation in recent years for producing fine scrummagers but lacking the flair to attack at pace and with the ball in hand. We were changing that reputation. But it was slow and it was hard work and I was interested to see whether the South Africans would be able to produce the expansive game they were talking.

Certainly, they had some talented backs. In the pint-sized coloured lad Breyton Paulse, they had a young wing who has the gas and the verve to punish teams if they give him any space at all and we were conscious of the threat from him. We knew, though, that he was defensively a little weak and also suspect under the high ball. Robbie Fleck was a centre with power and speed who we knew was capable of causing us problems in midfield. Chester Williams was another player we knew had the genius to spark off dazzling and dangerous moves and, while he was not the player he'd been in the mid-1990s – not having started a game since the 1995 World Cup, we knew we had to watch him if he came on late in the match. To cap it off, the Springbok back row was certainly one of the best in the world. Vos, the new captain, had a lot to prove. Venter is a big, athletic guy who I rate highly. Erasmus is more than competent, too, and both he and Venter can play on either side.

We knew their pack would work hard to provide time and space in which the backs could operate and, also, that they would be quick to close down our attacking options when we won the ball. It looked very much as though Hilly, Lol and myself were in for some hard graft.

Having said that, they had their weak links too. Joost van der Westhuizen was nothing like the player he had been although, in that typically arrogant Afrikaaner way that he has, he was refusing to accept the fact. Don't get me wrong. Van der Westhuizen had been a tremendous player, probably the best scrum-half in the world in the mid-1990s. But he'd missed most of the Super 12 season with his knee injury and, to me, he looked lacking in pace and confidence. I definitely felt his selection was a plus for us and Clive felt the same way. We decided we would pressurise him whenever the opportunity arose. Likewise, his half-back partner. I'd not seen much of

Braam van Straaten but what I had seen confirmed in my mind that he was an excellent goal kicker with very little else in his armoury. Not for nothing had he been nicknamed 'Braam van Statue' by some cruel South African journalists. My feeling was that if we let him get within range he would punish us on penalties but that he offered the South Africans little else. Certainly I couldn't see him making their game flow in the way they reckoned they wanted it to.

Our own side looked a little different from the XV which had lost to Scotland in the agony and the rain and the cold of Murrayfield just a few weeks earlier.

Garath Archer and Simon Shaw were out of the second row, replaced by Martin Johnson and my fellow Coventrian Danny Grewcock, both of whom had missed the Six Nations through injury. Arch and Shawsy had put in top performances during the early part of the year but I don't think anyone would argue with the suggestion that a fit Johnno is the world's finest lock. Once his Achilles had cleared up, he would obviously reclaim his place in the side and Clive obviously looked back at the great partnership he had built up with Danny – a very athletic jumper and a hard player who complements Martin – before their lay-offs. Johnno was also back as skipper, Daws having been ruled out by a shoulder problem. But one world class scrum-half had been replaced by another, Kyran Bracken slotting back in after 10-month absence, also caused by injury – in his case, a mysterious and agonising back complaint which had made playing impossible. I rate Kyran extremely highly as a scrum-half. He is a very confident, vocal guy which is something you need in a 'boss' position like No 9. He has explosive power and can make good, quick yards. He also has good vision and quick hands. Now he has been handed the captaincy of his club side, Saracens, I expect him to add leadership to an impressive list of qualities. Clive has shown a tendency to favour the man in possession which means that assuming Kyran stays fit and maintains his form, poor old Daws could face a battle to get back into the side. Looking on the bright side, having that sort of competition for a key position like scrum-half can only be good for England.

Julian White was in at tight-head – a hell of a game to make your debut. I didn't know Julian very well until we met up in South Africa. He was a bit of a mystery man, a 27-year-old who had come late to the squad. I soon found out that he didn't like being called 'Big Nose' – well, to quote the old line from Monty Python's *Life of Brian*, he has got a very big nose – and that he was embarrassed by his singing voice. It is a long-established tradition that new England caps sing a song for everyone else on the bus back from their first game. Julian was desperate not to sing, eventually mumbling something so indistinct I can't even remember what it was. On the other hand, I can hardly talk. After my first cap I sang a song I'd just learned off Dosser Smith's son. It went: 'Mrs Walls, toffee balls, la la la ... Mrs Walls, toffee balls, cha cha cha' It is still fondly talked of as the worst debutant song ever.

Finally, Dan Luger was back on the left wing.

Our coaching set-up was a little different, too. John Mitchell had gone and Andy Robinson had come into his position of forwards coach. The history between Robbo and myself is well-known – we'd been rivals for the England No 7 shirt years earlier. I remember a bust-up between us in a Leicester versus Bath game around 1992. Things boiled over a bit and I called him a 'has-been'. He spat back that it was better than being a never-been, which cut me dead since I hadn't been capped at that time. I was mildly interested, therefore, to see how he would react to me in our new relationship. He couldn't have been better. He took all the guys off into one-to-one situations, chatted to them about his hopes for them and for the team and generally impressed us all with his man-management and his attitude. In my case he told me he liked what I was doing and that he wanted me to play with freedom. I came away feeling very positive. Andy is a passionate, patriotic man who wants his team and his country to do well and the energy and ideas he has already brought to his role as forwards coach make it very clear that we've found the perfect replacement for Mitch.

Tactically, we had looked long and hard at the Springboks. In the World Cup we'd taken the decision to move Lawrence out wide at the kick-off, on the opposite side of the pitch from the rest of the forwards, to make sure we had defensive cover all over the park. Normally, Lol is used to take the ball up in the first phase following kick-off. Instead of someone like Hilly adopting his role, however, we kicked deep. In hindsight, this was a mistake. We reckoned that we'd be able to stop them with our defence when they ran back at us. By and large it worked because it was only de Beer's freakish kicking on the day and a dodgy try by van der Westhuizen which won the game for them. However, it did mean that their back three, the full-back and the wings, were able to stay back and take our return kicks in front of themselves, giving them time to exploit any 'match-ups' – where a back deliberately targets a more unwieldy forward in the defensive line.

For this game, we decided we would not kick possession away. Indeed, Robbo said he didn't want us kicking anything away until we hit our own 10 metre line. That meant that their back three would have to come up to defend and that, when we were ready to kick, the ball would be landing behind them. No-one plays well when he has to keep turning to fetch the ball. That was the plan.

As we've done too many times, though, we started slowly and were rocked by a sustained and ferocious attack by the Springbok forwards. Spurred on by a howling crowd of 41,150 who pelted us with oranges and, in Austin Healey's case, a plastic Coke bottle full of stones, they pinned us back for 20 minutes or so and were awarded a succession of penalties, which van Straaten took well. The Leicester full-back Tim Stimpson, selected on the wing in place of Austin Healey, who had moved to fly-half after Jonny pulled out, replied with a goal but after 24 minutes we were behind by 15 points to three.

We've worked hard on getting our mental game right and we were determined not to panic, but it was a worrying start.

The positional changes didn't help, of course. And Julian White, the young Saracens tighthead who was making his debut, was given quite a torrid time early on by Robbie Kempson. It's a big learning process and to come in at tighthead against one of the world's top packs was a tall order. But White showed he is a quick learner, with plenty of brain to go with a lot of brawn, and as the game wore on he began to impose himself, as did the whole England team.

If you reflect that the South Africans scored 15 points in the first 24 minutes but only managed to add three more in the remaining 81 minutes the referee played, you get some idea of how the balance shifted.

The big break came when the Springboks gave away a penalty at a scrummage. Instead of kicking for the three points, as the England of old would undoubtedly have done, we ran a quick tap-penalty back at them. De Wet Barry held up Phil Greening on the try-line but we retained and recycled the ball to have another go via Mike Tindall. He, too, was stopped, this time by Breyton Paulse. But we were stretching their defence and retaining possession and we felt it was only a matter of time. Finally, the try came when Dan Luger barged over for a score a forward would have been proud of. Stimmo, a superb kicker for Leicester, converted, making it 15–10 and we were well on top.

Shortly afterwards came the most controversial moment of the match. Mike Catt kicked the ball downfield and set up a chase between Stimpson and Andre Vos, the Springbok captain. Stimmo had beaten Vos over the try line but the ball bounced awkwardly over his head and, as he reached up to catch it, he was tackled without the ball.

How can that not be a penalty try? Ask Mark Lawrence, the video referee and, coincidentally, a South African.

Even ignoring that, as Tim went down, it looked to me as though he managed to get the ball under control and touch it down. If that was the case there was no controversy about the tackle because it was a try anyway. Amazingly, Lawrence ruled that Stimmo had knocked the ball on and awarded a scrum to

South Africa. You can't blame Vos. If he didn't make the tackle we were definitely going to score. His best hope was that Stimpson had the ball in his hands but that the tackle might force an error – maybe he would drop it. You can blame the video referee, however. He watched the action for several minutes from lots of different angles and I honestly can't see how he arrived at the decision he made. We watched the replays on the big screen and were confident that either the try would be given or we would be awarded the penalty try. The crowd were hushed and several of the Springboks' heads were down so it looked to us as though they felt the same way. I was stunned when the decision went against us. Not long afterwards, Stimmo slotted over for another three points but I felt very strongly that the try, which would have made it 15–15 at least, would have opened the game up for us and we would have won.

It was gut-wrenching, especially after Joost van der Westhuizen's try against us in the World Cup which was allowed, despite slow motion replays showing clearly that he had touched the corner flag – and was, therefore, in touch – before grounding the ball. It seemed that, where TV replays, England and South Africa were concerned, we were always going to come off second best.

Another controversial element was their somewhat questionable use of the blood replacement rule. Our defence was so hard that we were injuring them – they lost both centres, the flanker Erasmus and Vos, the No 8, at various stages. Vos went off with what was supposedly a blood injury but I saw no blood. It looked to me much more like a bang on the head and around 20 minutes later he suddenly reappeared. Very strange.

They popped another penalty over and stole the match 18–13. You could almost feel the sense of relief among their players and supporters. We trooped off, angry and upset but not downhearted. We'd out-tackled, out-thought and out-run them. We'd missed Jonny at fly-half, though Austin had put in an amazing performance considering he'd only been playing there in club rugby for a few months. We felt sure we'd take them in the next Test.

CHAPTER 18

Beating the Boks

OVER THE next few days, the South African media and the public we met on trips out to the local shopping malls and the gym made it quite clear that they, too, thought we'd been robbed. They're knowledgeable rugby folk and their loyalty to their team doesn't preclude straight-talking and honesty. The talk was that Nick Mallett's head was on the block and those fans we met left us in no doubt that they wanted him out.

The first Test may have seen an excellent, committed England battling and fighting every scrap of the way. We may have produced the only try (I still think 'tries') of the game. But we had still lost. And so as we headed for the second Test at Bloemfontein I felt even more than before that this was a must-win game. There could be no excuses.

We were missing Dan Luger, out with a bruised chest. His had been a sparkling performance of real class in the Loftus Versfeld encounter and I was sorry he was unavailable. However, Ben Cohen was on hand to step back in at No 11, showing the new-found strength in depth of the England backs.

If anything, though, the team was slightly stronger because we had Jonny Wilkinson back at No 10, fully recovered from his food poisoning. Incredibly, he'd lost almost a stone in weight since falling ill just before the First Test. Like me, Jonny's not a big guy anyway – he's around 5ft 10in tall and weighs something like 14 stones dripping wet – and for him to shed so much so quickly was bad news. A lot of guys would certainly not have been able to come back from that sort of problem as quickly as he did. He didn't start eating properly again until the Wednesday before the game and was nowhere near his fighting weight and strength on the morning of the match. It stands in testament to him and his character that he even made it onto the field – his performance showed he really is a world class player and pointed up how much we had missed him in the first game.

Ironically, Jonny's stomach bug occurred at the same time as a book came out alleging that the All Blacks *had* been poisoned a couple of days before their defeat in the 1995 World Cup final at the hands of South Africa. The All Blacks were hot favourites to beat the South Africans, following their defeat of England in the semi-final, but put in a lacklustre performance and lost to Joel Stransky's boot. There were all sorts of rumours that they'd been fed some dodgy food, leaving them weak and explaining their poor showing.

Rory Steyn, Nelson Mandela's bodyguard and the guy in charge of the New Zealand team's security, said in his book *One Step Behind Mandela*: 'There is no doubt that the All Blacks were poisoned two days before the final. When I got upstairs to the doctor's room it looked like a battle zone. Players were lying all over the place with the doctor and physio injecting them. What my eyes told me that night was that the team had been deliberately poisoned.'

Food for thought, if you'll excuse the pun. I make no allegation at all. All I will say is the All Blacks fell ill just before a big game in South Africa and so did a number of our key players – with our fly-half and captain being most seriously affected.

Wilkinson's return lifted us. We are very lucky just now to have so many very good players to fill every position, as demonstrated by the competition between Ben Cohen and Dan Luger on the left wing. In Jonny's absence, Tim Stimpson had shown his merits as a utility back in the first game and Austin had served us well at stand-off. But Jonny was our first choice fly-half and Healey perhaps just has the edge over Stimmo on the wing so the return to normality augured well.

At our luxurious Johannesburg retreat, we relaxed, training only twice in midweek. We needed to nurse our battered bodies. We were not the only guys capable of big hits in defence.

We talked in groups and as a team about our tactics. We didn't feel that we'd got too much wrong in the first game. A little luck and we would have won. One thing we did want to change, though, was our tendency to concede possession. We'd given the ball away 34 times at Loftus Versfeld. You can't play like that against top sides and expect to win and if it wasn't for the fact that our defence was so strong those turnovers might have cost us dear. This was an area we looked at during the week. Another area was penalties. The first half-penalty count had been 11–4 against us. Even though we felt the referee had been harsh, this was still something we wanted to tighten up.

Before the game, I went through my usual pre-match routine. We get into the dressing room about an hour and half before kick-off. Usually, it's a 2.30pm start, so we will arrive at about 1pm. If we are away, I find a space and drop my kit. If we are at home, we each have spots with our names above them. I always have both my ankles strapped before every game. It is a precautionary measure and not because they are weak. The strapping just gives your ankle more support so that it's harder for the joint to move in the lateral plain if you fall awkwardly. Out in South Africa, I was strapping my knee too, following the Ba-Bas game – that is always done if you have suffered an injury recently. Again, it's a question of supporting the joint. The England physiotherapist Kevin Murphy takes care of this, using white potassium tape and then a stretchy gauze covering.

Once strapped, I have a massage to loosen me up and, when Lawrence and Richard are ready, we all go out onto the pitch as a threesome. Other players come and go while we are out there. There is about an hour to go at this point, and the stadium will be starting to fill up. I like to have a look around to try to get a feel for the atmosphere as it builds.

Some people are in their tracksuits, some in their full kit. I always wear my England socks, the adidas boots I play in, my underwear, a training T shirt, and my tracksuit bottoms and top. I don't put my shorts and shirt on until 10 minutes before kick-off, after we have done the team warm up. It is not a question of superstition. I just like to go out for the match in fresh, clean kit. If there is a team photo before my individual warm-up, I will even put my shorts and shirt on for the snaps and then take them off again for my warm-up.

The three back rowers go through some stretching together. Then we normally circle half the pitch three times before meeting up back under the posts. The idea of this little run is to get the body's core temperature up which is important both in terms of performance and also as a means of avoiding injury caused by working with a cold body. Someone over there described it as being like three lions marking out their territory: a nice, if somewhat over-the-top simile. We will do some more stretching together under the posts, and a few sprint drills – three quarter pace, then full pace – before going back in to join the rest of the team. Some of them will not have bothered going onto the turf – they prefer to do their stretches and individual warm-ups inside in the aisles outside the dressing rooms.

Back in the changing rooms – at Twickenham they are white painted, with pictures of the players in action all over the walls and, in big letters, the words 'Think Who Has Stood Here' – guys are taking on lots of water or Lucozade Sport, keeping themselves hydrated. I usually have to urinate seven or eight times in the hour before the start of the game – and at half-time – though, luckily, I've never been caught short during play!

Forty minutes before kick-off, the players will be taking strong coffee or caffeine-rich drinks to increase their mental alertness. We are not advised to take caffeine – even tea – except on match day because it dehydrates you, so you get a surprising 'buzz' from this. Most people are quite quiet at this point. We are all trying to focus on the game and our role in it. I will run through a few defensive and offensive moves in my head and work my way through the line-out calls. Meanwhile, the stereo is banging out tunes.

Later, there will be a bit of conversation. I tend to take a lot of the defensive chats so I'll have a word with Johnno about the second row and also talk to Jonny and the centres, because 7, 10, 12 and 13 are your main defensive strength.

Clive tends to leave us alone – it is usually just the team and the replacements – though he walks around the room having a word with the odd individual. In the background, there is the usual changing-room sound of studs on a hard floor and a bit of noise from the crowd might start to filter down as the door opens and closes.

Some players will be really suffering with nerves as the time approaches. In the days when Cocker was in the England side he would have been vomiting now, throwing up in the sink or the shower. He is still sick before every game with Leicester – you just hear this 'Uurrrgghh!' sound somewhere in the distance. Neil Jenkins was the same on the Lions tour. A few senior players might be chatting to the less experienced guys, reassuring them, just checking they are feeling confident and ready.

Then we head out for our team warm-ups on the pitch.

The forwards and backs split into their groups and the pack will work on line outs and have a last chat about our tactics. The backs, meanwhile, are going through their moves, just passing the ball in hand, getting the feel of it, getting their handling slick. After a few minutes, we huddle together as a team and do some dynamic stretching and powerful movements – power squats and high, swinging kick-throughs, where you bring your leg up so the foot is level with your forehead and touch your toes. Again, this loosens you and readies you for the explosive activity ahead. Then we will get some tackle bags out and start to put in some big hits on one another, rehearsing our defensive patterns. There is a lot of aggression and a lot of shouting now.

Ten minutes before kick-off, we head back into the changing room fully warmed, sweating, and drink as much fluid down as we can. The back row will get our heads together. I'll be saying to Lol and Hilly: 'Right lads, it's up to us today'. A few feet away, the front row are doing much the same thing. We operate on a sort of 'teams-within-a-team' basis and each little grouping tries to take responsibility for the game ahead.

The front five as a unit are generally pretty physical by now – they will be very psyched-up, grinding their heads together and even punching one another with all the aggression and adrenalin and yelling at the top of their voices. Then the captain will make a few points and offer some words of motivation before we head back out.

*

Out on the field in Bloemfontein for the national anthems, the hairs rose up on the back of my neck. And not because of the chilly night air. We were facing not just 15 Springboks, desperate to silence their critics, but a baying, howling crowd of 37,000 Free Staters. It was a magnificent atmosphere of confrontation and aggression and I fed off it.

Again, we started poorly, giving away a couple of early penalties. But within minutes Jonny was starting to show flashes of brilliance and I just felt it was going to be our night. At only just 21, Jonny is, inevitably, not quite the finished article. As a positional and points kicker, he is second to none. Defensively he is the world's stand-out stand-off. As a running fly-half, he maybe has a little to learn. Like all of us, he has areas of his game which could be improved. That night, though, he produced an all-round display of such maturity, skill and composure that it was almost breathtaking. He scored all of our points through penalties and a drop goal. He marshalled and organised the backs like a guy of 31. He made breaks, he put in big hits and he threw some outstanding, long, floating passes. And the South Africans didn't have a clue how to stop him.

We led 12–18 at half-time and, after 80 minutes we were ahead 15–27. The Springboks threw everything they had at us but we held them, despite losing Jason Leonard and Lawrence Dallaglio to the sin-bin at crucial times.

There were moments of outstanding defence – Ben Cohen motoring across like a runaway train to smash Breyton Paulse into touch right by our line, Austin Healey calmly sidestepping three onrushing Springboks, again, right on our line, before punting coolly into the stands.

Ultimately, it took another mad decision by another South African video referee to get them even close to us. Earlier, the TV ref, Andre Watson, had made a decision in our favour when a combination of myself Lol and Kyran Bracken had prevented Krige from grounding the ball. In a similar situation five minutes later, Jonny Wilkinson and Ben Cohen stopped Robbie Fleck as he raced down the left-hand touchline. Supporting South Africans arrived and a mass of players collapsed on top of one another across our line. Austin Healey was at the bottom of the pile with the ball on his chest. It wasn't going anywhere. Suddenly, van der Westhuizen lunged into the middle of the pile with his hand and claimed a try. Watson studied the pictures and awarded the score. I will never know how. I defy anyone to see the ball from the replays we were shown. You can't see the ball and you can't see van der Westhuizen's hand properly either. There was no way it was a try. Once again, we'd suffered bad luck at the hands of the video ref.

When the whistle blew a few minutes later, though, none of that mattered. The feeling of elation flowing through me was incredible. To my mind, we'd won both Tests. Indisputably, we had proved ourselves the equal of this so-called Southern Hemisphere Superpower. It was only the third win we'd recorded on South African soil – and how appropriate that it should come in the City of Roses.

The local media were highly complimentary of us and Jonny in particular. 'Superb', 'sublime' and 'near faultless' were just three of the descriptions I read of his performance.

The win heralded some old-style boozing. We played drinking games, spoofing for shots of vodka, whisky and rum. Later, we went clubbing and the single guys discovered that South African girls found them quite attractive. We drank until 6am on the Sunday. That night and the next we carried on, boozing through till dawn once more. Tuesday night we recovered, wanting to save ourselves for an even bigger session on the Wednesday before we flew home. That evening, I came in like a pinball, bouncing from wall to wall along the hotel corridor and off every surface in my bedroom until I collapsed naked in my bathroom with my head down the loo. Where I awoke the following morning.

*

I think we did prove something in South Africa. We knew only too well that we had failed to take our chances at critical points and in major matches before then. This time we didn't retreat into ourselves and we played the kind of rugby that we knew we were capable of, the kind of rugby that wins matches and wins fans.

The only disappointment was that the Springboks started their subsequent 2000 Tri-Nations in such poor fashion. Their crushing first-up defeats at the hands of the All Blacks and the Wallabies meant that, in the eyes of some critics, we still had not passed the sternest test. That was upsetting. The South Africans are always tough to beat, even more so at home. We had done all that could be asked of us. When, later in that competition, the South Africans beat the New Zealanders, putting six tries past them in a thrilling match on their own turf, I felt that redressed the balance a little.

The big question, of course, is consistency. We could have beaten the Springboks two-nil in the series but it does not matter a jot if we can't do it again and again and again. I think the England side Clive Woodward and his staff are building will go on to beat the best in the world consistently, to actually be the best side in the world.

I just hope I'm around to be part of it when it happens.

CHAPTER 19

Our Changing Game

ON THE pitch, English rugby has come on in leaps and bounds in the last few years. Off it, though, squabbling, back-biting and unnecessary changes to the structure of the season and our League system threaten to undermine all that good work.

It is a shame, because right now the opportunities for rugby in England to grow as a sport are massive. I cannot believe that soccer can carry on gobbling up airtime, cash and interest at the rate it has done. Sooner or later, people are going to get sick of guys earning £50,000-a-week who are unable to control their tempers, who are incompetent by international stand-ards and who fall over in tears every time someone clips their ankle. Where will the fans turn? I think modern, flow-ing rugby has just the ingredients to attract the disgruntled soccer supporter. No longer the exclusive province of fatties and public schoolboys, it is now a sport dominated by fit, skilful, powerful athletes. Media coverage has increased as the England team has begun to look like a force to be reckoned with. This is benefiting the sport already: Premiership clubs are starting to attract bigger crowds to games which are more exciting.

Unfortunately, off the field it sometimes seems our admini-strators are failing to grasp the opportunities. The sports pages of the morning papers ought to be packed with good news about rugby. Instead, there are dozens of column inches filled with controversy, friction and uncertainty. As we started the 2000/2001 season, unbelievably, there were still wrangles to be sorted out.

One was the question of whether or not the winner of National Division One should be allowed automatic promotion to the top flight, swapping places with our bottom side. The answer seems obvious to me: of course they should. What is the point of Rotherham's players putting their bodies on the line week in, week out down among the mud and the studs in Division Two if the door to the next level is locked in their faces – as it was in 2002, with Leeds staying up and their Yorkshire neighbours staying down, despite thrashing all-comers in the division. Is that going to encourage their supporters – or those of any Division One clubs – to turn up every Saturday? Of course it isn't. Those clubs would wither on the vine. A few die-hard supporters might continue to turn up but their chance of attracting the big crowds and media interest that go with a promotion battle would vanish forever. And it would not be any good for the game higher up, either. The argument is that ring-fencing the Premiership will produce a stable financial situation, where the top clubs know where they were going to be for the next few years. But it would not do anything for the overall competitiveness of the Premiership if there were no ultimate sanction for coming last. And who decides who the 'top' clubs are, anyway? My home town side Coventry were a big team not so long ago. Now they languish in the second division. Bristol are another yo-yo side. If we are not careful we will arrive at something like the American football 'franchise' system. Over there, no-one really wins or loses because there is no drop to avoid. If you come bottom, you get first choice of the best players next year and if your owner decides he does not like New York he can just move his team 3,000 miles away to California.

Yes, there is a need for financial security in the professional era. At Leicester, we know that more than most. We do not have a money man behind the scenes. We have survived – and begun to prosper – with sound management on and off the field, good commercial people and good crowds. To a certain extent, we are lucky. Some clubs will struggle to get attendances above 4,000 at the moment and, therefore, they need someone to bankroll them in the meantime. But making the League more artificial is not the way forward.

This promotion-relegation argument was still raging as the insurance company Zurich tried to announce its new three-year, £15 million sponsorship of the Premiership in June 2000. Somehow this excellent news filtered through but it was largely lost in the sound of squabbling. That is a whole other issue, of course: how English rugby treats its sponsors. Tetley's Bitter, who helped me by sponsoring my column in the *Daily Mirror* for a long time, have ploughed a lot of cash into the game, not least with the Tetley's Bitter Cup. How have they been repaid? The run-up to the 2000/2001 season was full of stories of how the Cup was being phased out and how there might be a British Cup instead. Eventually, they decided on a February 24 final. Scheduling their final in the depths of winter sounds a strange way of repaying one of your most loyal backers.

The new points system in place for the 2000/2001 season was another mystery to me. I can accept a team picking up bonus points for scoring extra tries. But I cannot agree with sides getting a point for losing but coming within seven points of the winners. If you lose, you lose. End of story. In any case, I read an article in one of the papers where someone had applied the 2000/2001 points system to the 1999/2000 season's results and found that it would have had no effect on the top five places. Leicester were still top, by an even greater margin. Surely the lesson is if it ain't broke, don't fix it. And if you absolutely must fix it, fix it in a way which will make a difference.

Another bizarre change introduced was the play-off. The idea is that we go through the same full season as before but at the end the top eight clubs will then go forward to a new Zurich Premiership Plate competition, with the leading four sides earning the right to play at home in the mini-tournament. This is not some sort of tin-pot competition. The grand final winner earns a European Cup place for 2001/2002, a very valuable commodity.

Three thoughts occur to me.

First, which is the champion club in England – the winners of the Premiership or the winners of the Plate?

Second, we play far too many games already. Those guys lucky enough to be selected for the autumn internationals, the Six Nations and then the Lions will have played something like twice as much rugby in a year as their Southern Hemisphere counterparts.

Third, imagine you are fifth or sixth in the Premiership with a couple of games to go. You have no realistic hopes of finishing first but you know you will finish in the top eight, come what may. What do you do? The sensible coach rests all his top players and puts out a second team for the remaining Premiership-proper fixtures. That two or three week break gives his guys enough time to recharge their batteries at a point in the season when everyone else is knackered and that may well be enough to see them through to a Plate victory and a European place. Thus, a team which finishes, eventually, eighth in our domestic competition may go to Europe while a better side misses out. The implications are wider than that, though. Say it is tight at the top of the table, with Leicester heading the list from Bath and a tight group of other clubs. Imagine our final three games are against the third, fourth and fifth-placed clubs, Northampton, Bristol and Saracens – all sides with reasonable hopes of finishing in the top three of the Premiership and gaining automatic places in Europe. Meanwhile, let's say Bath's run-in is Wasps, Gloucester and Quins – occupying the sixth, seventh and eighth slots. The danger is clear: Wasps' best hope of Europe is to rest key guys like Lawrence Dallaglio, Joe Worsley, Josh Lewsey and Phil Greening in the hope of making a good showing in the Plate. Bath's chances of victory in that game, and the Premiership as a whole, are, therefore, vastly improved. The whole essence of League rugby could be skewed.

The administrators haven't got it all wrong, though. The salary cap is something I happen to believe in. That may sound strange, coming from a player, without being too big-headed, who would probably be among those earning more money if the cap were lifted. The fact is, without it, certain clubs would prosper because they could afford the best players and others would die. That is fine if you want to end up with rugby looking like Scottish soccer. I don't.

At Leicester, as far as I know, we adhere strictly to the cap. There are rumours rife around the Premiership that some other clubs, whether through creative accounting or 'legal' fiddles, are managing to get around it. EFDR was now paying £75,000 to have the accounts of the 12 Premiership clubs independently audited in an attempt to root out these alleged breaches. Penalties for miscreants include fines and expulsion from European competition. We must not allow a few clubs to suck up all the available talent and create a ghetto. I hope that the auditors do discover any misbehaviour that might be occurring.

*

The changes which have been made have not just been to the structure of the game off the field. Rugby's international administrators have introduced sweeping changes to the way the sport is played on the park in recent years.

Some of the new rules have been brought in to create a quicker brand with more excitement and more tries. It has not pleased everyone. Stephen Jones, a thoughtful critic whose opinions often carry a lot of merit, is one of them. He wrote a full-page article in the *Sunday Times* in March 2000 which was read by a lot of players. The headline was: 'GOING SOFT – *Rugby is now a game for wimps. From the ludicrous spectacle of unopposed lineouts to the shameful absence of grinding confrontation, it has renounced that which made it great.*'

What 'made it great', according to Stephen and some ex-players he quoted, was hard scrummaging, confrontation and physical fear of the opposition. 'Rugby is fast retreating from its roots and ethos.' he wrote. 'The elements of thunder and confrontation are disappearing without trace . . . It is time for rugby to stop this utter betrayal of itself. Currently, it is as hard as melting butter.'

Strong words, and sentiments shared by a lot of former stars.

I find this attitude strange, though. I certainly don't recognise modern rugby as a soft game. I had 57 stitches in my head in one season. Those gashes were not opened shaving. Among many other injuries, I have also damaged ligaments in neck, split my face open in numerous places, broken my collar bone and been knocked out. And I consider myself lucky.

I would love for Stephen or any of the past international players he quoted – Ireland and Lions captain and lock forward Willie-John McBride, the England and Lions flanker Mike Teague, Welsh prop Charlie Faulkener or French prop Gerard Cholley – to play in the modern game if they think it is non-competitive and not confrontational and there's no fear. These were great players and they are entitled to their views. But in some cases those views just don't stand up to scrutiny.

For instance, Willie-John McBride says the aggression has gone, claims the scrum is a waste of time because you are 99 per cent sure of winning your own ball and criticises the use of 'body armour'. Let's be clear that the aggression is still there: players at my club, like Martin Johnson, Darren Garforth and Richard Cockerill, would stand toe-to-toe with anyone from Willie-John's day. And this stuff about body armour is just nonsense. We're not talking American football pads, we're talking about 15mm of foam on the shoulders and the odd head guard. And even with this minimal padding, we still get plenty of broken bones and shoulder injuries. Unless something in the water is making our joints weaker than they were 25 years ago I think that proves we are still in a physical game. With all due respect to Willie-John, a legendary player and a renowned hard man in his era, he has no comprehension of the power and momentum which the modern player unleashes. It is just a fact of life that people are far fitter than in any previous era and they are also three stones heavier, and quicker and stronger too. The modern England pack would walk through any pack from 20 years ago. No question. Andrew Sheridan, the Bristol forward, bench-presses over 200kg – 440lb. Easily. I know scrummaging is not just a question of bench-pressing but that gives you some idea of the power of the modern athlete.

Gerard Cholley, an ex-French prop, said: 'Players don't even know fear any more. Everything is so strictly controlled that they can insult the opposition because they know nobody is going to risk taking any retaliation. In my day, retribution was not always instantaneous, but it would come.' When people start using the phrase 'In my day . . .' you tend to turn off. But Monsieur Cholley has a point. Yes, sometimes you do want to give a player a dig if he is winding you up. I have actually been known to do it myself on occasions (once in the Sistine Chapel in the Vatican, of all places: on a squad day out during an England under-21 tour, Harvey Thorneycroft accused me of knocking a tourist's camera to the floor. Harvey was actually responsible; I warned him to shut up but, like a school kid, he carried on yelling 'Backy knocked the camera off, Backy knocked the camera off!' So I chinned him).

However, I do not actually think it is good for the game for wholesale brawling to break out on the pitch. If you want to see punching, go and watch a boxing match. Secondly, if you do whack someone you will probably be caught. Unlike in the Holy City, and unlike in Willie-John's time, the TV cameras are now on you all the time and you will be cited if you are seen. If they had had the tools in 1975 they would have come down hard on foul play then too. And thirdly, if you do waste time scrabbling around on the ground with some opponent, the ball could well be out and over your try-line in the meantime. The game is now that quick you haven't got time for aggro.

Anyway, you ask any front row if it's still competitive, and fearful, and hard work. I think you will get a resounding 'Yes'.

It is perhaps significant that Stephen has chosen four ex-forwards. Ask a few of the backs who stood freezing on the wing for 80 minutes whether the game was better in the old days. Ask the fans who watched England win 9–6, in an awesome display of shoving, grunting and place-kicking. Yes, there is a time and a place for forward domination but when the only way England can score is via penalty kicks and the pushover try it is time to try something else.

To be fair, these guys did make some valid points. Willie-John was correct about the scrum. Referees should police the put-in. A crooked feed, and possession should change hands. In the line out it is also true that much of the individual skill has gone but in its place is a new team discipline. I do not agree that it is always uncontested; as people have got used to the change in the rules, teams have started winning opposition ball and we are all having to work to combat that. The result is a new style line-out which still requires athleticism but is more of a team effort, players working in almost choreographed synchronisation. Yes, smaller guys are being lifted up to heights they could not previously have attained. Having said all that, was the old line-out all it is cracked up to be anyway? Was Martin Bayfield a fantastically skilled line-out jumper or was he just a 6ft 10in bloke who could reach things no-one else could get to?

The journalist Ian Stafford has written a book which sees him going into action with different professional sportsmen and teams. He played in a Super League match, he played for Everton, he has rowed in a boat with Steve Redgrave and so on. He was working on a follow-up book and came out with Leicester in the summer for our pre-season week in Ireland. He played against Ulster for 10 minutes. He experienced what it is all about and he was absolutely wrecked – smashed black and blue – and totally exhausted by the end of the week. There's no reason why Stephen Jones couldn't come and have a go. Or if Gerard Cholley wants to come to training at Oval Park, we'll put him through a few line-outs and scrum sessions and show him how soft the modern game is.

I'm not trying to claim I have all the answers. I am wrong as often as anyone else. For instance, I thought that allowing replacements like soccer-style substitutes, rather than on the old injury basis, was a good idea. The thinking was that it would increase the pace of the game and that that would lead to a more entertaining spectacle for the fans. It created a whole new player: the 'impact' replacement. I have talked about these guys in this book – people like Victor Ubogu, who could be devastating in the final quarter.

In fact, the rule has been shown to be a bad one. Boxing is a useful analogy. There, you may have two fighters who are pretty well-matched. During the course of their fight, the man who is slightly stronger, fitter or technically more skilful will eventually come out on top and win. It would be rather absurd if, in round eight, he could leave the ring and his mate could hop over the ropes and take over. Unfortunately, that is almost what we now have in rugby. Now, when guys are getting tired, you just bring in another fresh body. This makes it harder for the better side to kill off the weaker opposition, particularly up front. Traditionally, games were won in the last quarter because one pack got on top of the other. In theory, the other side could now bring almost a new pack on if they had put seven forwards on the bench.

It is all very well striving to 'increase the pace of the game' on the assumption that it will 'lead to a more entertaining spectacle'. But our fans are not mugs and they don't like contrived results.

I am not sure, though, that there is any way back. Coaches and teams have become used to the idea of substitution and I believe that if we returned to the old injury replacement rule it would be abused. People would just fake injuries to come off. You might argue that that happened before. Maybe, but I doubt it. The ethos was different then. You didn't want to be replaced. Now it is acceptable and stuffing that genie back into his bottle would be a tall order.

There is a sense in which the replacements rule is now essential, of course. If you are going to stop the clock every time the ball goes out of play then what was once an 80 minute game is instantly transformed into a 105–110 minute affair. This was what happened in South Africa during our summer 2000 tour. Great for the paying public – they really get their money's worth. But it is hell for the players and very testing on our fitness levels. Without the replacements rule, which gives us 22 men to share the workload, I think some guys would be dropping like flies with the demands of the game now.

Another rule change which I at first welcomed but which has now been shown to be ill-conceived is the video referee. It has worked well in cricket and rugby league and I assumed that you could transfer that success. But in cricket, the video umpire is judging easy line decisions – a bat behind the popping crease, a fielder in contact with the boundary rope. Rugby league is similar, in that the defences tend to be strung out so that try decisions involve a ball and four or five guys.

In rugby union, you can have a total pile-up, involving 15 or twenty players, and this can reduce the role of the video ref to farce as we saw with Joust's 'try' in South Africa. Furthermore, if the IRB plans to continue with it, neutral video referees are a must. I am not suggesting that the South African viewing the tapes in the two Tests down there was biased. But the fact that he was South African added to the controversy and that was neither fair to him nor good for the game.

One alternative would be to introduce touch judges in the in-goal area, similar to those used in Sevens competitions. This would give the ref a little help. It is very rare that the main official gets in front of the play and having an extra pair of eyes located at either end might help with try-scoring or defensive movement decisions.

One thing to ponder, though: the fans seem to enjoy the tension brought about by the wait for decisions. I think it has added interest, for instance, to international cricket. We are in the entertainment business. If the crowds want it, and the wrong decisions can be kept to an absolute minimum, maybe we should keep the video.

Many of the rule changes over the years have actually improved the game and generally I have agreed with them. The law which was introduced to stop flankers breaking off the scum before the ball has come out was a good innovation which allowed the quicker, fitter and more skilful player to triumph over a guy who just broke early. I'm in favour, too, of the new ruck law which states that players have to approach from behind the back foot of your own team. In theory, this should allow a quicker game because it gives the attacking side slightly more time to pick it up and recycle before a pile of bodies forms over it. It also prizes the speed of a player like myself – as long as referees ensure that the tackled player releases the ball as he should.

Of course, if you introduce all these new laws you must make sure the structure is in place to enforce them. I'm not convinced it is right now. Policing of the game needs to be tightened up.

The blood rule is a case in point. In these days of AIDS, the rule has to be in place. There is a danger, however, of abuse. In one of our summer Tests against South Africa, André Vos was taken off, supposedly with a blood injury, and returned to the fray a long time later. None of our guys saw any evidence of blood on Vos. Maybe it was there, but it looked more to us as though he was woozy after a big tackle and that he was taken off to give him the chance to recover. The facts of that particular case are irrelevant, though. What is important is that someone is on hand to check on blood injuries. They should not just be a chance for a key player to have a quick rest. I am not convinced the present scrutiny is watertight.

'Grannygate', in which Wales and Scotland selected players on the basis of what later turned out to be erroneous claims about their ancestry, also demonstrated the need for better policing. These guys said they qualified by dint of having Welsh and Scottish grandparents. It turned out, of course, that they did not have these antecedents and they were prevented from playing again. The Unions and coaches took their supposed antecedents at face value. This was farcical. Someone, some-where, should have the responsibility of checking passports, birth certificates, whatever it takes, to establish the facts. It was highly embarrassing for all concerned and damaging to rugby in general because it made the sport look amateurish and careless.

We have yet to have this problem in England and I doubt, now, that we will. Mike Catt and now Robbie Paul apart, I don't think any of our players has even got serious connections to any other country. And I believe that is the way it should be.

Take Shane Howarth, one of the Grannygate figures. I cannot understand how Shane could have been happy playing for Wales. Even assuming he had a Welsh grandparent and was, therefore, qualified, the fact is he was a New Zealander by any other definition. Personally, I could not have played under those conditions. If I had an Australian grandparent and had been asked to pull on the green and gold I would have said no. I cannot imagine wanting to play for any country other than England. Before the 1999 World Cup there was talk that Joel Stransky – who was England-qualified – might be called up by Clive to solve what was then perceived to be a problem at fly-half. Clive later said it was never an option and this was something I was pleased to hear. I would not have been happy if Stranners had played for England, even though he was a great player and is a great friend. I did not think it was right, especially since he had already played international football for another country – something which, under new rules, would now bar him from selection anyway.

*

Professionalism has been good to me. It has given me a good living and allowed me to concentrate on my rugby, my skills and my fitness. Suddenly, there was no work to interfere. For some guys that has been a strange thing to grasp and some still have problems with it five years on. My old Leicester coach Bob Dwyer said fairly recently: 'I'd say 50 per cent (of Premiership players) are professional, 40 per cent are less than professional and 10 per cent are unacceptable.'

Bob spent a lot of time over here with the Tigers and with Bristol and I have to say he has a point. In the England squad, now, I would say that everyone is 'on-message'. We all have excellent fitness levels, we all watch our diets and we all put in 100 per cent in training and in matches. In Premiership One rugby, in my opinion, there are guys who are coasting. There are young players at the Tigers with masses of talent but who just do not have the right attitude as yet. During the 1999/2000 season I had a word with the flanker Paul Gustard, for instance. I told him he had everything – natural ability, size, strength, pace – but that he needed to improve his commitment. Fair play to Guzzy, he listened to my thoughts, went away over the close season and came back a changed guy. He had worked hard on his pre-season fitness and looked sharp and up for it in training and our early games. That sort of response is what is needed.

The demon drink has long been associated with rugby and some guys have had difficulty cutting down on their boozing. Pre-professionalism, even top-level rugby was much closer to the junior club game. A lot of the guys would go out together on the Saturday after the game and really get stuck in to the beers. That is something we have had to forego. When Roz Kadir was taken on as the England nutrition adviser, we all had to go down to Harley Street, individually, to see her. One of the questions she asked was how much alcohol we drank. I was able, quite honestly, to say very little: many weeks, I would not touch a drop. Occasionally I would have a glass of wine. My big sessions are always saved until the end of the season. In South Africa, for instance, during our four-night celebration, I drank more then than I would in the rest of the year. One current England player, who shall remain nameless, answered that he drank 20 pints.

Roz was a little surprised but thought that three pints a night, while too much, was not the end of the world.

'No, no,' says the player. 'Twenty pints on a *Saturday*.'

Having said that, the guy in question is one of the most committed and respected members of the side, which goes to show, I suppose, that the rule book is not always correct.

The effects of professionalism have filtered down to junior clubs. I think they should recognise that the game at that level is, essentially, about fun. You want to win but you should not want to win at all costs. Leave that to the guys whose livelihoods depend on it. Lower down, players have the luxury of playing the game as it used to be played: hard, but fair and with a pint and a laugh beckoning in the bar. Instead, I heard recently how one club four divisions below Premiership level was offering £20,000-a-year packages and trying to attract foreign players. Even further down, guys are hopping from club to club to get an increase in match fees. It has all become too serious. And it is turning off the casual, social players. A huge number of players are drifting away from rugby. It is quite frightening. Clubs are folding or drastically reducing the number of teams they can put out. That cannot be good for the health of the game.

At the higher levels, professionalism is inevitably putting greater strains on players. We do get more time to train and better recovery but play a massive number of games.

What is the solution? I am a big believer in central contracts. The serious money in the English game comes in via the England team. The RFU's Twickenham gate receipts, TV revenues and sponsorship income are huge compared with those even at a successful club like Leicester. Rugby as a game will only really go mainstream if the England team can win against top opposition on a regular basis. And that won't happen while the players are being ground down by a diet of constant rugby. The solution seems obvious: take some of the RFU money and contract 30 or so key players centrally. Loan them out to their clubs but restrict the number of games they play.

When the sport turned professional four years ago, the Southern sides went the right way and up here we went the wrong way. The Australian, New Zealand and South African Unions all contracted their top players. They are in charge. International rugby comes first. Club rugby comes second. They restrict the number of games their men play and they can take them away whenever necessary for squad training and so on. Over here, the RFU has no real say in how many games Martin Johnson or Lawrence Dallaglio play. They have to ask Leicester or Wasps for them if and when they are required. Naturally enough, Deano and Nigel Melville want Martin and Lol to be available for as many club games as possible because their first loyalty is to their employers. Thus, these key guys, and every other international in the Northern Hemisphere, have to play in every club game they possibly can. And we play far too many games. I will play twice as many matches in a season as Josh Kronfeld or Andre Venter. You cannot keep going forever. I draw the comparison with a 100 metre sprinter. If he has to run 30 times a year he's likely to run better than if he has fifty races. He doesn't have to peak so often.

I know the clubs are against this but I think the benefits for them would be substantial.

Imagine the situation at Leicester if the RFU contracted its England players. The club would be relieved of a wage bill of over a million pounds a year. The management could then use those resources to help develop the club. They would know they had the England players for, say, 20 fixtures each and they could plan the season accordingly. They would also be able to bring on new players. How else will they get the chance to shine? Leicester did tremendously well during the World Cup considering we were missing 10 or 11 players. They were forced to give young guys a go. Lewis Moody who plays in my position was named Player of the Month while I was away. He's a great young talent and it was fortunate for me he was injured by the time the World Cup ended! Dean brought on a young half-back, Andy Goode, who kept his place after the internationals returned. Those opportunities would never have arisen if the World Cup hadn't taken place when it did. And, unless the timing of future tournaments eats into our domestic season again something I doubt will happen it won't recur. But if the internationals were not available for every game, guys like Goode would get their chance quicker.

Another concern is the quality of games we play. The top league matches like Leicester against Northampton or Bath, where you've got good players, a decent crowd and plenty of pride and needle, are tough enough and intense enough but, in general, we're not playing Super 12 standard rugby. There are too many meaningless fixtures. They still take it out of you physically and you can still pick up injuries but you learn nothing. You aren't stretched. Maybe we could consider a provincial-style set-up a bit like those in the Super 12 and, closer to home, in Ireland, with four regions; North, South, East and West. North would be made up of the best players from Newcastle, Sale and Rotherham. South would be those from Quins, Wasps and Sarries. East would be Leicester, Northampton and London Irish and West, obviously, Bristol, Bath and Gloucester. I know there are holes in this concept: London Irish are not in the east, for a start-off, and until this season Rotherham would have been Bedford (if that makes sense!). But something must be done to ensure the quality of rugby goes up while the quantity goes down.

*

But even central contracts and a Northern Super 12s are not a cure for all English rugby's ills.

In Coventry, where I grew up, lots of the state schools played the game. That number is diminishing. All sport is suffering. Children over here spend their lives eating junk food in front of the television or the computer screen. They'd rather watch soccer than play it.

If you go to South Africa or Australia the kids are outside surfing, playing sports. In Durban, for instance, they're on the beach before school and straight back after school. They're physically fitter. All the gyms are full of people of all ages. They have special areas set aside for youngsters with weights to suit them. In Australia I went to one gym and it was packed with 60-year-olds all working out, doing aerobics and keep-fit.

Unbelievable. I'm sure it happens here in isolation but it's not commonplace as it is down there.

And there's the wider question of foreign involvement in the English game. Where younger overseas players have come over, they've been great for the game. They've improved the domestic standard, brought in fresh ideas, shown the way forward with their discipline and commitment. I've nothing against that. In fact, I'm in favour. At Leicester, guys like Fritz and Log were immense for us. Other clubs have had far bigger names. Guys like Thomas Castaignède, Tim Horan, Jason Little and David Wilson joined the Premiership this season and they will surely draw crowds. These guys are coming to the ends of their careers but have enough gas in the tank to give value for a while, as long as the clubs do not keep on playing them beyond their sell-by date to recoup their investment. That happened with Francois Pienaar at Saracens. He was obviously a world class player and was great for them in the first year. After that, when he was being played ahead of Hilly, it was a joke.

But I am more concerned about the players who are already past it when they come. You can't blame the blokes themselves: they get a lot more money for playing here than they would at home and they've got to take the opportunity. Frank Bunce at Bristol was a case in point. One of the best All Black centres ever, no question, but he just came along for a big payday and was no longer good enough. When Leicester played Bristol he made no impact at all. I've no idea what these players are earning but I would guess it's around £150,000. With money like that on offer, even Campese was talking about coming back. In their own countries, these guys wouldn't be tolerated. They'd have been retired and gone because the fans and the clubs wouldn't put up with sub-standard performances. Over here, you've got a game which has suddenly gone professional, where money men have come in to run clubs, in some cases men with little real idea about rugby, and they know that signing a big name player is a short-term solution to getting more people through the turnstiles. It's a shame and it's no good for the English game.

CHAPTER 20

Captain of England

TO SAY a lot has happened since I started work on the first edition of this book some three years ago would be the understatement of the century.

Leicester have been beaten just once at home – by Bristol, right at the end of the 2001/02 season, after we had already won the Premiership twice more – and have won and then become the first team to successfully defend the Heineken Cup.

I made it onto the plane for that second Lions tour . . . and what a six weeks that turned out to be.

England have beaten South Africa, Australia and every side in the Northern Hemisphere . . . and *still* not won that elusive Grand Slam.

And I've achieved two goals I once thought were millions of miles away – my 50th international cap and, best of all, the captaincy of my country.

I was not surprised, if I am honest, to make the 2001 Lions party. I was taking nothing for granted but I would have been shocked not to have been chosen. I still rate myself as the best openside in British Isles rugby, though David Wallace, Budge Pountney and Martyn Williams are all fine players and the man who seems destined, eventually, to replace me with England, Lewis Moody, is also a class act. So there were no tears of joy this time; just elation and a little sadness. Another summer away from Olivia and Ali.

We knew the Australians would be tough opposition; as World and Tri-Nations champions, they had nothing to prove. The early tour games, however, were against poor opposition that Premiership sides would beat easily. It was not exactly a waste of time – you need match fitness and it gave the boys a chance to run out in opposed matches – but there was little chance to evaluate players' performances and we would have preferred better opposition. Because Australia lacks a strong middle tier of rugby, there were no real alternatives. It is amazing how good the Australian side is in a country which has so few decent rugby teams, and is symptomatic of their attitude to sport in general: millions of dollars are poured into the facilities, to the coaching systems, to ensure they are number one. It is an admirable approach which has had great spin-offs; the whole country feels good about itself because its sports teams do well.

It was a marvellous feeling to pull on the shirt for my first game, against Western Australia in Perth. I cannot put into words how fantastic it feels to wear a Lions jersey. It is an honour very few men experience and the pride and emotion are extraordinary. I performed well and, as my good form continued, I looked to be heading for a place in the first Test team. Then I got injured playing in a pre-Test match. It was a tear to my external oblique muscle – an abdominal which is important for core stabilisation – which came as I attempted a 20-metre pass off my left hand. I had been feeling some soreness for five or 10 minutes but suddenly, as the ball left me, there was an agonising pain in my gut and I went down like I had been shot. I was helped from the field and was immediately iced up and had some ultrasound therapy, which is aimed at helping the tissue repair itself. I knew straight away that my appearance in that Brisbane clash was in doubt and feared for the whole of my tour. Next day, the decision was made for me; Johnno, our doctor James Robson and Andy Robinson came to my room to break the bad news that I would not be considered for the first

Test. I was absolutely gutted but it was the right decision. I could perhaps have started the match but would have struggled, and probably would have had to come off at some point. Then my tour would certainly have been over.

It was a very low point for me. I phoned home and spoke to Ali. She was supportive and concerned but, at a distance of 12,000 miles, there was not much she could do other than sympathise. Then I called Craig Mortimer, a friend throughout my Leicester playing days and, more importantly, an excellent physio, and chatted to him. Craig, who is available 24 hours a day, seven days a week for me, gave me some good, though obvious, advice: don't stretch, don't move too much, keep it iced as much as possible. Icing involves sitting with a big pack of crushed ice strapped to the affected area for periods of 10 to 15 minutes. It is a shock when it first goes on but you soon get used to it. Finally, I rang Darren Grewcock, someone I always turn to in a crisis, and asked his advice. What training could I do? He was reassuring. 'You're in great condition,' he told me. 'Just do nothing. If you don't do any work other than playing between now and the end of the tour, you will be able to perform well. Don't stress yourself about it.' He put my mind at rest – I always turn to Grewy when I have a crisis – but my appetite for work meant I had to do something; I spent time on aerobic and endurance work on cross training machines.

Shortly afterwards, a tragedy occurred which put my problems into perspective. Some of the players and Anton Coia, our kit bag and odd-job man, had gone on a fishing trip. They had all had a few beers and, as the boat neared the shore, Anton dived off and started to swim to the beach. He started waving and the boat moved off but he suffered a massive heart attack and died in the water. The sea was full of kids surfing on boogie boards and they found him after about five minutes and dragged him out. I was with Jonny Wilkinson in our hotel. We could see a commotion down on the beach and there were people running about down there. Louise, one of the admin girls in our party, came back up looking very shocked and pale. Jonny and I ran down to the beach and there he was, laid out on the sand, clearly dead. A group of people were gathered around and we stood and watched from a few yards away. An ambulance was pulling up and there was nothing we could do. It was a great shame; he was such a lovely bloke, he would do anything to help and was a big loss to the tour party. It certainly made me think that a muscle tear and a missed Test match were not the most important things in life.

The tear was improving, meanwhile. I have always, touch wood, had a good record of recovering quickly from injury and so it was this time; towards the end of the week, I was getting to the point where at least I could run so I started to feel I would be alright for the second Test. Missing that first encounter was difficult, though. To keep me involved, Graham Henry and Andy Robinson miked me up so I could relay messages between coaches and players. That took my mind off things a bit as the game got underway.

And what a game it was. The boys displayed amazing passion and togetherness and really went for the Australians. The Wallabies had changed their gameplan from that which they had pursued in the Tri-Nations; they tried to play it wide, threw a lot of passes, and it did not come off. Defensively, we were very aggressive, went forward and put them under a lot of pressure and, as they crumbled a little, we took our chances. It was almost hard to believe what was happening as we cut them to pieces time and time again. Although they came back into it towards the end there was only going to be one outcome. I will always be disappointed not to have been in the side, given the way the Lions played that day, but I try first and foremost to be a team man and I felt I contributed as much as I could, encouraging the guys from the sidelines and helping out where possible. Afterwards, the squad went out for a few beers but I stayed behind, nursing my injury and hoping to get the call for the second Test.

We all felt that would be the decider. If we won – and we

thought we would – then, obviously, the series was ours. If the Aussies came back at us, then going to Sydney at one-all, with the psychological advantage switched to them, would be tough. The ARU had been shaken by the massive support we had enjoyed at Brisbane – it was like a home game – and had been dishing out gold t-shirts and scarves to people in the bars and streets of Melbourne as the game approached. Our supporters were taunting them good-naturedly, singing: 'You're only wearing yellow 'cos it's free!' and it smacked a little of desperation on the part of the Australians.

The match, at the magnificent indoor Melbourne Colonial Stadium, turned into one of the most disappointing of my career. It started so well. I scored a Leicester-style drive-over try from a rolling maul early on. After my injury, that was a fantastic feeling and it meant we went in ahead. The Wallabies were virtually out on their feet, they looked in despair and I felt they were mentally gone. I remember thinking the series was ours if we could keep going like this. There was a massive buzz inside our changing room but we were not over-confident. After dominating the first half, we knew we should have been further ahead but we had missed some opportunities to really screw them down. Then, almost as soon as we ran out we were behind: Joe Roff scored off Jonny Wilkinson's speculative pass inside our 22. They converted and suddenly they were ahead. All our first half pressure was gone, they scored quickly again and the game was lost.

Why did Jonny throw that pass so deep in our half? I don't know. We had said it was up to them to play all the rugby: they had to catch up, we just needed to play for territory and make them run it back at us from their half. We would turn them over, force errors, win penalties, build the score. We had played a wide and expansive game in the first Test and it had come off and perhaps Jonny felt we should be doing that again. I do not blame him; he was one of the series' major successes. If the ball had gone to our hand, we would have made a lot of ground. But it did not and that was the turning point of the whole series.

Credit must be given to Australia. They seized on that one moment and switched everything around. They have great mental strength and they deserved their win.

Along the way, we lost Richard Hill for the second half and the final game to concussion from a blatant forearm in the face from Nathan Grey. Grey should have been cited but losing Hilly was a bigger worry to us. I felt he had been our man of the match in the first Test – awkwardly, from a personal point of view, in my position – and it was a savage blow. Martin Corry was a great replacement but Richard is a special player.

It was a low dressing room but we consoled ourselves with the knowledge that all was not lost. They were perhaps now favourites but we still had the opportunity to beat them the following weekend. We had been the best team in three of the four halves in the games so far. We had to be as upbeat as possible.

We were competitive in that last match. The score flipped this way and that and right at the death we were awarded a line-out near their line. A Lions score would have won us the match. It seemed a foregone conclusion; Keith Wood to Johnno, rolling maul, myself or Tom Smith would score and the game and series were ours. I thought destiny was with us. Amazingly, Johnno lost the line-out, they cleared the ball and our dream was destroyed. It just was not to be. I will never play for the Lions again and that loss was devastating. Massive. Awful. The worst thing is that I believe we should have won the Test series. I think we had a better set of individual players in our squad than the Wallabies had in theirs and, despite the 12,000-mile journey, we had better support, too.

So what went wrong?

A variety of things. Firstly, we were all absolutely knackered; to go on tour with the British and Irish Lions only a few days, in some cases, after you have finished a hard, 10-month domestic season is lunacy. Speaking for myself, I was exhausted, as were all the Leicester boys. We had played over 40 games and had lost only once since Christmas. You have to be working hard to achieve that. Add the Six Nations games and then the physical, emotional and mental effort involved in winning the European Cup and you can begin to imagine just how shattered we were. A few days' rest, wave farewell to the family and you are catapulted right back into it. I felt drained, physically and mentally, and probably needed some Caribbean sunshine and total relaxation rather than six more weeks of graft, even though I would have hated to miss the trip. It was not just Tigers players. Plenty of guys were getting on that plane who should really have been booking themselves into hospital. Neil Jenkins was one who was held together with sticking plaster and Sellotape before we even took off and who was effectively walking wounded for the whole time. Lawrence Dallaglio was another who could have done with a summer off after damaging his knee towards the end of the season. Other players had postponed operations. By the time the third Test came along, people took to the field in a condition in which they would certainly not have played for their clubs and probably not for their countries. For instance, Rob Henderson and Brian O'Driscoll, both tour heroes, were shot to bits. I am not criticising them. Lions tours come twice, maybe three times, in your career and you cannot blame them for playing. But taking on the World Champions, in Australia, requires mental sharpness all of the time. Top level professional rugby is about executing everything perfectly. In the final analysis, we could not do that.

Secondly, the tour management's communication skills were poor. Two simple examples spring to mind. First, selection. They must have known the likely make-up of the Test squad before we left the UK. While there would have been some doubt around one or two positions – Scott Quinnell or Lawrence Dallaglio at No8, Rob Howley or Matt Dawson at scrum-half – I am sure Graham Henry, Donal Lenihan and Andy Robinson knew in their hearts of hearts who they wanted even in those spots. Other choices were more straightforward still; for instance, Keith Wood was sure to be our starting hooker, Jonny Wilkinson was a cast-iron certainty at outside-half and Brian O'Driscoll was guaranteed the No13 shirt.

Unfortunately, there were some guys on the tour who seemed to feel they had a right to be in the final 22 when possibly other players had more to offer. Given that, I feel the management should have been open with everyone from the start. They should have managed expectations, explaining to the party and to individuals that, on a very short tour like this, not everyone may get a fair crack of the whip. The make-up of the Test squad was not set in stone and obviously there would be opportunities for guys to come into the frame but those currently outside the preferred 22 were going to have to hit the ground running and perform really well to break in.

Undoubtedly this would have hit some people hard and it might have impacted on their ability and desire to perform. But since that is what happened anyway, once players worked out where they were in the pecking order, he would have lost nothing. Indeed, I think he would have gained in two ways: firstly, players like and respect coaches who are prepared to be open with them; secondly, speaking for myself, if I had been one of those told he had work to do, you can be damn sure I would have done it. I was in a similar position on the 1997 tour to South Africa, where I was very much an outside bet for the openside spot, with Richard Hill ahead of me. To me, though, this provided a massive incentive – as though you should need one on a Lions tour – to run my socks off in the hope of breaking through.

However, none of this was done, and it was left to us all to work out what Graham and the management were thinking by the make-up of their sides as the Tests drew nearer and the selection patterns for big games emerged.

Some people did take it badly when they realised they were not in the frame for the Tests. Colin Charvis was one. Colin is a very gifted footballer and a big, strong lad with plenty of pace. Above all, he is a top bloke – I roomed with him on the first week of the tour and we really got on well. On his day, he would be up there with the best. Unfortunately, he was competing with an absolutely world class player in Richard Hill. If

Scott Quinnell were to play No8, a fit Lawrence Dallaglio would also be in the mix. To my mind, Colin should have put all his energy into playing as well as possible to help his chances. Instead, he let his head go down a little. Natural talent will only take you part of the way; the rest is in your head and your heart. Darren Morris was another who, I think, just expected to be in the Test side. In his case he had Graham Rowntree, Tom Smith and Jason Leonard to compete with, three of the best and most-experienced looseheads in world rugby. Darren has good hands and a surprising turn of speed but he was possibly not at peak fitness and, again, it was in his hands to force his way into the starting side.

Both Colin and Darren were on their first Lions tours and each certainly has more than enough ability to make it on to the next, to New Zealand, and to star there. But they, and others, have to ensure they have the right attitude. Martyn Williams was a guy who got it right. Relatively new to international football, young and a bit untried, Martyn must have felt he was probably third choice for the No7 Test shirt ahead of Richard Hill and myself. Despite this, I thought he played some superb games and that put pressure on me to perform well. He was a top lad with a really professional attitude.

Another area where Graham and the management failed to communicate properly and, again, manage expectations, was in their plans for training. A lot has been said and written about the amount of training we did, and at times it did verge on the excessive. We worked very hard, usually twice a day, almost every day for the first four weeks. It was really demanding but I could see why we needed to do it, although I believe the sessions could have been shorter, sharper and more intense than they were. Some of the players were behind in their general fitness and condition and there were gaps, too, in areas like defence which we needed to work on if we were going to be competitive. Putting in the hours of hard graft early on would mean, in theory, that we could taper down our training to light work once the Tests started. Our international weeks back home are, effectively, a microcosm of this: go for it Monday, Tuesday and Wednesday, rest on Thursday and have a short team run the day before the match. As it happened, because we were trying to play to an English-style defensive pattern that was new to the other guys, and because some were slow to catch on to it, we unfortunately ended up having to eat into Test week with more training than would have been ideal.

Graham should have explained all this, calling a squad meeting on the day we all met up in Hampshire and pointing out to everyone how much they were going to have to do and why they would be doing it. We were going to train tired and play tired, leg-weary even, in order that we could wind down at the crucial period, and we would just have to get used to it. It was not rocket science. Despite this, there were people who really did need everything spelling out for them. It might sound incredible but there it is. Henry's failure to do so meant some members of the squad were wholly unprepared for the work we would have to do and grumbling and moaning soon set in – even, in one case, before we left England.

This attitude problem did get worse as the tour wore on. I felt that there were two types of player. There were those who regarded it as an honour to be in the party, who worked hard and who put the squad first. And there were the others who you saw in the gym rarely, if at all, and who, in my opinion, did not take correct care of themselves. I do not want to name names but I came away from the tour thinking that, collectively, England were literally miles ahead of the other Home Nations in terms of what needs to be done to be the best. The mental toughness and the attitude towards training, gym work and diet was much better in the English players, on the whole.

Let me give two examples. At one point, one non-English guy said: 'I haven't done any weights since Christmas.' Bearing in mind it was now the summer, I found that unbelievable. Admittedly, it is not as though the guy in question needs to work on strength and power. He is naturally a very big and strong bloke – on one occasion after a match he lifted a nightclub doorman above his head for a laugh. But there is more to being in the gym than mindlessly smashing big weights away. A balanced programme can help with core stability and injury prevention, just working on isolation weights, for example. I do not want to name the player: he is a great bloke, someone I would call a friend and a naturally talented player who was one of the undoubted stars on the tour. But he has suffered with his injuries and I wonder if more gym work and a more professional approach would help. It is just frustrating to me to think how good he could be. Then again, I would have to play against him now and then and he is hard enough to deal with as it is.

Another occasion, early in the tour, also sticks in my mind. Most of the English players and some other guys were in the gym putting in the weights work, which we were expected to do unsupervised. After an hour or so of really hard graft we were walking back to our hotel and we passed a Hungry Jack's – an Aussie fast food chain. We looked in through the window and there were half a dozen other players, having a burger and chips. To me, that told a story.

The unfortunate thing was that a lot of this was almost officially sanctioned. Steve Black, the Lions' fitness coach, is a really good bloke and someone for whom I have tremendous respect. He knows his stuff and has some very unusual but effective ideas about training. But I think he made the mistake of assuming that because he was dealing with professional sportsmen, who played for their countries and had now been selected for the Lions, the ultimate team in world rugby, they would have totally professional attitudes. Early on, Steve had said to us: 'I'm not going to tell you what to eat and when to eat it. I just want you to do what you normally do.' He also expected players to know about and follow recovery techniques, post-training or -playing. But there was little or no mention of this – beyond 'take a stretch in the pool' – and a lot of guys did not even bother to do that. Again, Steve told us: 'I'm not going to tell you what to do in terms of training or when to do it.' The problem was that there were some guys on that tour who needed firm direction and Steve's approach gave them the excuse they needed to do nothing.

I will probably get hate mail from non-English fans for singling out their players. Before they put pen to paper let me say that guys like Rob Howley and Daff James were exemplary in their attitudes, as were the likes of Keith Wood and Tom Smith. And I am sure not every English player was perfect. I am generalising. But our performances, generally speaking, against Wales, Scotland and Ireland in recent years bear me out. I would love nothing better than to see a strong Six Nations. It would be great for the game in the UK and Northern Hemisphere and great preparation for us against the Southern Hemisphere sides. But if the indications from that Lions tour are accurate, the other Home nations have some work to do.

There was a lack of professionalism in the really small things, too. If the management called a meeting, the English players were there 10 to 15 minutes ahead of time. With the national squad, we work on 'Lombardi time' – 10 minutes early for everything – after Vince Lombardi, the legendary American football coach who had an obsessive insistence on punctuality. Out in Australia, we just carried it on. It soon became apparent that other people did not view meetings in the same way; guys were turning up five or 10 minutes late. It might sound petty but it delayed and irritated everyone else and was unprofessional. Amazingly, the management were just as bad. It would be five or 10 minutes past the hour we had agreed to meet and Donal and Graham would be chatting among themselves with a few stragglers arriving in the background. It got so frustrating that it became a standing joke: Will Greenwood would say 'When is the session scheduled for... am or pm?' To me it is pretty simple. You are on tour with the British and Irish Lions. You get into the gym, you do not eat fast food and you get to meetings on time. It is black and white. Isn't it?

Other issues had a part to play. Selection was interesting. It was hard for Graham because he was a national coach and after the Lions tour he had to go back to work with Wales. It was not the same for Ian McGeechan; he took Tim Rodber and Matt Dawson with him to South Africa but he was able to justify not taking many Northampton players because they weren't playing international rugby. With Graham's situation, for every non-Welsh player he took he had someone in his squad thinking: 'Henry obviously doesn't rate me that highly.' I am sure that must have influenced his selection of so many guys from Wales. In my own position, I thought Budge Pountney would be in the party, though I was later told he was not even close. David Wallace was another openside who was perhaps unlucky not to make the original group. Elsewhere, Martin Corry's omission was a big mistake, as he showed once he finally arrived. Dorian West is a fine and underestimated hooker and Denis Hickie, the Irish winger, might have been included too. Gregor Townsend, for his sheer unpredictability, would have been worth a spot.

Perhaps the biggest reason for our eventual defeat, though, was that we were strangled by Graham Henry's obsession with detail. There is not the space here to go into great detail but Henry wanted us to stick to a pre-determined gameplan for six, seven, eight, even nine phases of play. Literally, you were supposed to memorise where on the field you should be after that number of phases – and be there. Maybe it was because he felt we did not have enough time to gel together, to know each other to the point where we could play more instinctively. On the other hand, one of the Welsh boys told me: 'When we played you (England), Graham wrote nine phases up on the board, showing where people had to be for each phase.'

That is totally unrealistic and ignores the basic realities of life, never mind rugby. Rugby is organised chaos: people miss tackles, get hurt, the opposition does something unexpected. You can plan for maybe three phases – line-out, move the ball one way, come back the other and ensure the team retains its width – but after that you have to take it as it comes. It was almost as though Graham did not trust us to play with our heads up, to make our own decisions. Our fantastic First Test victory was not the result of good coaching and tactical planning;

it was 22 players, all fired up, playing for the Lions, *forgetting* almost everything Graham had told them and relying on their natural footballing skills and ability. Jason Robinson cutting down the left wing and skinning the Australian full-back, Brian O'Driscoll jinking past tacklers to score perhaps the greatest ever Lions try . . . that is down to individual genius and excellence, backed by a team playing it as it sees it. That sort of brilliance is instinctive, spontaneous and startling: it cannot come from rigid gameplans.

Despite all this, I respected Graham as a coach. His knowledge and understanding of the game was superb and he was very enthusiastic – I am sure that he would love to be playing still. And maybe a modern Lions tour is too much for one head coach and a couple of advisers? Unlike, for instance, the England environment, he did not have a raft of specialist coaches; it was just himself, Andy Robinson and Phil Larder. Towards the end of the tour you could see him almost frazzling under the pressure. More time, more coaches, more professionalism from the players – that is not a bad template for success in New Zealand in 2005.

I do not hold with the almost personal criticism Graham suffered after the tour and, later, after he resigned from the Welsh national coaching position. If that second Test had gone our way, history would judge Graham Henry and the rest of us differently. Instead of picking over the bones of the tour and dissecting what went wrong, a lot of the grief would be glossed over and we would all be talking about what a tremendous time it was. People have this picture of the 1997 tour that it was all sweetness and light and camaraderie but, looking back, we had some absolutely mindless sessions: 50 scrums, hitting the machines as hard as we could, live lineout and scrum sessions that boiled over into fights because we were all so wound up. Morale probably *was* a little better, perhaps because we had a longer tour and much more free time together to bond and relax away from the rugby pitch. There was time to build a togetherness which was perhaps missing in Australia. But the key factor was that we won. What a hero Graham would be now if he had come back with a winning side.

*

With the disappointment of the Lions' tour smouldering in the back of my mind, it was great that England had the chance to play Australia almost immediately. Our autumn had got off to a bad start with the defeat against Ireland, however. Following our Grand Slam-losing defeats to Wales and Scotland in earlier seasons, we once again had a whitewash in our sights. We had beaten all four other sides fairly convincingly, with a new style of running rugby that was exciting the crowds, the media and the players. Guys like Iain Balshaw and Jason Robinson had burst onto the scene and cut defences to pieces. With a solid forward platform, we were looking something like the finished article. Then foot-and-mouth intervened and the Irish game was called off. If we had played them when it was scheduled, during the spring, we would have stuffed them. They have some great players, particularly O'Driscoll and Wood, but we were steaming. As it was, we were not quite the same team. Three key guys – Lawrence Dallaglio and Martin Johnson and Iain Balshaw – were either out of the team or out of sorts. The first two were missing with injury and Balsh had gone into his shell a little after the Lions tour. During the Six Nations, he was very confident, everything he did came off and I believe he was playing at a world class level. Out in Australia, the gameplan was different, defences were a bit tighter and his youth and inexperience showed a little; he desperately wanted to make the same impact out there as he had back home and, when it did not happen instantly, he started trying too hard instead of just concentrating on doing the simple things well. It became a spiral: the more he tried things, the more they didn't work. In the end he was badly affected by it and had still not properly recovered in time for Dublin – though he will be back, I am sure.

For some reason, the whole side failed to fire and we went down in a scrappy match to a committed Ireland side. The most irritating thing about the defeat was that we had identified the exact danger that led to the crucial score. Earlier in the week, Dorian West suggested Keith Wood might throw in near our line, then run round to receive the ball and try to barrel his way over or offload to support runners. Westy pointed this up because it is something we watch for at Leicester; normally he or Cocker will be there with Johnno to guard against it. My job will be to watch the support runners or put pressure on the 10. Somehow, Westy's warning was forgotten and, come match day, there I was trying to stop Woody from two metres out at full velocity. Impossible. He should have been taken down before he even came round the edge of the lineout. Not playing Dorian that day was, in hindsight, possibly a rare selection mistake. He is a bit old school in terms of his diet and training and, like a few of the players I mentioned earlier, he could probably improve further if he took on some modern ideas. But he works hard on his game, particularly his throwing in. Most times he will hit his man and that is important. Win 95 per cent of your lineouts, scrums and kick-offs and you will probably win the game. He is also a stronger scrummager than Phil Greening and would have put pressure on Keith Wood in the tight. I would have introduced Phil as an impact player later in the game, once it had loosened up. As it was, our lineout did not function too well and it was a factor in the defeat. That said, we still should have beaten the Irish.

The loss put even more pressure on us as we prepared to face the Wallabies. We had beaten South Africa recently but our record against Australia was less impressive. And the pressure on me in particular was about to increase dramatically. With Martin Johnson unavailable, Clive Woodward rang. He had previously called me one afternoon ahead of the Dublin match to ask how I would feel about skippering the side for that game in Johnno's absence. In the event, chose Dawson instead.

I was not delighted, obviously, but I told him I respected his decision. Later that night, I could not sleep. It was preying on my mind. Eventually I texted Clive: 'I am gutted about the captaincy. I would love to have done it. But I will give Matt 100% support.' After I had got it off my chest I managed to sleep.

Once we had lost against Ireland, and once it was clear Matt – who was injured – and Johnno were out of the frame, I was hoping and expecting to get another call. I knew I could do the job; I stand in for Martin for the Tigers when he is out and we have only lost one game at the club with me as skipper for Leicester.

Every cap is an honour. Every game for Leicester is an honour. The Lions was a big thing in my life. But nothing compares to that phone call. At the back of my mind, I know I would not have been given the job if everyone had been available – and that does take some of the gloss off – but it is still a huge honour and something I had always dreamed of.

As soon as the phone went down, I thought, *This is your opportunity to prepare for a Test match the way you think it should be done*. I went down to the coaches' meeting on the Sunday afternoon to sit in and explain how I wanted us to work. Instead of starting with a general team run, I wanted training to be more specific; right from the first session on Monday, we would work on the set plays we had identified as those we would use: first kick-off, first lineout, first scrum and so on. I also insisted that, at training, no-one went onto the pitch or touched the ball before we were ready to start. Normally there is a bit of throwing the ball about, laughing and joking, people on the pitch doing their stretches. I wanted us to treat the pitch and the ball seriously. When we crossed that paint we were to be switched on and concentrating; no balls were to hit the deck and no errors were to creep in. Short, sharp, concentrated training was the order of the day.

Finally, I also stressed that we should be very direct. I wanted us to be absolutely ruthless, to be intimidating, to smash them off and away from the ball. I wanted us to play with pace and variety, in their half, and to create close targets initially just to get into them and rough them up. Against Ireland we had been a bit too lateral and we played with a lot of flash and no bash. I wanted more physicality, I wanted domination of the contact area and the breakdowns. And it was very gratifying that that was how it happened on the day. At the end we were direct almost for too long because when there was space out wide we were still passing the ball inside into collision areas. Irritatingly, we let them score a pair of tries but there was no argument over which was the better side on the day.

We did a job on George Smith, too. We targeted him and he was subbed after 50 minutes and dropped for the next game. Nothing personal against George, but that gave me a good feeling. A lot of people had questioned my form during the Lions series and had suggested I had been outplayed by George Smith, the Wallaby wing-forward. Smith is undoubtedly a fantastic player but I do not feel he got the better of me out there. Often, for a No7, it is out of your hands to an extent. It is the kind of position where you tend to shine in a team which is going forward. Look at the first Test. Richard Hill outplayed him as the Lions ran riot. He hardly had a look-in in the first half of the second Test, either; once they got on top and we were on the back foot, he came into the game more. In the third Test, I would say honours were even – pretty much as the game was.

*

I do wonder sometimes whether some of the critics are watching the action they report on. Several times I have been named Man of the Match in games where I do not feel I have performed particularly well. On other occasions, I'll get a 'five out of 10' rating in the papers when I have come off thinking – knowing – I have had a good afternoon. Maybe it is inevitable, given my position. With a winger, it is pretty easy to judge his perform-ance; he beats players and hits his tackles or he does not. Out there in the wide open spaces, it is all on view. Most of my work is by definition hidden; I will be scrapping for the ball with three guys stamping on my back and other two or three lying all over me. With the best will in the world, it is hard for the journalists to see what is happening.

The other irritating thing which has started creeping into newspaper reports about me is references to my age. 'Back, who is nearly 33,...', they will write. I cannot deny my age as I could not deny my size. I am not stupid. I am obviously getting older and I cannot play until I am 40. I am at the end of my career rather than the beginning, at that point where every match is a bonus and I am really able to appreciate my career in a way you cannot when you are younger. None of us will play for England forever. Those occasions are very special and should be treated as a first cap would be. No-one should get too comfortable in that changing room because as soon as you start thinking the seat is yours, you are history. But while I fight complacency every day and recognise that we all must retire, I am, in my opinion, playing as well as I ever have. The game against Wales in the 2002 Six Nations was a case in point. A lot of the articles ahead of the game talked about how I was the oldest and most-capped player in our side. Wales were not great but we scored 23 of our points directly off turnover ball. Who stole all that Welsh ball? Not only that, Phil Larder's stats – which often differ from those produced for the TV but are more accurate and clearly more important – showed I was our top tackler and in the top five ball carriers. That is despite the fact that it is not my primary job to carry the ball – I am supposed to support other players who make breaks, aid continuity and help clean up the mess if they get into trouble.

Clive Woodward and Dean Richards, I would, say, know more about rugby, about their sides and about me than most of the critics. Maybe one or two of the writers should ask Clive or Dean why they have carried on picking me to date? I got a good ride from the papers early in my career. Maybe it is just my turn to get some stick.

To win my first game as captain was a massive relief. We had helped to avenge the Lions defeat and, coming off a bad loss, had also made amends for that, and in a really big game. I had sensed earlier that vultures were beginning to circle. It was a match that we could have easily have lost and I honestly felt that another loss would mean another captain and, quite possibly, another No7. Defeat might well have spurred Clive on to think about some changes, with a 'soft' game against Romania the following week. Lewis Moody was being widely talked about as the next England openside; for a while it has been a question of when, not if. Lewis had burst onto the international scene during England's tour to the USA that summer. He had been on the verge of leaving the club after Leicester signed Josh Kronfeld but Dean had persuaded him to stay and work for his place and it has been good for him, good for me and good for the club. Good for Lewis because he has forced his way in, good for me because Josh and occasionally Lewis have shared the No7 burden with me and good for the club for obvious reasons. However, I did not want to give up my international place to him just yet.

Romania was my second game in charge. It was all a bit sad. They were once a proud rugby nation but they were hopelessly outclassed and, while we used the game well, it was never a contest. Again, I wanted the team to be ruthless and we ran up a record score. I believe the RFU is involved in initiatives to rebuild Romanian rugby; I wish them all the best because rugby needs to spread its grip around the world.

With Johnno back in the frame for South Africa the following week, it was time to hand back the captaincy. To be honest, I did not want to. Those two games had boosted my confidence and I had enjoyed having more of a say in matters on and off the pitch. Coaches are often reluctant to change a winning team and I know Clive considered the possibility of keeping me in charge. He phoned me and asked me how I would feel about captaining the side even if Johnno was back. We had a very frank and honest conversation. I said: 'I would be delighted, as long as Johnno is happy with it. Otherwise, I think it would be a bit harsh on him. He has done nothing wrong and it might feel like a kick in the teeth.' We agreed to talk again after 24 hours and when he called me back he said he had decided to retain Martin, with me as vice-captain. I felt relieved and rueful at the same time, but Clive went out of his way to let me know he thought I had done a good job. He has always treated me well: he does not mess around, he is straight and to-the-point and honest and I respect that.

South Africa was a massive game and, in the end, a bit of an anti-climax. We played well, to the point where we made them look ordinary. They are in something of a trough at the moment, with their Super 12 sides faring badly and key players leaving to go to club rugby overseas and I felt they were suffering a lack of belief. Our forward play was outstanding and the backs deserved more than Dan Luger's length-of-the pitch breakaway score at the end.

That victory gave us a great recent record against the Southern Hemisphere nations and a good springboard into the 2002 Six Nations. After tremendous victories over Scotland, Wales and Ireland, though, we came unstuck against France. Our kicking game was poor and, for once, our defence let us down. France, meanwhile, were on top of their game and went on to take the Grand Slam. It was another desperate disappointment – I said when this book was first published that I had won nothing with England and, discounting a few Triple Crowns and non-Slam championships, that remains the case – but there is no hex on an English Grand Slam, as some people seem to think. Before Paris, the popular theory was that we could not win big pressure games without Johnno. We had lost to Scotland and then Ireland with him on the sidelines. Then we went and lost to France with Martin in the side, so that scotched that one. The fact is that there is no secret hoodoo, no psychological weakness, no key that will unlock the door; we lost to Wales, Scotland, Ireland and France because we played badly and the other side, at home (well, Wembley *was* 'home' for the Welsh!), played well. That happens in sport. It is just a coincidence that, on two of the three occasions, we were going for the Grand Slam. It is insulting to the other sides, in my opinion, to suggest that if only the real

England turned up on the day it would be a foregone conclusion. These are proud, talented, international rugby sides and they are going to beat us from time to time.

If only England could produce the sort of consistency the Leicester have been able to show. In 2001/02, we retained our Premiership title for a fourth consecutive season, we win many more games than we lose and we headed into the European/ Heineken Cup final at the Millennium Stadium in Cardiff to play Munster as defending champions. What a match that turned out to be, in more ways than one.

Munster gave it their all, as we knew they would, and though we scored two tries and kept them from crossing our line, it could have gone either way, with Ronan O'Gara kicking superbly for them. Our defence was staunch, however, and probably the key to the game. Some of the press, though, would prefer to focus on a little incident in the dying moments of the match. Munster had a vital, last-ditch scrum under our posts but lost possession when my hand, shall we say, dislodged the ball from their scrum-half Peter Stringer's grip at the put-in. It was, I admit, an infringement but was not spotted by the referee. We held out for a 15–9 victory, becoming the first side to win the trophy twice.

I was slated afterwards in some quarters for disrupting Stringer's throw. I can only repeat what I said to reporters immediately afterwards: this game is all about little edges, especially in finals, and about doing what you have to do to win. That was a crucial scrum and I did what I had to do. There had been plenty of fouls, penalised and not penalised, on both sides, as there are in any game. Top-level sport is played on the edge; that's why we have referees, linesmen and video replays. As Deano was quick to point out, 'If you cast Neil as a cheat, then everyone who gave a penalty away on the field is a cheat too.' Interestingly, one of the Munster guys said that if I had been playing for them and had done the same thing, I'd have been made Lord Mayor!

Leicester's success is down to professionalism: hard work, commitment and guts. A lot of the good things about England's recent performances have come from the side's Leicester contingent. We are driven by a fear of failure, by a desperation to prove ourselves to our team-mates, our coaches and our fans that I do not think exists at every club. At Leicester, we win week in, week out. If we lose a game it is a major problem. If we lose two games on the trot – as we did this season for the first time in years – it is a genuine disaster and we have a real inquest, with strong views exchanged. Some of my England colleagues play in teams that are losing three or four games in a row and leaking tries all over the place. They are great players but their club ethos is mediocre and that has to rub off on them. With the Tigers, if someone breaks our line there is a real urgency, a desperation, to get back and stop them scoring. I am not sure quite that desperation exists in all English clubs.

So what does the future hold – and do England have any chance of winning the next World Cup?

A few months ago, people were writing us up as world-beaters. We even topped the computer-generated list as best team in the globe at one point. After the loss to France, that all changed. I never thought we were the No1 side and losing that tag was not a problem. But I do think we have a better hope of success than we had in either 1995 or 1999, perhaps the best chance we have ever had. Three years ago our forwards were among the best in the world but, as I have said, our backs lacked penetration. Now, with the likes of Jonny Wilkinson, Matt Dawson or Kyran Bracken, Dan Luger, Ben Cohen, Austin Healey, Will Greenwood and Jason Robinson playing at their best we can compete with anyone. Add in Mike Tindall, Leon Lloyd and any of a number of really quick young lads coming up on the rails and the future looks bright. New Zealand, Australia and France will be the teams to beat but any one of us, with perhaps South Africa and Ireland, can win.

But if we are to stand any chance we need an experienced squad; that means more than 30 players with international experience. If we do not win our group we will have a mid-week match before the quarter-finals, assuming we make it that far. We would need to rotate our squad and that is hard if you have 22 guys with a lot of games between them and a bunch of others who have little or no experience at that level. Clive has recognised that and that is why he has given opportunities to guys like Lewis Moody, Charlie Hodgson, Ben Kay and Steve Thompson. Ben and Steve, and to a lesser extent Lewis, have actually come in and made places their own. When you factor in the likes of Lawrence Dallaglio, Martin Corry, Mike Catt, Iain Balshaw and Matt Perry, guys who, for one reason and another, have not played much recently, then we do have good strength in depth.

Will I be in that final squad? Only Clive Woodward can tell you that. All I can do is keep myself fit, keep playing well and keep my fingers crossed.

And what then for Neil Back? If I am fortunate enough to make it to the World Cup I will probably have surpassed Peter Winterbottom's record of 58 openside caps for England. To go past a true great like Wints will be some achievement; a massive honour and one I and many others never thought I would reach. I think that would be an appropriate moment to stand aside and let someone else have the honour of that precious No7 jersey.

I will carry on for Leicester, probably for another season, perhaps two, and then hang up my playing boots for good. I like the idea of coaching and I think I will have something to offer in that department.

Of course, international retirement might be forced upon me earlier than that. I will be terribly disappointed if I get that call from Clive because I genuinely think I am still the best openside in England. But I will thank him for the opportunities he has given me and bow out as gracefully as possible. Where once it would have been the end of the world, now it would be...well, bearable. The hunger and desire is still there and I am still in search of the perfect game but I am now a much happier, more fulfilled man.

A gorgeous wife, a lovely daughter (with another baby on the way), two European crowns and 50 or more England caps – and England captain. How much better could it get anyway?

Neil Back: Career Statistics

(supplied by Stuart Farmer Media Services Ltd, Hinckley)

TIGERS CAPTAINCY RECORD

No	Date	Opponents	Result	Game
1	17 Oct 92	At Moseley	L 14–20	44th
2	17 Aug 93	At Zululand	W 15–8	60th
3	5 Apr 97	Orrell (CL)	W 36–14	139th
4	28 Feb 98	At Bristol (ADP)	W 27–24	163rd
5	16 Jan 99	London Scottish (ADP)	W 24–12	187th
6	5 Dec 99	At Saracens (ADP)	L 20–36	203rd
7	18 Dec 99	Glasgow Caled (EC)	W 34–21	205th
8	26 Dec 99	At Bath (ADP)	W 13–3	206th
9	29 Dec 99	Harlequins (ADP)	W 29–17	207th
10	22 Jan 00	Saracens (ADP)	W 48–20	208th
11	25 Jan 00	At Wasps (ADP)	W 29–20	209th
12	29 Jan 00	At London Irish (TBC4)	L 7–47	210th
13	6 Jan 01	At Harlequins (TBCQF)	L 18–22	234th
14	13 Jan 01	At Pau (EC)	W 20–3	235th
15	5 May 01	Northampton (ZP)	W 17–13	242nd
16	3 Nov 01	Perpignan (EC)	W 54–15	251st

TIGERS MILESTONES

Game	Date	Opponents	Result	Notes
1st	1 Sep 90	Bedford	W 57–6	Scored a try
20th	13 Apr 91	London Irish	W 54–16	Scored a try
50th	28 Dec 92	Barbarians	W 41–23	
100th	16 Sep 95	At Sale (CL)	W 16–12	
150th	27 Sep 97	Leinster (EC)	W 47–22	
200th	13 Nov 99	Wasps (ADP)	W 28–9	Scored a try
250th	27 Oct 01	At Perpignan (EC)	W 31–30	

MOST TRIES IN A GAME

Tries	Date	Opponents	Result	Game
3	16 May 99	West Hartlepool (ADP)	W 72–37	198th
3	21 May 00	Bath (ADP)	W 43–25	217th
3	19 Apr 02	Leeds Tykes (ZP)	W 31-10	265th

TIGERS SEASON BY SEASON

Season	Club	League			Cup			All Games		
		App	T	Pts	App	T	Pts	App	T	Pts
1988/89	Nottingham		1	-	-			16	8	32
1989/90	Nottingham		6+1	2	8			21	2	8
Tigers Debuts		*22 Sep 90 v*			*26 Jan 91 v*			*1 Sep 90 v*		
		Gloucester			*Wasps*			*Bedford*		
1990/91	TIGERS	9	-	-	1	-	-	22	4	16
1991 tour	TIGERS							2	1	4
1991/92	TIGERS	10	1	4	3	1	4	17	5	20
1992/93	TIGERS	8	1	5	5	3	15	18	6	30
1993 tour	TIGERS							2	-	-
1993/94	TIGERS	13	7	35	4	2	10	18	9	45
1994/95	TIGERS	13	-	-	4	1	5	18	1	5
1995/96	TIGERS	15	4	20	4	-	-	25	8	40
1996/97	TIGERS	14	3	15	4	1	5	23	5	25
1997/98	TIGERS	18	8	40	2	-	-	27	10	50
1998/99	TIGERS	22+1	16	80	2	3	15	25+1	20	100
1999/00	TIGERS	14	7	35	1	-	-	20	9	45

2000/01	TIGERS	12+1	8	40	2	1	5	25+1	13	65
2001/02	TIGERS	9+5	6	30	0+1	-	-	15+8	10	50
Tigers Totals		157+7	61	304	32+1	12	59	257+10	101	495

ENGLAND CAPS

Cap	Date	Opponents	Venue	Result	Notes
1	5 Feb 94	Scotland	Murrayfield	W 15–14	
2	19 Feb 94	Ireland	Twickenham	L 12–13	
3	27 May 95	Argentina (RWC)	Durban	W 24–18	Replacement
4	31 May 95	Italy (RWC)	Durban	W 27–20	
5	4 Jun 95	Western Samoa (RWC)	Durban	W 44–22	Try. replaced
6	22 Nov 97	New Zealand	Manchester	L 8–25	Replacement
7	29 Nov 97	South Africa	Twickenham	L 11–29	
8	6 Dec 97	New Zealand	Twickenham	D 26–26	Temp replaced
9	7 Feb 98	France	Paris	L 17–24	Try
10	21 Feb 98	Wales	Twickenham	W 60–26	Try
11	22 Mar 98	Scotland	Murrayfield	W 34–20	
12	4 Apr 98	Ireland	Twickenham	W 35–17	
13	14 Nov 98	Netherlands (WCQ)	Huddersfield	W 110–0	4 tries
14	22 Nov 98	Italy (WCQ)	Huddersfield	W 23–15	
15	28 Nov 98	Australia	Twickenham	L 11–12	
16	5 Dec 98	South Africa	Twickenham	W 13–7	
17	20 Feb 99	Scotland	Twickenham	W 24–21	
18	6 Mar 99	Ireland	Dublin	W 27–15	
19	20 Mar 99	France	Twickenham	W 21–10	
20	11 Apr 99	Wales	Wembley	L 31–32	
21	26 Jun 99	Australia	Sydney	L 15–22	
22	21 Aug 99	United States	Twickenham	W 106–8	2 tries
23	28 Aug 99	Canada	Twickenham	W 36–11	
24	2 Oct 99	Italy (RWC)	Twickenham	W 67–7	Try
25	9 Oct 99	New Zealand (RWC)	Twickenham	L 16–30	Replaced
26	20 Oct 99	Fiji (RWC)	Twickenham	W 45–24	Try
27	24 Oct 99	South Africa (RWCQF)	Paris	L 21–44	

28	5 Feb 00	Ireland	Twickenham	W 50–18	Try
29	19 Feb 00	France	Paris	W 15–9	
30	4 Mar 00	Wales	Twickenham	W 46–12	Try
31	18 Mar 00	Italy	Rome	W 59–12	Drop goal
32	2 Apr 00	Scotland	Murrayfield	L 13–19	
33	17 Jun 00	South Africa	Pretoria	L 13–18	
34	24 Jun 00	South Africa	Bloemfontein	W 27–22	
35	18 Nov 00	Australia	Twickenham	W 22–19	
36	25 Nov 00	Argentina	Twickenham	W 19–0	
37	2 Dec 00	South Africa	Twickenham	W 25–17	Temp replaced
38	3 Feb 01	Wales	Cardiff	W 44–15	
39	17 Feb 01	Italy	Twickenham	W 80–23	Replaced
40	3 Mar 01	Scotland	Twickenham	W 43–3	Replaced
41	7 Apr 01	France	Twickenham	W 48–19	
42	20 Oct 01	Ireland	Dublin	L 14–20	
43	10 Nov 01	Australia	Twickenham	W 21–15	CAPT
44	17 Nov 01	Romania	Twickenham	W 134-0	CAPT. Replaced
45	24 Nov 01	South Africa	Twickenham	W 29-9	Temp replaced
46	2 Feb 02	Scotland	Murrayfield	W 29-3	
47	16 Feb 02	Ireland	Twickenham	W 45-11	
48	2 Mar 02	France	Paris	L 15–20	Temp replaced
49	23 Mar 02	Wales	Twickenham	W 50–10	CAPT
50	7 Apr 02	Italy	Rome	W 45–9	CAPT. Replaced

LIONS CAPS

Cap	Date	Opponents	Venue	Result	Notes
1	28 Jun 97	South Africa	Durban	W 18–15	Replacement
2	5 Jul 97	South Africa	Johannesburg	L 16–35	
3	7 Jul 01	Australia	Melbourne	L 14–35	Try
4	14 Jul 01	Australia	Sydney	L 23–29	